# Surprised by C. S. Lewis, George MacDonald, & Dante

## An Array of Original Discoveries

# Kathryn Lindskoog

Mercer University Press 2001

ISBN 0-86554-728-9
MUP/H546

© 2001 Mercer University Press
6316 Peake Road
Macon, Georgia 31210-3960
All rights reserved

First Edition.

*Library of Congress Cataloging-in-Publication Data*

Lindskoog, Kathryn Ann.
Surprised by C.S. Lewis, George MacDonald, and Dante : an array of original
discoveries / by Kathryn Lindskoog.—1st ed.
p. cm.
Includes bibliographical references and index.
ISBN 0-86554-728-9 (alk. paper)
1. Lewis, C. S. (CliveStaples), 1898-1963—Criticism and interpretation.
2. MacDonald, George, 1824-1905—Criticism  and interpretation.
3. Christian literature, English—History and criticism. 4. Children's stories,
Scottish—History and criticism. 5. Fantasy literature, English—History
and criticism. 6. Fantasy fiction, Scottish—History and criticism. 7. Dante
Alighieri, 1265-1321—Influence. 8. English Literature—Italian influences.
I. Title.

PR6023.E926 Z7815 2001
823'.912—dc21

                                    2001018014

Some of these essays have appeared earlier in the following periodicals:

*The Canadian C. S. Lewis Journal*

*The Christian Century*

*C. S. L., Bulletin of the New York C. S. Lewis Society*

*The Lamp-Post*

*The Lewis Legacy*

*The Mark Twain Journal*

*Mythlore*

*Perspectives*

*Radix*

# TABLE OF CONTENTS

*Dedicated to Kristin Carmody,*
*fellow lover of C. S. Lewis and George MacDonald*

# SIMPLE PLEASURES

# 1

## WHO IS THIS MAN?

*A surprising answer to the question "Who Is This Man?" appears below the list of clues.*

1. Educated at the University of Oxford.
2. An instructor at the University of Oxford.
3. A brilliant and innovative scholar.
4. Wrote important scholarly books.
5. Born in the 1800s.
6. His father was a successful professional man.
7. His mother died prematurely, in her forties.
8. His father never remarried.
9. Loved to teach people things he knew.
10. Witty, and believed in the value of humor.
11. Lived frugally and gave generously.
12. His first name began with C.
13. Published books under a pseudonym.
14. Used the name Lewis.
15. A sincerely devout Christian.
16. Prayed for people.
17. Sometimes wrote and delivered sermons.
18. Was interested in George MacDonald.
19. A prodigious and delightful letter writer.
20. Never had any little children.
21. Sent charming letters to little children.
22. Published extremely successful fantasies for children.
23. Highly quotable.
24. Has been translated into many languages.
25. Died in his mid-sixties, just days before his birthday.
26. Has sold millions of books and is world famous.

27. There is a society for his literary fans.
28. A favorite of Kathryn Lindskoog.
29. 1998 was observed as his centenary year.
30. Featured on a 1998 British Royal Mail stamp.

*Answer: C. S. Lewis (1898–1963),*

*and Charles Dodgson (Lewis Carroll) (1832-1898)*

# 2

# C. S. LEWIS AND PETER RABBIT

*Few people are aware of the following connection between C. S. Lewis and Beatrix Potter.*

On September 4, 1893, five years before C. S. Lewis was born, a young woman wrote a letter to three-year-old Noel Moore because he was ill. She began, "My dear Noel, I don't know what to write to you, so I shall tell you about four little rabbits whose names were Flopsy, Mopsy, Cottontail and Peter..."

Everyone knew that Noel got his name from the fact that he had been born on Christmas Eve. Likewise, Noel and his family knew that Peter Rabbit got his name from Beatrix Potter's pet rabbit named Peter Piper who went everywhere with her. She was a nature lover and an amateur artist, and so she sprinkled illustrations in her letter.

Noel and his sisters treasured all their mail from Beatrix Potter, and when Noel was about ten Beatrix asked to see the Peter Rabbit letter again. She copied it out, added some garden adventures to make it longer, and titled it *The Tale of Peter Rabbit and Mr. McGregor's Garden.* Then months went by as she sent it off to at least six publishers, one by one, and they all rejected it.

On September 25, 1901, Beatrix wrote a letter to Noel's little sister Norah, beginning, "I believe that his name was Nutkin and that he had a brother called Twinkleberry, and this is the story of how he lost his tail." That was the origin of *The Tale of Squirrel Nutkin,* a book which would profoundly influence C. S. Lewis.

With Christmas coming, Beatrix went ahead and paid a printer to produce 250 inexpensive copies of her first book, titled simply *The Tale of Peter Rabbit.* They were ready on December 16, 1901, and those that she didn't give away sold quickly. Arthur Conan Doyle, author of the Sherlock Holmes stories, had one for his children and liked it. Beatrix was so pleased with the book's reception that she paid to have another 200 copies printed.

At that point her friend Hardwicke Rawnsley, a rector in the Lake District where she vacationed, tried to help her find a publisher. He had written a popular book titled *Moral Rhymes for the Young,* and he thought her story might be accepted if it rhymed. He rewrote it for her, beginning:

> There were four little bunnies
> — no bunnies were sweeter
> Mopsy and Cotton-tail,
> Flopsy and Peter.

His version of the story ended:

> They sat down to tea
> too good mannered to cram
> and ate bread and milk
> and sweet blackberry jam.

Rawnsley got the Frederick Warne company interested in "the bunny book," as they called it, but they decided that the black-and-white illustrations must be colored. Furthermore, they decided that the story should not be rhymed after all. So Beatrix put the words back into good order and painted the pictures during her summer vacation.

On October 2, 1902, *The Tale of Peter Rabbit* was published; and all 8,000 copies were ordered in advance. In the meantime, Beatrix had written another story called *The Tailor of Gloucester,* and had paid a printer to produce 500 copies. The Warne company decided to publish both *The Tailor of Gloucester* and *The Tale of Squirrel Nutkin* before Christmas in 1903. By the end of 1903, over 50,000 copies of *Peter Rabbit* had already been sold; and by the end of 1904, 30,000 copies of *Squirrel Nutkin* and *The Tailor of Gloucester* were in print. Beatrix Potter was famous.

C. S. Lewis was five years old when *Squirrel Nutkin* was published. According to his 1961 book *An Experiment in Criticism*, at that age he was even more fascinated with the idea of humanized animals than most children are. And because his only exposure to art was in book illustrations, "Those to Beatrix Potter's *tales* were the delight of my childhood." As an adult he also admired what he called "the classic economy and finality of her writing."

Over 50 years after discovering *Squirrel Nutkin*, Lewis recounted his first three experiences of what he called Joy ("unsatisfied desire which is itself more desireable than any other satisfaction"):

> The second glimpse came through *Squirrel Nutkin*, and through it only, though I loved all the Beatrix Potter books. But the rest of them were merely entertaining; it administered the shock, it was a trouble. It troubled me with what I can only describe as the Idea of Autumn. It sounds fantastic to say that one can be enamored of a season, but that is something like what happened; and, as before, the experience was one of intense desire. And one went back to the book, not to gratify the desire (that was impossible—how can one *possess* Autumn?) but to reawake it. And in this experience also there was the same surprise and the same sense of incalculable importance. It was something quite different from ordinary life and even from ordinary pleasure; something, as they now say, "in another dimension. (From *Surprised by Joy*.)

By the end of 1910 Beatrix Potter had sixteen books in print and was the mainstay of the Warne company. In 1912 *Peter Rabbit* was published in French; he became Pierre Lapin and his sisters became Flopsaut, Trotsaut, and Queue-de-Coton. By 1934 *Peter Rabbit* had been translated into six languages, and Beatrix Potter was known around the world. In 1943 alone, in spite of World War II and paper shortages, her books sold 219,000 copies. Since then sales have increased so much that in 1987 the total was seven million. The three places where *Peter Rabbit* is most popular today are the United States, Britain, and Japan, in that order.

Always a shrewd businesswoman, in 1902 Beatrix made a Peter Rabbit doll out of white velveteen. She designed Peter Rabbit and

Benjamin Bunny wallpaper. She designed special fold-out picture-strip booklets for little children. *Peter Rabbit's Painting Book* came out in 1911, followed by *Jemima Puddle-Duck's Painting Book* in 1925. She designed *Peter Rabbit's Almanac for 1929.* A set of twelve table mats featured scenes from *Jemima Puddle-duck.* There were Peter Rabbit slippers, and white Peter Rabbit bookshelves to hold sets of her books.

Although she would not tolerate the slightest copyright infringement, Beatrix gladly allowed the Invalid Children's Aid Society to use Peter Rabbit as its symbol; and she sometimes donated illustrations for that charity's Christmas cards.

What did Londoner Beatrix Potter do with all her money? She bought more and more rolling farmland in the Lake District, married her real estate lawyer William Heelis, and turned into a devoted farmer. When she died in 1943, she left over 4,000 acres of Lake District property to the National Trust, to be preserved for the people of England. Her little house, called Hill Top Farm, was kept exactly as she had it and is now a popular museum and tourist attraction.

In 1980 two other developments occurred. First, the quaint old city building that Beatrix pictured in her other 1903 book, *The Tailor of Gloucester,* was purchased and turned into a Beatrix Potter shop that sells an array of products including dishes, puzzles, books, pencil sharpeners, slippers, dolls, figurines, baby pajamas, and pillows. Second, a Beatrix Potter Society was formed to promote the serious study and appreciation of all aspects of her life, promising a quarterly newsletter, an annual lecture, and a biennial study conference. Of the two projects, crusty Beatrix would have preferred the former.

What of Noel Moore, the sick child who received a Peter Rabbit letter from Beatrix in 1893? He grew up, became an Anglican priest, and went to work in inner city London.

And what of C. S. Lewis, a little boy in Belfast who discovered the Beatrix Potter stories in 1904 or 1905? He grew up to become an Oxbridge professor and one of the most beloved Christian writers of all time. In 1944 he happened to write a letter to little Sarah Neylan, the daughter of a student he had led to God. He told Sarah a true story about a wild rabbit he had befriended and named Baron Biscuit.

One day he stood up on his hind legs and put his front paws against me, he was so greedy. I wrote this about it:

A funny old man had a habit
Of giving a leaf to a rabbit.
  At first it was shy
  But then, by and by,
It got rude and would stand up to grab it.

In his 1956 autobiography *Surprised by Joy*, Lewis recalled "Then came the Beatrix Potter books, and here at last beauty." In 1956 Lewis had just completed his seven tales of Narnia, and by the end of the century he would would join Beatrix Potter as one of the world's favorite writers for children.

# 3

# UNEXPECTED TREASURE

*This account of C. S. Lewis's childhood and the origin of his Narnian Chronicles is written in story form for children. Aside from the chronology, the data is all factual, including the hitherto-unknown treasure-hunting incident.*

There were once two brothers who lived in a big house in Ireland and always played with each other. This was back in the days before radio and television. The boys had a home teacher and didn't go to school; so their main job was to keep themselves busy, and they loved it.

The Lewis family had many silly nicknames. Their mother often called their father "Old Bear," and when they got older the boys secretly called him "Potato," as he pronounced it—"Pudaita." The boys were named Warren and Clive, but when they were little they were usually called "Badgie" and "Babs." Most boys wouldn't like to be called Clive or Babs very well, and when Clive was only four years old he announced "I'm Jacksie!" Jack was the only name he would answer to from that day on. When he grew up and became a famous writer, he signed his books C. S. Lewis. But his friends and relatives called him Jack all his life.

One day the two boys decided to dig for treasure. Digging was harder work than they thought it would be, but they kept at it until they had quite a big hole in the broad path that ran from the road to their front door. They had expected to find at least a little gold or a few jewels, but they found nothing in the ground except dirt. Finally they gave up and went inside to do something else until supper. Little did they guess that they had dug themselves into deep trouble.

When their father came home from his day at the office, the sun was already going down. He was striding up the path, thinking about his law business and hungry for supper, when suddenly—whoosh! His briefcase went flying. He found himself on his hands and knees in a damp, dirty hole. He struggled up and brushed some of the dirt off his good shoes and his good suit and tie. His hands were scraped and dirty, and his temper was on fire. He marched into the house, informed his wife Flora that her sons had almost broken his neck, and gave them a spanking they never forgot.

That's how the brothers learned that it's dangerous to dig a hole where people might fall in. But that certainly wasn't the end of their good and bad adventures. It was only the beginning.

These boys liked to get on their bicycles and roam along quiet little roads that ran mile after mile through the green countryside near their house. They were always looking for things to discover. One cloudy day they were planning to go farther than ever and explore a different road, when—split—splat—split-split—splat-splat—splitty-split-split—splatty-splat-splat, it started to rain.

"Oh, no, not again!" the older one cried.

"Hurry!" the younger one shouted.

They wheeled around and pumped for home as fast as they could. One of their mother's strictest rules was that they couldn't be out in the rain. It rained often in those days, and so they were used to rushing home fast.

"What'll we do now?" the younger one gasped as they tumbled back into the house and pulled off their damp jackets.

"I know," his brother answered. "Let's make a new page for our story about Animal Land. I'll beat you upstairs."

Through the stately living room full of books they ran, up the curving staircase, past the great bookcase on the landing, on up the stairs, down the hall, and into their favorite little attic room. Everything was scattered about waiting for them just as they had left it the day before. Lots of paper, a jar of paste, a ball of string, dip-pens and ink, pencils, erasers, water-color paints and brushes, a ruler, and scissors. And of course their very own book that they were making.

They eventually finished the first book and started a second. The Animal Land stories kept growing, and so did the boys. Life seemed to go along the same happy way forever. Every summer their mother took them for a vacation at the beach, and one year she took them on a boat all the way to the beach in France. But that was their last summer vacation, because when the brothers were nine and ten years old, their mother became very sick and died. Then everything changed.

One day their father put them on a boat because he had decided to send them to live at a boys' school in England. When they finally got to the tall, narrow house that was their school, they hurried up the steps hoping for a good hot supper and a soft warm bed. Inside they found several unhappy-looking boys who lived there with the teacher and his timid little wife. The teacher was a huge, rough man with dirty hair, who warned them to behave if they didn't want a beating. It was soon supper time, and the boys all sat at the student table waiting for their helping of meat, thick gray gravy, boiled potatoes, and over-cooked cabbage.

"Ugh!" the younger brother whispered. "What's the matter with this meat?"

"Sh!" the boy next to him warned. "Don't let them hear you complain. We call the meat here slime balls. Just choke it down." So he did.

The two brothers loved going back home on the boat and spending vacations in their big house in Ireland. But their father never believed that he had accidentally sent them to a bad school until the police finally closed it down and locked the teacher away. Their father put them in better boarding schools, but the younger brother, Jack, never liked any of the schools very well. He was glad when he finally got to move in with a wise old teacher who lived out in the English countryside. There he studied hard and went hiking for miles every afternoon to see what he could discover.

One day when Jack was 16 years old, he was surprised by a picture that suddenly popped into his head—a little goat-man carrying packages in a snowy wood. Years passed, and he became a professor and lived in a house out in the country. One day he was walking in the snowy wood behind his house. He was thinking about the girls from London who had come to live with him. (Many children had been sent to live in the country to get away from wartime bombing.) In the summer the children could swim in his pond and row his boat and hike in his woods, but in the wet winter they had to stay indoors most of the time.

Suddenly he imagined one of these girls meeting a little goat-man with packages out in his snowy wood. He went to his desk and started to write a story about that, but after a few chapters he stopped because the story became boring. Writing a dull story was like digging a hole that didn't uncover any treasure.

Then one day after the war was all over and the children had gone home to London, he started the story again. The name of the place was Narnia. To his surprise, a great Lion named Aslan seemed to leap into the story of his own accord this time. Writing this story was like discovering a great treasure. He finished the book quickly and called it *The Lion, the Witch and the Wardrobe*. Now millions and millions of people know about the Lion named Aslan and the funny little goat-man in the snowy wood.

# 4

# THE SPLENDID LANDS

*This pastiche is an imitation of C. S. Lewis's short story "The Shoddy Lands," in which Lewis found himself exploring the world inside someone else's head. At the end he asked, "And how if some other time, I were not the explorer but the explored?" As I finished rereading the story once, I lifted my eyes to a framed photo of Lewis on my desk and wished I could explore the world inside Lewis's head. So I did that in my imagination, drawing together a variety of Lewis's quotations that show how the world looked to him. The ending of this story is patterned on the ending of* The Great Divorce.

Being, as I believe, of sound mind and normal health, I am sitting down at 8:30 A.M. (with everyone fed and off to school) to record the curious experience I had last night.

It happened at my desk in the den, where I am now writing. I was browsing in my C. S. Lewis books at about 9 P.M., and I happened to get involved in the delightful volume *Of Other Worlds,* which begins with Walter Hooper reporting Lewis's statement "You can't get a cup of tea large enough or a book long enough to suit me."

I couldn't resist rereading Lewis' peculiar short story "The Shoddy Lands," which begins on page 99. There Lewis tells about his strange journey into the mind of a frivolous girl named Peggy. For a few seconds he had inadvertently explored the second-rate world that existed within her mind. It was miserable. When he snapped back into his real world, he was silly with joy. His conclusion was, "What if this sort of thing were to become common? And how if some other time, I were not the explorer but the explored?"

As I finished the story, I leaned on my desk and gazed at the large framed magazine photo of C. S. Lewis I keep there. He held his glasses in his right hand, leaned his head on his left hand, and peered back at me enigmatically in grainy shades of gray. His collar was rumpled, his head balding, and the pouches under his eyes showed clearly. His eyes, dark, deep, and twinkly, were what fascinated me. I stared into them for some time.

The pleasant darkness of those eyes gradually enveloped me; I didn't notice as the room became dim. But I did notice when a cheerily cold sea breeze blew into my face. To my dismay, I suddenly realized that I was not leaning on my desk any more, but on the railing of a ship.

Perhaps I had died and was on my way to heaven, I thought giddily. I saw the phosphorescence of the ship's wash, the mast unmoving against the stars although the water rushed past, and then the long salmon-colored rifts of dawn on the horizon of cold gray-green water. A steamer's horn blew in the distance. Then there was the astonishing behavior of land as we approached it, the promontories that walked out to meet us, the complex movements and final disappearance of the mountains further inland. The salt water washing past looked rather like beaten copper.

Before I knew it I had somehow disembarked and was walking all alone on the beach without a soul in sight, watching the great green ginger-beer colored waves. I remember one long sunlit wave in particular, creamy crested and arched with emerald, that came on nine feet tall, with roaring and with terror and with unquenchable laughter. It seemed as if I had never really seen and heard the surf before, although I have spent much time there.

What awaited me inland? I soon discovered grass and primroses and orchards in bloom, deafened with bird songs and astir with running water. In the distance were blue ridges against the horizon. The mere smells were enough to make me tipsy—cut grass, dew-dabbled mosses, sweet pea, autumn woods, wood burning, peat, salt water. The senses ached. I was sick with desire; that sickness better than health. The whole land seemed cool, dewy, fresh, exuberant. And there was one flowering currant bush alone which all by itself nearly broke my heart.

I entered a wood where the light breeze carried cool, delicious scents my way. The larches and birches were covered with green, the laburnums with gold. Under the delicate, transparent leaves of the beeches the light itself became green. A bee buzzed across my path. This wood was very much alive. All I can say is that it was a rich place—as rich as plum-cake.

Then I came to a hilly area bleak in comparison. The few woods there were only small trees, rowan and birch and small fir. The fields were small, divided by ditches with ragged sea-nipped hedges on top of them. There was a good deal of gorse and many outcroppings of rock. Small abandoned quarries, filled with cold-looking water, were numerous. Wind whistled through the grass, and gulls wheeled overhead. The soil had no rich chocolate or ocher here. It was pale, but the grass was soft, rich, and sweet, and single-storied whitewashed cottages with blue slate roofs lit up the whole landscape like white-caps on a summer sea. At my feet there was pale, soft sunlight on the grass and dew, crowing cocks and gaggling ducks On the horizon I watched a line of pointed, toothed and jagged mountains— sometimes blue, sometimes violet, and sometimes transparent like sheets of gauze.

I didn't think that I was in heaven, and soon I saw that I was right. On the flat floor of the valley at my feet, a forest of factory chimneys, cranes, towers, screeching trams, clatter of traffic, and the smoke and stir of a city arose. I was down there in no time.

At first my mind seemed numb down in the city. Cars that went by me in the street were shapeless and dingy; I couldn't identify any of them. I paused at a clothing store window and tried hard to get my eyes back into focus. No use. The clothes inside were marked with high prices, but they looked shoddy and rumpled, without any particuar style or color. Then a large old tabby cat wandered by, vivid in whisker and paw; so I knew my eyes were working fine after all. Next I passed a movie theater and couldn't quite make out the titles on the posters nor the names of the stars. Newspapers at a stand were mainly smudges. A queer city indeed. I hadn't happened to meet any people yet.

Then it happened. An elderly lady stepped out of a shop onto the walk before me, and I fell to my knees in awe. She was clearly a royal person, from her silver hair down to her sturdy walking shoes. She had a beautiful motherly face and ordinary clothes, with no jewels at all; but there was an aura of greatness about her. I was overwhelmed with the honor of seeing her close and wondered who in the world she was. She counted the parcels in her shopping bag and walked on down the street alone.

Next, two boys sauntered up the street and I stayed where I was on my knees because they, too, struck me as people of overwhelming importance. Princes, perhaps, out for fun in someone else's old clothes? They eyed me curiously as they walked by, and I got up uncertainly and started walking. From then on it was one magnificent, mysterious person after another. Every person I saw was obviously of inestimable value in some way or other and had some kind of fame and power. Fame with whom, I couldn't tell, and power for what, I didn't know. Some were likable and some were not. I can't recall just how their importance radiated from them, but it was undeniable and, after a while, unbearable. Too many near-gods and near-goddesses were wearing on my nerves.

I turned into a library to get some privacy. I had noticed several beautiful bookshops along the way, full of shining titles, and I decided to browse a bit. (Strangely, I never saw a single bank.) The books had a mild radiance of their own. There were many of them, from Plato to Beatrix Potter, from St. Augustine to Dorothy L. Sayers. Many were in languages I don't know, and many were from the medieval and Renaissance eras. They all looked loved. I checked to see which titles were there by my favorite author, C. S. Lewis. I found rich volumes of all the works of George MacDonald, Charles Williams, and G. K. Chesterton, but only a few scrubby little books by C. S. Lewis himself, almost illegible. They weren't even very solid to the touch. I didn't see a librarian or I would have complained. By then I was getting tired, irritable, and hungry.

As I passed one snug little home I could smell trout frying, and so I watched through a window while the family sat down to eat. There was a jug of creamy milk for the children and a great lump of deep yellow butter in the middle of the table from which everyone took as much as he wanted to go with his potatoes. And everyone said that there' s nothing to beat good freshwater fish if you eat it when it has been alive half an hour ago and has come out of the pan half a minute ago. And when they had finished, they brought out of the oven a great and gloriously sticky marmalade roll, steaming hot, and after the marmalade roll they each leaned back and had a cup of tea. I swear that these children with sticky faces looked like future kings and queens. And the mere sight of their cozy meal calmed my hunger, as if I had eaten with them.

At another house I heard the hissing and smelled the delicious smell of sausages—real meaty, spicy ones, fat and piping hot and just the tiniest bit burnt. There were great mugs of frothy chocolate on the table, and roast potatoes and roast chestnuts, and baked apples with raisins stuck in where the cores had been, and then ices just to freshen you up after all the hot things.

Next I passed a lavish picnic in a public park. I could smell sides of roasted meat, and there were wheaten cakes and oaten cakes, honey and many-colored sugars and cream as thick as porridge and as smooth as still water, peaches, nectarines, pomegranates, pears, grapes, strawberries, raspberries—pyramids and cataracts of fruit. Then came the wines: dark, thick ones like syrup of mulberry juice, and clear red ones like red jellies liquefied, and yellow wines and green wines and yellowy-green and greenish-yellow.

To save myself, I cannot remember the witty talking I overheard there—plays upon words, plays upon thoughts, paradoxes, fancies, anecdotes, theories laughingly advanced yet (on consideration) well worth taking seriously. There was gay intellectual duel, each side capping the other, each rising above the other, up and up, like birds or airplanes in combat. If only I could remember what they said. For never in my life have I heard such talk—such eloquence, such melody (song could have added nothing to it), such toppling structures of double meaning, such sky-rockets of metaphor and allusion.

Still, something was missing. I left the party and walked on past the center of the city, past very real pubs and shrubs and aged university buildings. I walked over a bridge and up a long hill and round about. Then I saw what I was looking for—a simple stone church. Perhaps in that dim interior, alone, I could find myself. I walked up the time-worn steps, pulled open the door, quickly slipped into a back pew, and picked up a prayer book.

Then I noticed a bulky man kneeling in a front pew. He was the only person I had seen in this land who didn't look at all important. I could tell that, even from his back. He evidently hadn't heard me come in, for he began to speak aloud in a resonant voice.

"And this is the marvel of marvels, that he called me Beloved" he said. Just then the soft glow above the altar became a blinding light and some kind of burning joy, too much for my senses, seemed to explode the building. I think I may have screamed as the brightness pierced me.

\* \* \* \* \*

Instantly only soft lamplight and shadows surrounded me. I was sitting at my desk and the old uncolored photo of C. S. Lewis was before me, and his book was in my hands. The room seemed very small. I was trembling, and I could have cried. But whether from sadness or joy, I cannot say.

## SOURCES

1. *That Hideous Strength* (Macmillan, 1946) p, 385.
2. *Surprised by Joy* (Harcourt Brace, 1955), pp. 11, 149- 50.
3. *That Hideous Strength,* p. 387.
4. *Surprised by Joy,* pp. 72, 118-19, 7, 16.
5. *The Lion, the Witch and the Wardrobe* (Macmillan, 1950), p. 98
6. *The Magician' s Nephew* (Macmillan 1955), p. 26.
7. *Surprised by Joy,* pp. 153, 156, 154.
8. *The Weight of Glory* (Eerdmans, 1965), pp. 14-15.
9. *Lion, Witch and Wardrobe,* pp. 59-61.
10. *The Silver Chair* (Macmillan, 1953), pp. 195-96.
11. *Prince Caspian* (Macmillan, 1951), p. 177.
12. *That Hideous Strength,* pp. 380-81.
13. *The Last Battle* (London. Bodley Head, 1956) p. 167; *The Four Loves* (London: Geoffrey Bles 1960), p. 159; *The Weight of Glory,* pp. 11-14.
14. *That Hideous Strength,* p. 383.

# 5

# WHERE IS THE ANCIENT CITY OF TASHBAAN?

*Six of the seven Chronicles of Narnia are set in a magical land reminiscent of medieval England. But* The Horse and His Boy *is set in a surprisingly different medieval location: Uzbekistan .*

In the world at the back of C. S. Lewis's magic wardrobe, Tashbaan is located on a fruit-growing island in a river at the edge of the great desert between Calormen and Archenland. Dangerous adventures take place there in *The Horse and His Boy.*

In the world on this side of the wardrobe, Tashkent is located on a fruit-growing oasis on the Chirchik River in the midst of one of the largest deserts in the world. It was conquered by Alexander the Great in the fourth century, by Arabs in the eighth century, by Mongols in the thirteenth century, by Russians in the nineteenth century, and by the Soviet Union in the twentieth century. It is the capital of Uzbekistan in Central Asia.

In 1950, when C. S. Lewis wrote *The Horse and His Boy,* Tashkent was populated by about a million Muslim or Communist Uzbeks and Russians; many Koreans lived there also, brought there by Stalin. The native Uzbek people are a mixture of Mongol and Middle Eastern ancestry; thus their skin is light brown and their faces look slightly Asian. Since Uzbekistan became independent in 1991, many Russians able to do so have left, but their language and bureaucracy remain firmly in place although the country is again Islamic with Uzbek its official language. (Uzbek is a branch of the Turkic language family, which spans the Middle East and Central Asia.)

*Tash* is a Uzbek word that means stone, and Lewis used it for the evil god Tash as well as the city of Tashbaan. The great Uzbek hero Amir Timur is called Tamarlane in English; perhaps that is where Lewis got the name of the evil race called Telmarines. The name Aravis might be a variation of Avaris, which was the capital of the Hyksos, a nomadic semitic tribe from around Turkey that ruled Egypt in 1600 B.C. and introduced horse-drawn chariots there.

In Samarkand, Uzbekistan, there is an observatory built by Ulugh Beg circa 1420, and the museum there shows what military clothing and equipment of that era looked like; they reportedly match Pauline Baynes' portrayal of the Calormenes. She is an illustrator who does careful research for the sake of accuracy.

In the nineteenth century the English had taken a great interest in the colorful culture of Central Asia and its history, which helps to explain Lewis's interest in it in the twentieth century. But Lewis had a more immediate reason for his interest. From 1945 to 1948 he had a Middle Eastern student at Oxford named M. A. Manzalaoui, and Lewis supervised his thesis about eighteenth century English translations from Arabic. Lewis evidently re-read the *Arabian Nights* to equip himself for that task and drew on it when he wrote *The Horse and His Boy*. In fact, in 1952 he explained to an inquirer that he had discovered Aslan, the Turkic word for lion, when he was reading about the *Arabian Nights*.

Perhaps Lewis learned that in Northern Syria there is actually a town called Aslan-Tash; it's on the map. (One can imagine a rock formation there that resembles a crouching lion.) In *The Last Battle* the Ape explained, "Tash and Aslan are only two names for you know Who. That's why there can ever be any quarrel between them. Get that into your heads, you stupid brutes. Tash is Aslan: Aslan is Tash." Soon the Ape had changed the name of Aslan to Tashlan.

Lewis would no doubt have been amazed and delighted to hear that forty-five years after he wrote *The Horse and His Boy*, it was actually for sale in Tashkent in Russian translation, along with the rest of the Chronicles. Thus it is that of the two million residents of Tashkent, some have read about a city named Tashbaan in the world at the back of C. S. Lewis's magic wardrobe.

*Note: Thanks to Brad Brenneman for some of this information.*

# 6

# C. S. LEWIS AND CHRISTMAS

*Christmas is the holiday that was a recurring theme in C. S. Lewis's life and thought.*

Our earliest description of Christmas from C. S. Lewis is a bitter one. The year was 1922. As usual, C. S. Lewis and his brother Warren spent the holidays with their widowed father in his big house outside Belfast.

"It was a dark morning with a gale blowing and some very cold rain," Lewis reported in his diary. Their father Albert awakened his two sons, both in their mid-twenties, to go to early Communion service. As they walked to church in the dawn light, they started discussing the time of sunrise. Albert irritated his sons by insisting that the sun had already risen or else they would not have any light. He was an illogical and argumentative man.

Saint Mark's church was intensely cold. Warren wanted to keep his coat on during the service, and his father disapproved. "Well, at least you won't keep it on when you go up to the Table," Albert warned. Warren asked why not and was told that taking Communion with a coat on was "most disrespectful." Warren took his coat off to avoid an argument. Not one of the three Lewis men had any interest in the meaning of Communion. The two sons hadn't believed in Christianity for years.

"Christmas dinner, a rather deplorable ceremony, at quarter to four," Lewis continued in his diary. After dinner the rain had stopped at last, and Albert urged his two sons to take a walk. They were delighted to get out into the fresh air and head for a pub where they could get a drink. Before they came to the pub, however, some relatives drove by on the way to their house for a visit and gave them an unwelcome ride right back home.

After too much sitting and talking and eating and smoking all day in the stuffy house, Lewis went to bed early, dead tired and headachy. He felt like a flabby, lazy teenager again. It had been another bad Christmas.

In 1929 Albert Lewis suddenly died of cancer. There would be no more coming home for Christmas. Within a couple of years of their father's death. both Warren and C. S. Lewis privately made some major shifts in their ideas about religion. They were separately moving toward Christian faith.

It was 1931. In Shanghai, where he was serving as a British military officer, Warren got up at 6:30 on Christmas morning. There was bright sun, frost on the ground, and what Warren called a faint keen wind. For the first time in many years Warren went to church to take Communion. He was deeply excited about it.

Warren couldn't help thinking about the old days when he had attended Christmas Communion at home in Ireland. "The kafuffle of the early start, the hurried walk in the chill half light, Barton's beautiful voice, the dim lights of Saint Mark's and then the return home to the Gargantuan breakfast—how jolly it all seems in retrospect!" It hadn't seemed jolly at the time. Warren felt great sorrow about the past, but his sorrow was outweighed by gladness and thanks that he was once again a believer in the Christmas story.

On that very day, Christmas of 1931, C. S. Lewis sat down in Oxford to write an eight-page letter to Warren. He began by warning that because of his teaching duties he had done, read, and heard nothing for a long time that could possibly interest Warren. Then he proceeded to write one of his usual entertaining letters full of humor and ideas and bits of news. In the middle of the letter he mentioned that it was a foggy afternoon, but that it had seemed spring-like early that morning as he went to the Communion service. That is how he admitted the big news that he had taken Communion for the first time in many years.

At that point in the letter, C. S. Lewis recounted a couple of things he had heard in recent sermons. In a sermon on foreign missions the preacher had said, "Many of us have friends who used to live abroad, and had a native Christian cook who was unsatisfactory.

Well, after all, there are a great many unsatisfactory Christians in England too. In fact I'm one myself." In a different sermon, that preacher had declared that if early Christians had known they were founding an organization to last for centuries, they would have organized it to death. But because they believed that they were making provisional arrangements for a year or so, they left it free to live. Lewis thought that was an interesting idea.

A neighbor had remarked shortly before Christmas that he objected to the early chapters of Luke, especially the story of the Annunciation, because they were *indelicate*. Such prudery left Lewis gasping.

That Christmas letter from C. S. Lewis found its way to Warren on January 19, 1932, and he wrote in his diary, "A letter... today containing the news that he too has once more started to go to Communion, at which I am delighted." Had he not done so, Warren reflected, they would not have been quite so close in the future as in the past.

From 1931 to the end of his life, C. S. Lewis looked at Christmas from a Christian point of view. In 1939 Warren was on duty away from home again, and on Christmas Eve C. S. Lewis wrote that he had been thinking much that week about Christmas cards. Aside from the absurdity of celebrating the nativity at all if you don't believe in the Incarnation, "what in heaven's name is the idea of everyone sending everyone else pictures of stage-coaches, fairies, foxes, dogs, butterflies, kittens, flowers, etc.?"

Warming to his topic, Lewis asked his brother to imagine a Chinese man sitting at a table covered with small pictures. The man explains that he is preparing for the anniversary of Buddha's being protected by the dragons. Not that he personally believes that this is the real anniversary of the event or even that it really happened. He is just keeping up the old custom. Not that he has any pictures of Buddha or of the dragons. He doesn't like that kind. He says, "Here's one of a traction engine for Hu Flung Dung, and I'm sending this study of a napkin-ring to Lo Hung Git, and these jolly ones of bluebottles are for the children."

Aside from thinking about Christmas cards, Lewis had enjoyed himself in two ways that week. He was back at work on his book *The Problem of Pain*, and he was able to enjoy good winter walks. The pond on his property had a thin skin of ice. The beautiful frozen days had been of two kinds: "those with bright yellow suns, turning at sunset to red cannon balls, and those with deep dark-grey fog through which the ridges of the grass loom up white." Near the end of his letter he said, "Well, Brother, (as the troops say) it's a sad business not to have you with me to-morrow morning...." That meant church.

During World War II C. S. Lewis gave a series of talks about Christianity on BBC radio, and later he brought these out as his book *Mere Christianity*. There Lewis summed up Christmas and Christianity in one memorable sentence: "The Son of God became a man to enable men to become the sons of God."

In his 1950 book for children, *The Lion, the Witch and the Wardrobe,* Lewis made it clear that he was all for merry times and good gifts and Christmas pudding. The land of Narnia was under the spell of a wicked white witch who made it always winter and never Christmas. When the great gold lion Aslan brought the thaw that spelled her doom, Father Christmas came at last.

In 1954 Lewis published a very different kind of fantasy about Christmas, "Xmas and Christmas." It is an essay about the strange island called Niatirb (Britain spelled backwards) and the winter festival called Exmas that the Niatirbians observe with great patience and endurance.

One of the customs that fills the marketplace with crowds during the foggiest and rainiest season of the year is the great labor and weariness of sending cards and gifts. Every citizen has to guess the value of the gift that every friend will send him so that he may send one of equal value whether he can afford it or not. Everyone becomes so pale and weary that it looks as if calamity has struck. These days are called the Exmas *Rush*. Exhausted with the *Rush*, most citizens lie in bed until noon on the day of the festival. Later that day they eat far too much and get intoxicated. On the day after Exmas they are very grave because they feel unwell and begin to calculate how much they have spent on Exmas and the *Rush*.

There is also a festival in Niatirb called Crissmas, held on the same day as Exmas. A few people in Niatirb keep Crissmas sacred, but they are greatly distracted by Exmas and the *Rush*.

On December 17, 1955, Lewis wrote to an old friend that he was pleased by the card the man had sent him, a Japanese-style nativity scene. But, he continued, Christmas cards in general and the whole vast commercial drive called "Xmas" was one of his pet abominations. He wished they would die away and leave the Christmas observance alone. He had nothing against secular festivities. But he despised the artificial jollity, the artificial childlikeness, and the attempts to keep up some shallow connection with the birth of Christ.

In 1957 C. S. Lewis published "What Christmas Means to Me." He claimed that three things go by the name of Christmas. First is the religious festival. Second is an occasion for merry making and hospitality. Third is the commercial racket, a modern invention to boost sales. He listed his reasons for condemning the commercial racket. First, it causes more pain than pleasure. Second, it is a trap made up of obligations. Third, many of the purchases are gaudy rubbish. Fourth, we get exhausted by having to support the commercial racket while carrying on all our regular duties as well. "Can it really be my duty to buy and receive masses of junk every winter...?" Lewis demanded plaintively.

Two years later C. S. Lewis was featured in the Christmas issue of the *Saturday Evening Post*. The issue, dated December 19, 1959, bore on its cover a 15-cent price, a picture of a man struggling clumsily to get a package wrapped, and the announcement of a new Screwtape letter by C. S. Lewis. Inside was a life-size, close-up photo of Lewis's face and his essay "Screwtape Proposes a Toast." This was a kind of Christmas gift to the public from the editors.

In 1963 the *Saturday Evening Post* featured C. S. Lewis in its Christmas issue for the second time. This time the price on the cover was 20 cents and the picture on the cover was of a children's choir. Inside was Lewis's article "We Have No 'Right to Happiness'" with the heading "Is happiness—in particular sexual happiness—one of man's inalienable rights? A distinguished author attacks the brutality of this increasingly common notion." In the upper right-hand corner is the announcement, "As this article went to press, its author died at his home in Oxford, England. The article is his last work."

Since Lewis's death on November 22, 1963, a number of his writings from earlier years have become more widely available. A few not published at all in his lifetime have now found their way into print. One of these is his undated poem "The Nativity," available in his book *Poems*. In this brief poem Lewis shows what the nativity scene meant in his own prayer life.

First, Lewis likens himself to a slow, dull ox. Along with the oxen he sees the glory growing in the stable, he says, and he hopes that it will give him, at length, an ox's strength. Second, Lewis likens himself to a stubborn and foolish ass. Along with the asses he sees the Savior in the hay, and he hopes that he will learn the patience of an ass. Third, Lewis likens himself to a strayed and bleating sheep. Along with the sheep in the stable he watches his Lord lying in the manger. From his Lord he hopes to gain some of a sheep's woolly innocence.

One of the earliest photos of C. S. Lewis shows him as a very little boy posed with a Father Christmas doll. The half-smile caught forever on his plump young face seems balanced between anxiety and pleasure. He looks thoughtfully attentive. It is fitting, because he half smiled at Christmas the rest of his days. We might do well to pause in the "kafuffle" and "Exmas *Rush*" and look into the manger with C. S. Lewis.

# 7

# ALL OR NOTHING:
# A NEWLY DISCOVERED LEWIS ESSAY

*Unlikely as it sounds, in the year 2000 Perry Bramlett came across an old book that contained an essay by C. S. Lewis that had never been discovered before. Lewis had been dead for thirty-seven years, and the essays published in his lifetime had been painstakingly sought out and gathered and entered in his bibliography. (If this essay had come to light soon enough, it would have fit perfectly in the collection* God in the Dock.)

In 1943, in the midst of World War II, an Anglican priest named James Patrick Stevenson obtained thirty-four brief essays about Christianity from a variety of military chaplains, priests, ministers, and at least one layman, C. S. Lewis. (Lewis's essay had already appeared in an obscure publication named *Think.*) Stevenson's collection was aimed at servicemen, and it was published in 1944 by the Society for the Promotion of Christian Knowledge (SPCK). The austere wartime dustjacket was tan, but the binding was bright red and essays were excellent. C. S. Lewis's was ninth in the book and among the briefest of the lot. It is apparently the most evangelical essay that Lewis ever wrote, and it may be a sample of the talks he gave to servicemen during the war. It can't be published here because of copyright restrictions, but it can be closely paraphrased.

Some people say that religion doesn't appeal to them; in fact, a girl I knew at one time said that religion is all right if it doesn't go too far. People like that assume that religion resembles football or music in that it interests some of us and not others, and it's appropriate to be only moderately interested in it. But more mature thinkers realize that this is poppycock.

Christianity isn't an avocation or a tonic. It claims that there is a God, that humankind is damaged, that God became a human, that this human alone can repair all other humans, and that those who aren't repaired will go into the trashcan. If these claims are true, they are of importance to no one. It's either nothing at all or infinitude. The Christianity wire is either dead or alive with an unlimited amount of electrical current. It's impossible for Christianity to be fairly important.

This God does not desire some particular thing from you; he wants all there is of you. And that's understandable because he created you and became a human to repair you. (Think of your becoming a cow for a long time.) It is God who gives you life hour by hour. Every second you count your own is really a gift from him. He owns you and wants you for his own, but there are enemies of his and yours that want you also. You must belong either to him or to them; there is no middle ground in this war. If you don't choose to be on God's side, the enemy will have you.

Some people think that because our world is such a small spot in the cosmos it couldn't be important to God. But a small spot can be of great importance in a war; Stalingrad is a small spot on a world map. So we are asking you to join God's side completely and immediately. Wherever you are, tell God right now that you are reporting for duty. I'm convinced that if you do this sincerely you won't ever regret it. (On the other hand, most people who don't join God's side come to feel slightly uncertain that their choice was correct.)

Many good people are not Christians, but many good people get the wrong train. The trains may look alike, no matter where they are going, and they may seem to be going in the same direction for quite a while. But they won't end up taking you to the same destination. And it's the destination that matters.

# HIDDEN CONNECTIONS

# 8

# C. S. LEWIS'S ANTI-ANTI-SEMITISM IN *THE GREAT DIVORCE*

*When I had tea with C. S. Lewis and told him my favorite book of his was probably* The Great Divorce, *he beamed with approval and called it his Cinderella. What I didn't realize then was that hidden in his Cinderella was an attack on anti-Semitism.*

Ꮖn 1933, the year Hitler was elected chancellor of Germany, Lewis published his allegorical *Pilgrim's Regress*. There he warned of a tribe of black-shirted dwarfs named the Swastici, who were vassals to a bloodthirsty northern tyrant named Savage.

On November 5, 1933, Lewis wrote to his friend Arthur Greeves, "...nothing can fully excuse the iniquity of Hitler's persecution of the Jews, or the absurdity of his theoretical position. Did you see that he said 'The Jews have made *no contribution to human culture* and in crushing them I am doing the *will of the Lord*.' Now as the whole idea of the 'Will of the Lord' is precisely what the world owes to the Jews, the blaspheming tyrant has just fixed his absurdity for all to see in a single sentence, and shown that he is as contemptible for his stupidity as he is detestable for his cruelty. For the German people as a whole we ought to have charity; but for dictators, 'Nordic' tyrants and so on— well, read the chapter about Mr. Savage in the *Regress* and you have my views."

(Readers of the collected letters of Lewis's friend J. R. R. Tolkien find that on July 25, 1938, he wrote a defiant letter to his German publisher when asked about his racial heritage. "But if I am to understand that you are enquiring whether I am of Jewish origin, I

can only reply that I regret that I appear to have no ancestors of that
gifted people.")

One evening after the fall of France in June, 1940—when the
invasion of England seemed imminent—Lewis and some of his friends
were thinking of passages in their writings that could mark them for
elimination under Nazi occupation. Lewis recalled ominously his
subhuman dwarfs in black shirts called the Swastici. As Robert Havard
put it later, that was not their happiest evening.

On April 15, 1944, Lewis published his little-known essay "What
France Means to You" (a response in French to that question) in the
journal *La France Libre*. His brief essay is, in my opinion, a
masterpiece of ironic discretion and double meaning. When he speaks
of the "worst cancers of the modern world" taking up residence in
France, and "the idol of Stupidity" being raised in what used to be
the country of Reason, he is overtly referring to modern decadence;
but in my opinion he is also tacitly referring to Nazism. After all,
when he wrote this the liberation of France had not yet begun.

On November 10, 1944, C. S. Lewis published the first chapter of
his serial novel "Who Goes Home?" in a national church-related
newspaper called the *Guardian*. The story ran, chapter by chapter,
until mid-April, 1945; and shortly thereafter it was released as the
book Lewis called his Cinderella, *The Great Divorce*. In that story
Lewis finds himself in a desolate grey city (hell) waiting for a bus that
is headed for the outskirts of heaven. The second person Lewis meets
on the bus is an intelligent-looking businessman in a round bowler
hat. Anyone who has read Lewis's 1927 "Easley fragment" would recognize this accidental traveling companion of 1944 as a new version
of Lewis's (Dr. Easley's) accidental travelling companion of 1927;
both are outgoing, greedy, materialistic businessmen who wear round
bowler hats. But the encounter in the Easley fragment takes place on
a boat, and that companion is an Ulster Irishman; the encounter in
*The Great Divorce* takes place on a bus, and that companion is a Jew.

Almost everyone overlooks Lewis's single clue that "the Intelligent
Man" (called that in chapters 2 and 6) is a Jew. This clue is the fact
that the Big Man, a spiteful fellow-traveller, calls the Intelligent Man
"Ikey" (a term of insult derived from the name Isaac). Needless to
say, Lewis is expressing for alert readers his opinion of anti-Semitism;
the anti-Semite ("the Big Man") has already proved himself an ob-

noxious and violent bully. Nevertheless, the fact that Lewis's Intelligent Man fits a negative Jewish stereotype will concern some readers in the era of Political Correctness. (In *Reflections on the Psalms* Lewis mentions the roots of this common stereotype: "For us the very name Jew is associated with finance, shop-keeping, money-lending and the like. This however, dates from the Middle Ages when the Jews were not allowed to own land and were driven into occupations remote from the soil. Whatever characteristics the modern Jew has acquired from millenia of such occupations, they cannot have been those of his ancient ancestors. Those were peasants or farmers.")

*The Great Divorce* is C. S. Lewis's miniature replica of Dante's *Divine Comedy*, and in chapters 12 and 13 of *The Great Divorce* he presents his transcendently beautiful version of Dante's Beatrice. This Lady radiates the joy and splendor of heaven, and many readers find her the loveliest of all Lewis's fictional characters. But to his surprise Lewis learns that on earth she was no famous saint. His mentor George MacDonald tells him "Her name on earth was Sarah Smith and she lived at Golders Green." Most readers naturally assume that this information has no particular significance; Sarah Smith is an ordinary name, and Golders Green is an ordinary section of London. (On 26 November 1942, Lewis preached his sermon "Miracles" at St. Jude on the Hill Church in Golders Green.)

But according to James O'Fee of Belfast, "London is a city of villages—Southall is Asian, Notting Hill is mainly black, Camden is largely Irish. Thirty years ago I lived in London, and I had a university friend of Jewish background from Hendon in North London, close to Golders Green. The Jews themselves would joke about Golders Green and its Jewishness. [According to a Jewish friend who is aware of the usage of Lewis's day, they sometimes called it Goldberg's Green.] England had small Jewish communities for centuries, but the great wave of Jewish immigrants from Eastern Europe arrived before the First World War, and many settled in the East End of London. By 1944, when Lewis wrote *The Great Divorce*, the Jewish character of Golders Green would have been established." Why, O'Fee asked, did Lewis have Sarah Smith come from Golders Green? Was it a gaffe on his part, or was it deliberate?

Just as Ikey is the only nickname used in *The Great Divorce*, Golders Green is the only location used in *The Great Divorce*. And just

as Ikey indicates Jewishness, so Golders Green indicates Jewishness. I
propose that beautiful, saintly Sarah Smith (Abraham's wife Sarah was
the mother of Isaac and foremother of the Jews) is in fact a foil to
Ikey, the stereotypically greedy Jewish businessman—and the strong-
est possible rebuke to anti-Semitism.

In the reader's last glimpse of Sarah Smith, Bright Spirits are
celebrating her in a 172-word song that echoes Psalm 91. (The
similarity to this particular Psalm was pointed out to me by Joshua
Pong of Hong Kong.)

> The happy Trinity is her home; nothing can trouble her joy....
> The invisible germ will not harm her: nor yet the glittering
>    sunstroke.
> A thousand fail to solve the problem, ten thousand choose
>    the wrong turning: but she passes safely through....
> She may walk among Lions and rattlesnakes: among dinosaurs
>    and nurseries of lionets.
> He fills her brim full of the immensity of life: he leads her to
>    see the world's desire.

How is it that a Jewish woman is celebrated in heaven in a
paraphrase of Psalm 91 that incorporates the Christian Trinity? I
assumed that her felicity there might simply echo that of Pipheus in
Dante's *Divine Comedy* and foreshadow Emeth's in Lewis's *Last Battle*.

I ended my first draft of this essay with the following statement:
"C. S. Lewis's life was itself a kind of rebuke to anti-Semitism. Twelve
years after publishing *The Great Divorce*, he married Joy Davidman
Gresham, an ethnic Jew from New York city."

Joe Christopher (of Texas) read the first draft and added his own
idea that Lewis might have conceived of Sarah Smith as a converted
Jew. He pointed out that two years before their marriage, Joy
published *Smoke on the Mountain* and Lewis wrote the preface.
Obviously referring to Joy herself, he said "In a sense the coverted
Jew is the only normal human being in the world. To him, in the first
instance, the promises were made, and he has availed himself of them.
He calls Abraham his father by hereditary right as well as by divine
courtesy....Everyone else is, from one point of view, a special case,
dealt with under emergency regulations." Perhaps Lewis had his

fictitious Sarah Smith in mind along with his friend Joy when he wrote that.

And perhaps Lewis had Sarah Smith in mind again when Joy died. We know he had her predecessor in mind, because in the last line of *A Grief Observed*, he quoted in Italian the last thing Dante said about Beatrice in the *Divine Comedy*: "She turned from me to the eternal fountain."

# 9

# C. S. LEWIS AND DANTE'S *PARADISE*

*One of C. S. Lewis's favorite works of literature was* The Divine Comedy, *but even he may not have been consciously aware of all it meant to him.*

The strong influence of Dante's *Paradise* in the life and writing of C. S. Lewis has gone almost unnoticed until now.

## I. Dante's *Paradise* in the Life of C. S. Lewis

C. S. Lewis read Dante's *Inferno* in Italian when he was in his teens, and he read Dante's *Purgatory* in the hospital when he was recovering from wounds he received in the inferno of World War One. When he was twenty-three he mentioned in his diary that he disbelieved in immortality and that Dante's "facts" were outdated. (At that time his brother Warren was reading Dante.) Six years later, in the spring of 1929, Lewis reluctantly decided that there is a God; but he did not yet believe in Christianity or an afterlife.

At the beginning of January in 1930 C. S. Lewis visited his friend Owen Barfield for a few days, and the two did "some solid reading together." After lunch they would take a walk, then read Dante's *Paradise* (in Italian) the rest of the day.

Afterward, Lewis described this experience to his friend Arthur Greeves: "[*Paradise*] has really opened a new world to me. I don't know whether it is really very different from the *Inferno* (B. says it is as different as chalk from cheese—heaven from hell, would be more appropriate!) or whether I was specially receptive, but it certainly seemed to me that I had never seen at all what Dante was like before. Unfortunately, the impression is one so unlike anything else that I can hardly describe it for your benefit—a sort of mixture of intense, even crabbed, complexity of language and thought with (what seems impossible) *at the very same time* a feeling of spacious gliding movement, like a slow dance, or like flying. It is like the stars—endless mathematical subtility of orb, cycle, epicycle and ecliptic, unthinkable & unpicturable yet at the same time the freedom and liquidity of empty space and the triumphant certainty of movement. I should describe it as feeling more *important* than any poetry I have ever read."

Lewis suggested that Greeves might try it in English translation, but warned him "If you do, I think the great point is to *give up any idea* of reading it in long stretches... instead, read a small daily portion, in rather a liturgical manner, letting the images and the purely intellectual conceptions sink well into the mind.... It is not really like any of the things we know."

Six months later, Lewis told Greeves he had visited Barfield again and they had finished *Paradise*. "I think it reaches heights of poetry which you get nowhere else; an ether almost too fine to breathe. It is a pity I can give you no notion what it is like. Can you imagine Shelley at his most ecstatic combined with Milton at his most solemn & rigid? It sounds impossible I know, but that is what Dante has done."

The year after he first read *Paradise*, C. S. Lewis became a believing Christian, and he was clearly influenced by Dante for the rest of his life. There are traces of *The Divine Comedy* throughout his writing, from *The Pilgrim's Regress*, his first Christian book, to *Letters to Malcolm*, his last.

## II. Dante's *Paradise* in the Writings of C. S. Lewis

### The Pilgrim's Regress

C. S. Lewis became a believing Christian in 1931, wrote *The Pilgrim's Regress* in 1932, and published it in 1933. Early in this allegory a man named John awakens in a wood and realizes that he wants out. After an adventurous journey in which he learns many lessons, he approaches at last the true object of his deepest desire. That is not an original plot outline; it is the outline of Dante's *Divine Comedy*.

In Book 10, chapter 3 of *Regress* Lewis included his perfect triolet quoting Canto 2 of *Inferno,* "God in his mercy made," then summarizing the second stanza over the gate to Hell.[1] There is also a specific allusion to *Paradise* within *Pilgrim's Regress,* and it is highly significant. In Book 9, chapter 1, of *Regress,* the sleeping pilgrim is awakened by the light of a woman who introduces herself as Contemplation and says "Rise and come with me." They travel far through the air together in a sphere of light that is finally swallowed up in an ocean of light (reminiscent of the ocean of light in *Paradise*). There light runs down like a river too bright to look at, and it sings with a very loud voice. Many people are traveling with them with happiness on their faces, moving together toward great castle gates at the summit. This journey is obviously composed of images from *Paradise*.

In *Regress* the journey with Contemplation is only a dream, and the pilgrim awakens to his old terror of death; his real arrival at his destination comes a bit later in the story, in Book 10. Thus Lewis's allegorical dream journey with Contemplation is a thinly veiled account of his contemplative foretaste of Christian faith in 1931 when he read *Paradise*. (Hence, Lewis is allegorizing Dante's allegory.)

## *Out of the Silent Planet*

C. S. Lewis published his first novel, a tale of space travel, in 1938. He apparently had both the beginning of Psalm 19 and the beginning of Canto 27 of *Paradise* in mind when he described the heavens in the fifth chapter of *Out of the Silent Planet*: "He [Ransom] had read of 'Space': at the back of his thinking for years had lurked the dismal fancy of the black, cold vacuity, the utter deadness, which was supposed to separate the worlds. He had not known how much it affected him till now—now that the very name 'Space' seemed a blasphemous libel for this empyrean ocean of radiance in which they

---

[1] Visiting Hell, Beatrice told Virgil, "God in his mercy made me so that your misery does not touch me, and the flame here does not burn me."

swam. He could not call it 'dead'; he felt life pouring into him from it every moment. He had thought it barren: he saw now that it was the womb of the worlds, whose blazing and innumerable offspring looked down nightly even upon the earth with many eyes... Older thinkers had been wiser when they named it simply the heavens—the heavens which declared the glory..."

This eyewitness account by Ransom agrees with the eyewitness account by Dante in Canto 27: "All Paradise began to ring with the sweet strain 'Glory be to the Father, to the Son, and to the Holy Spirit!'—which intoxicated me. I seemed to see the entire universe smile, and I was enraptured by both sound and sight. O joy! O indescribable ecstasy! O life of perfect love and peace! O endless unlimited riches!" Dante was consciously portraying Psalm19:1, "The heavens declare the glory of God; the skies proclaim the work of his hands," and C. S. Lewis would have realized that.

In 1931 Lewis had written to Arthur Greeves, "I think [*Paradise*] reaches heights of poetry which you get nowhere else." In 1938 he published *Out of the Silent Planet*. And in 1958 he published *Reflections on the Psalms*, where he said of Psalm 19, "I take this to be the greatest poem in the Psalter and one of the greatest lyrics in the world."

## The Problem of Pain

The final chapter in Lewis's first book of straightforward Christian apologetics, *The Problem of Pain* (1940), is also the first of his evocative descriptions of Heaven. There he wrote of "that something which you were born desiring": "All the things that have ever deeply possessed your soul have been but hints of it—tantalizing glimpses, promises never quite fulfilled, echoes that died away just as they caught your ear. But if it should ever really become manifest—if there ever came an echo that did not die away but swelled to the sound itself—you would know it. Beyond all possibility of doubt you would say 'Here at last is the thing I was made for'."

From Canto 1 to Canto 33 of *Paradise*, that promise was Dante's theme. In Canto 33 Dante said "Anyone who sees that Light becomes a person who would not possibly consent to turn away to any other sight; for the good that is the object of all desires is ingathered there in its fullness, and elsewhere it falls short of its perfection."

## "The Weight of Glory"

C. S. Lewis delivered his famous sermon "The Weight of Glory" in 1941, eleven years after first reading *Paradise*; and "The Weight of Glory" is like a vivid summary of Dante's most important points in *Paradise*. Lewis stresses that God wants us to strongly desire our own blessedness, glory and joy. The sermon is obviously based on Corinthians 4:17, "For this slight momentary affliction is preparing for us an eternal weight of glory beyond all comparison..."

Lewis explains at length the nature of our personal glory in Heaven. "I suddenly remembered that no one can enter heaven except as a child; and nothing is so obvious in a child—not in a conceited child, but in a good child—as its great and undisguised pleasure in being praised. Not only in a child, either, but even in a dog or a horse.... Perfect humility dispenses with modesty." Dante clearly demonstrated this humility in Canto 24 after being quizzed by St. Peter about faith. "Like a master who embraces his servant as soon as he hears good news that causes him to rejoice, so the light of that apostle at whose command I had spoken circled me three times, blessing me in song. That is how much my answer pleased him." Like a child, Dante was happy that St. Peter glorified him with song and dance in response to his correct answers.

Lewis warns that it may be possible to think too much of one's future glory in Heaven, but it is hardly possible to think too often or too deeply of the future glory of other people ("everlasting splendours"). "The load, or weight, or burden of my neighbour's glory should be laid daily on my back, a load so heavy that only humility can carry it, and the backs of the proud will be broken." This is like Dante's initial reaction to Peter and James in Canto 25. There James told Dante "Look up and be confident, for it befits anyone who ascends here from the mortal world to ripen in our radiance." As Dante told it, "This comforting word from the second flame caused me to lift my head up toward the mountains that had bent me down with their great weight." This mountain image is an allusion to Psalm 120:1, "I will lift up my eyes to the mountains, the source of my help." Peter and James were the mountains Dante was looking to for help, but he was in such awe of their radiant majesty that he had bent his head as if the weight of their light was more than he could bear.

(In Lewis's 1948 essay "Imagery in the Last Eleven Cantos of Dante's 'Comedy'" he says, "...the weight of the mountains (or of the Apostles, for they are momentarily one) which weighs upon the soul is equated with the actual weight which bends the bearer double." He continues, "...how immensely venerable the Apostles have become first by the mountain image and then by the image of weight which, as it were, grows from it. No direct praise of their wisdom or sanctity could have made us respect them half so much.")

In the last paragraph of "The Weight of Glory" Lewis concludes that we should conduct all our earthly relationships with awe and circumspection. "There are no *ordinary* people. You have never talked to a mere mortal. Nations, cultures, arts, civilization—these are mortal, and their life is to ours as the life of a gnat. But it is immortals whom we joke with, work with, marry, snub, and exploit—immortal horrors or everlasting splendours." In *The Divine Comedy* Dante showed how awesome all people really are. In *Inferno* they were immortal horrors, and in *Paradise* they were everlasting splendours. (In *Paradise* people who had been competitors or opponents on earth rejoiced with each other. One example of this is the heavenly relationship of Aquinas and Siger of Brabant in Canto 10.)

Lewis's single main point in "The Weight of Glory" is that we are born with a longing for heaven, but that we tend to misinterpret it. "Now, if we are made for heaven, the desire for our proper place will be already in us, but not yet attached to the true object, and will even appear as the rival of that object." He elaborates, "If a transpersonal, transfinite good is our real destiny, then any other good on which our desire fixes must be in some degree fallacious, must bear at best only a symbolical relationship to what will truly satisfy." In the third sentence of *Paradise* Dante referred to our awareness approaching "the object of its deepest desire," and later in Canto 1 Beatrice explained that our true desire is often "wrenched aside to earth by some fallacious pleasure."

Lewis tries to imagine what it will be like to reach the true object of our deepest desire. "What would it be to taste at the fountain-head that stream of which even these lower reaches prove so intoxicating? Yet that, I believe, is what lies before us. The whole man is to drink joy from the fountain of joy." Dante wrote all of *Paradise* to say that.

## Perelandra

C. S. Lewis published his second space-travel novel, *Perelandra*, in 1943. In a note at the end of her essay "Dante's Vision of Heaven" Barbara Reynolds states, "C. S. Lewis, who knew Dante's poem well, has used the concept of the Great Dance of the universe in the last chapter of *Perelandra*, which is in fact a descant upon *Paradise*." The Great Dance of the Universe was epitomized by Dante in Canto 28: "In the two next-to-last rings of dancers Principalities and Archangels whirl; and the last is made up of Angels frolicking."

## The Great Divorce

Lewis's *Great Divorce* (1945) is a profound little fantasy about a bus trip to the outskirts of Heaven. (Lewis told an inquirer that the busdriver is the same angel that descended in *Inferno* to help Dante on his way.)

In *The Great Divorce* a resident of Heaven, George MacDonald, assures Lewis that visitors from Hell to Heaven can stay if they want to. "Aye. Ye'll have heard that the emperor Trajan did." Readers of *Paradise* would have heard so. In Canto 10 of *Purgatory* Dante recounted the kindness of the pagan emperor Trajan to a widow, and in Canto 20 of *Paradise* he located Trajan in Heaven: "...the one closest to the beak consoled the widow for her son. Now he knows from his experience of this sweet life and its opposite the price of not following Christ." (According to a medieval tradition, after Trajan spent time in Hell he had a chance to enter Heaven and did so.)

In addition to surprises about who gets into Heaven, according to Lewis and Dante, there will be surprises about the ranking in Heaven. In *The Great Divorce* Lewis describes a woman named Sarah Smith who had no high position or prominence in her first life. In Heaven she is a great saint: "Love shone not from her face only, but from all her limbs, as if it were some liquid in which she had just been bathing." She is brisk, beneficent, and free from sentimentality. Likewise, on earth Beatrice had no high position or prominence, but in heaven her face was indescribably radiant with love. In Canto 31 she was seated forever in the third highest row; "if you look up at the third row from the top you will see her again, on the throne her merit reserved for her."

## Till We Have Faces

At the end of C. S. Lewis's finest novel, *Till We Have Faces* (1956), Orual says "I know now, Lord, why you utter no answer. You are youself the answer. Before your face questions die away. What other answer would suffice?" Although she did not get the kind of explanation of God's justice she sought, her real underlying question was answered. (In my opinion, that question was "God, are you good? Do you love us? Can I trust you?" The answer was a resounding yes.)

In Canto 19 of *Paradise*, Dante was deeply concerned about the fate of virtuous unbelievers. The eagle rebuked him; "Who are you to sit in a judgment seat a thousand miles away when you can't see farther than a handbreadth?.... O earthly animals! O doltish minds! The Primal Will, goodness itself, never deviates from itself, which is Supreme Good. All that is just harmonizes with it; it does not approximate any created good, but gives rise to that good by beaming forth its rays."

When Dante wrote Canto 19 of *Paradise* he was consciously echoing the crux of the book of Job, and when Lewis wrote *Till We Have Faces* he was consciously echoing both Job and *Paradise*. In all three accounts, the answer to rational human questions about divine justice is a transrational revelation of the wisdom and goodness of God.

## The Last Battle

In 1956 Lewis published his seventh Narnian Chronicle, *The Last Battle*. There a virtuous pagan soldier named Emeth dies bravely and awakens to find himself in Heaven with the very God he has been taught to oppose. In my opinion, Lewis had in mind Dante's claim in Canto 20 of *Paradise* that a virtuous pagan soldier named Ripheus was taken to Heaven, saved by God's inscrutable grace.

At the end of *The Last Battle* the children are in Heaven and one of them says, "I see... world within world, Narnia within Narnia... " "'Yes,' said Mr. Tumnus, 'like an onion: except that as you go in and in, each circle is larger than the last.'" Perhaps Lewis has in mind Canto 28 of *Paradise*, where Dante discovered that each of the nine concentric spheres was larger than the sphere enclosing it, and the Point in the very center enwrapped them all.

### "A Panegyric for Dorothy L. Sayers"

Dorothy Sayers died in December 1957, and C. S. Lewis wrote a tribute to be read at her memorial service in January 1958. In it he said, "She died instead; went, as one may in all humility hope, to learn more of Heaven than even the *Paradiso* could tell her."

### A Grief Observed

After the death of C. S. Lewis's wife in 1960, he kept a heartwrenching journal that he published under the title *A Grief Observed*. The last paragraph ends with a sentence from *Paradise*: "How wicked it would be, if we could, to call the dead back! She said not to me but to the chaplain, 'I am at peace with God.' She smiled, but not at me. *Poi si tornó all' eterna fontana.*" This is from Canto 31, where Dante described Beatrice looking at him for the last time in *Paradise*: "So I prayed; and as distant as she was, she smiled and gazed at me. Then she turned back to the Eternal Fountain."

### Letters to Malcolm

In C. S. Lewis's last book, *Letters to Malcolm* (1964), he is still referring to Dante's *Paradise*. He reflects "But when Dante saw the great apostles in heaven they affected him like *mountains*. There's lots to be said against devotions to saints; but at least they keep on reminding us that we are very small people compared to them. How much smaller before their Master?" Here Lewis also connects the crushing weight of the mountains' light with the intolerable weight on the backs of the proud on the First Terrace of Mount Purgatory (see Canto 13 of *Purgatory*). There Dante feared that his own back would be bent double someday because of pride, his besetting sin. In my opinion, the comforting words of St. James in Canto 25 of *Paradise* were an assurance to Dante that his pride had been replaced by humility, obviating his need to be cleansed of pride after death. Like Dante, Lewis considered pride to be his own setting sin.

(In Lewis's 1948 essay "Imagery in the Last Eleven Cantos of Dante's 'Comedy'" he says, "...the weight of the mountains (or of the Apostles, for they are momentarily one) which weighs upon the soul is equated with the actual weight which bends the bearer double." He continues, "...how immensely venerable the Apostles have become first by the mountain image and then by the image of weight which, as it were, grows from it. No direct praise of their wisdom or sanctity could have made us respect them half so much.")

In additon to Lewis's overt reference to Dante's *Paradise* in *Letters to Malcolm,* there are at least five specific correspondences between the two books that may or may not be significant:

(1) In chapter 13 Lewis describes the paradoxical nature of grace in an untitled poem about prayer. (Lewis's version of this poem does not appear in his posthumous poetry collection.) The first kind of grace is God's actively reaching out to His beloved creature, and the second kind of grace is God's helping the beloved creature to reach back. In Canto 20 of *Paradise* Dante made a fleeting reference to these two kinds of grace in explaining the salvation of Ripheus: "[Ripheus], by the grace that wells up from such a deep spring that no created eye has ever plumbed the depths of its source, set all his love below on righteousness; and therefore, by grace on grace, God let him see our future redemption."

(2) Lewis observes, "God is not in space, but space is in God." Dante made this concept famous by depicting it in Cantos 28-30 of *Paradise*. In Canto 30 he referred to God as "the Point... which seems to be enclosed by what It encloses."

(3) Lewis says, "Joy is the serious business of Heaven." Dante's entire *Paradise* is a mounting crescendo of that joy. In Canto 31 Dante declared, "And even if I had a wealth of words and an imagination to match, I would not endeavor to describe the smallest part of that delight."

(4) Lewis claims, "The angels never knew (from within) the meaning of the word *ought*, and the blessed dead have long since gladly forgotten it." Dante's final sentence in *Paradise* (and the entire *Comedy*) ends with "but my desire and will were being turned already, like a wheel in perfect balance, by the Love that moves the sun and other stars." In Heaven Dante's desire and will were miraculously conformed to the will of God.

(5) C. S. Lewis speculates about time and timelessness in heaven: "I certainly believe that to be God is to enjoy an infinite present, where nothing has yet passed away and nothing is still to come. Does it follow that we can say the same of saints and angels? Or at any rate exactly the same? The dead might experience a time which is not so

linear as ours—it might, so to speak, have thickness as well as length. Already in this life we get some thickness whenever we learn to attend to more than one thing at once. One can suppose this increased to any extent, so that though, for them as for us, the present is always becoming the past, yet each present contains unimaginably more than ours. I feel... that to make the life of the blessed dead strictly timeless is inconsistent with the resurrection of the body." Although Dante describes Heaven as beyond time and space, his saints there seem to experience time. In Canto 32 St. Bernard says to Dante, "But since the time for your vision grows short, let us stop here, like a careful tailor who cuts out a garment according to the amount of cloth he has..."

There is one more rather poignant connection between *Letters to Malcolm* and *Paradise* that I have noticed. Just as Dante died before there was time for *Paradise* to be copied and read, C. S. Lewis died before there was time for *Letters to Malcolm* to be published and read. Both books were completed when their authors were unaware that they were on the very brink of the eternity they were both describing.

# 10

## Spring in Purgatory
## Dante, Botticelli, C. S. Lewis,
## and a Lost Masterpiece

*C. S. Lewis would have been greatly surprised and delighted to learn of the hidden connection between two of his favorites— Dante and Botticelli. And he would have been amused by the fact that the discovery was made by someone he had met and encouraged.*

For slightly over five hundred years, the most famous and popular illustration of Dante's *Divine Comedy* has remained effectively "lost"—although millions have seen it and admired it. It is right out in plain sight and one of the world's most beloved paintings.[1]

### Botticelli's "Primavera"

C. S. Lewis first read Dante's *Inferno* at some unknown date in his youth. He first read *Purgatory* in 1918, when he was nineteen and found himself in a hospital recovering from wounds received in the inferno of World War One. He was an atheist.

Four years later, in 1922, Lewis had just received his B. A. at Oxford and was ready to start the graduate studies that would eventually culminate in a professorship of Medieval and Renaissance

---

[1] About 30 illuminated manuscripts of *The Divine Comedy* and some superb frescos have survived from the 1300s and 1400s, but not one of their sometimes exquisite depictions has ever been widely known and warmly loved by the general public. See *Illustrations to Dante's Inferno* by Eugene Paul Nassar (Cranbury, New Jersey: Associated University Presses, 1994).

Literature. Fortunately, in August he started to keep a diary, and he wryly recorded an experience he had on August 28 in London:

> I took the desperate resolve of entering the National Gallery, where I finally came to the conclusion that I have no taste for painting. I could make nothing of the Titians. The only thing (besides portraits) that I cared for much were Botticelli's Mars and Venus with satyrs, and Veronese's... "Unfaithfulness" in which I liked the *design* tho' I confess the actual figures always seem dull to me. However, the Italian rooms are nothing like so boring as the English.[2]

Although Lewis eventually appreciated Titian,[3] he never took any great interest in paintings; but his early affinity for Botticelli continued for the rest of his life. He commented upon Botticelli paintings (specifically "Mars and Venus" and "Primavera") in *The Allegory of Love, Rehabilitations, English Literature in the Sixteenth Century, An Experiment in Criticism, Studies in Medieval and Renaissance Literature,* and *Spenser's Images of Life.*

Eight years after Lewis's first recorded encounter with Botticelli, he first read Dante's *Paradise*; he was thirty years old and on the brink of belief in Christianity. In 1931 he became a believer. From then on, there are traces of *The Divine Comedy* throughout his writings, from *The Pilgrim's Regress,* his first Christian book, to *Letters to Malcolm,* his last.[4] Lewis twice presented papers at meetings of the Oxford Dante Society, and one of those papers was devoted to an aspect of the last twelve cantos of *Purgatory*.[5] So there is no doubt that Lewis would have been keenly interested in the following discovery related to the last four cantos of *Purgatory.*

Sandro Botticelli painted "Primavera" ("Spring") circa 1478 as a huge (roughly 6' by 10') wall decoration for Villa di Castello, the

---

[2] *All My Road Before Me: The Diary of C.S. Lewis 1922-1927* (London: Collins, 1991) 95.

[3] *That Hideous Strength* (London: John Lane, 1945) 372.

[4] See "C. S. Lewis and Dante's Paradise" by Kathryn Lindskoog in *The Canadian C. S. Lewis Journal,* Vol. 22, No. 3, Spring 1999.

[5] C. S. Lewis, "Dante's Statius," *Studies in Medieval and Renaissance Literature* (Cambridge: Cambridge University Press, 1966).

elegant home of Lorenzo (Lorenzino) di Pierfrancesco, a young member of the Medici family.[6] Although it is painted in tempera on a wood panel, the design is much like that of a medieval tapestry. The painting is one of the most beloved treasures of the Uffizi Gallery in the heart of Florence, but its meaning remains a puzzle to art experts as well as to the general public.[7] It seems to depict an odd mixture of figures from ancient Greco-Roman mythology.

But "Primavera" is not the mysterious and wistful tribute to paganism it is commonly assumed to be. Instead, it is an intentional Christian allegory as orthodox and ultimately joyful as John Bunyan's *Pilgrim's Progress.* It is above all a depiction of Dante's sacred Garden of Eden in *Purgatory,* cantos 28-31. (Dante's Purgatory is a transitory region of Heaven; everyone there is already saved and is moving on into the fullness of God's peace and joy.)

Set apart in the center of the painting, like a serene but childless Madonna, Dante's beloved Beatrice (who led him to God) presides benevolently over the tableau, adorned with a cloak of red and a patterned halo of sky light. Her right hand gestures acceptance, just as Mary's does in Botticelli's "Annunciation." (Art critics identify her as an unusually circumspect Venus, goddess of love and beauty.) At Beatrice's left hand, her friend Matilda has been gathering wildflowers as in Canto 28. (Most critics identify this figure as Flora, goddess of spring, who is scattering flowers.) At Beatrice's right hand, three maidens, Faith, Hope, and Charity, dance in a circle as in Canto 30. (Critics identify them as the Three Graces, daughters of Zeus.) The luminous equanimity of Beatrice and her four companions is paradisaical. Dante's leafy canopy spreads overhead, and his carpet of grass and flowers spreads underfoot. As Matilda says, "Here spring is everlasting."[8]

---

[6] In his 1989 volume *Sandro Botticelli: Life and Work*, Ronald Lightbown contests the 1478 Villa di Castello tradition; he believes that Botticelli painted "Primavera" circa 1482 for a room in Lorenzo's town palace.

[7] "The Primavera ... is probably one of the best known, as well as doubtless the most puzzling and disputed, of Botticelli's paintings, and its many layers of meaning still have not been satisfactorily explained." (*The Art of the Italian Renaissance*, edited by Rolf Toman [Cologne, Germany: Conemann, 1995], p. 279.)

[8] C. S. Lewis's 14-line poem "Chanson D'Aventure" (*The Oxford Magazine.* February 10, 1938) is about hope for everlasting spring. It expresses our natural

Who is Matilda? Botticelli was no doubt well aware that before Dante wrote *The Divine Comedy* he had memorialized a young Florentine woman called Primavera. In Part XXIV of *La Vita Nuova*, Dante told about a specific encounter he once had with her: "I saw approaching me a gracious lady, renowned for her beauty, who for a long time had been the beloved of my closest friend [Guido Cavalcante]. Her name was Giovanna [Joan, the feminine form of John], but some say that because of her beauty she was nicknamed Primavera, that is, Spring, and this is what she was usually called. And coming after her, as I looked, I saw the miraculous Beatrice. They passed by quite close to me, and Love seemed to say to me in my heart, 'The first is called Primavera, and the sole reason for this is the way you see her walking today, for I inspired him who gave her this name of Primavera, which means that she will come first (*prima verrá*) on the day Beatrice appears after the dream of the one[9] who serves her faithfully....."[10]

There can be little doubt that the historical Joan (Primavera) in *La Vita Nuova* appears as the allegorical Matilda (Primavera) in *The Divine Comedy*.[11] Charles Williams says, "It is sufficient to think of Matilda [in *Purgatory*] as we thought of Joan, Primavera [in *Vita Nuova*], who resembled the Precursor [John the Baptist]."[12] And so

---

desire to escape human mortality and futility, the cycle of life and death, and the mutability of all earthly joys; thus it is about the longing for heaven. This theme is also suggested in "Aslan Is Nearer," chapter 11 of *The Lion, the Witch and the Wardrobe*.

[9] This is Dante himself, who had recently had a soul-shaking dream about Beatrice.

[10] Barbara Reynolds, translator, *La Vita Nuova* by Dante Alighieri (Harmondsworth, Middlesex, England, New York: Penguin Books, 1969) 70-71.

[11] From Dante's point of view, there is a kind of triple meaning in Matilda's statement "Here spring is everlasting." Primavera's life on earth was brief, but in the next life she (bearer of the nickname) and her beauty (the meaning of the nickname) and the season (the source of the nickname) are indeed everlasting.

[12] Charles Williams, *The Figure of Beatrice: A Study in Dante* (New York: Noonday Press, 1961) 175. Just as John the Baptist preceded Jesus in premature death, so Joan preceded Beatrice in premature death. And just as Joan had once preceded Beatrice into Dante's presence on a real-life street in Florence, so in Canto 28 of Purgatory she precedes Beatrice into Dante's presence in his allegorical Garden of Eden. Williams continues, "The Active Life and the Contemplative are here almost like girls together; and all the learning which

it is that Joan/Primavera. who appeared as Matilda in *Purgatory*, appears as Primavera in the painting named after her.

Like the center panel in a triptych altarpiece, Botticelli's serene portrayal of Beatrice, Matilda, and the three Theological Virtues is flanked by two related scenes. On the far right a disheveled Eve lurches vulnerably, with a broken sprig dangling from her mouth. This depicts the lines in Canto 29 where Dante deplores Eve's primordial disobedience in the Garden: "A sweet melody ran through the luminous air; and a corresponding wave of indignation caused me to condemn the recklessness of Eve, who, alone and inexperienced in this place where heaven and earth obeyed God, was unwilling to wear her veil of obedience under which, if she had been faithful, I would have enjoyed these indescribable delights far earlier and longer."[13]

Eve is being steered and perhaps propelled toward Adam by a winged Satan, who hovers in some trees with his garment curving like a large snake. Critics often identify Eve as the nymph Chloris, and Satan as Zephyr, the West Wind. Indeed, this Satan figure resembles Botticelli's West Wind in "Birth of Venus;" but in "Primavera" he is facing the opposite direction, and if he is a wind he seems to be blowing from the East. This correlates with the westward movement of the breeze in Canto 28 of *Purgatory* and the westward movement of the divine pageant in Canto 29. Critics all note this general sense of movement from right to left (east to west) in "Primavera." (The viewer of "Primavera" is in the same position as Dante the pageant viewer, facing north.)

On the far left a jaunty, casual, unfallen Adam gazes upward and reaches as high as fruit on a nearby orange tree. In Canto 28 Matilda deplores Adam's loss of this happy Garden full of laughter and play, which was a foretaste of eternal peace: "Through his own fault he lived here only briefly; through his own fault he exchanged spontaneous laughter and sweet play for tears and labor."[14] According to Genesis, Adam was not only the first man and the first resident of Eden, but also Eden's caretaker, the first agriculturist.

---

Matilda first [in *Purgatory* 28] and Beatrice [in *Purgatory* 29-33] after pour out on Dante cannot make them other."

[13] Kathryn Lindskoog, *Dante's Divine Comedy, Journey to Joy: Purgatory* (Macon, Georgia: Mercer University Press, 1997) 166.

[14] Lindskoog, *Dante's Divine Comedy, Journey to Joy: Purgatory,* 162.

I suspect that Adam's martial costume is meant to suggest Mars (god of war) more than Mercury (god of commerce). Mars was originally the Roman god of agriculture and fruitfulness rather than war; thus he is a highly appropriate figure in an archetypal garden. His sword and wingless helmet are appropriate for Mars, and he strongly resembles Botticelli's Mars in "Mars and Venus." Because Mars was the unfortunately appropriate city god of Florence, he had special significance for Dante, Botticelli, and the owner of "Primavera." Furthermore, the month of Mars, March, is the time of the vernal equinox, when Dante makes his allegorical journey through Hell, Purgatory and Heaven at the beginning of earthly spring.

As a literate Christian, Botticelli was almost surely familiar with the Old Testament symbolism for war and peace. Joel 3:10 speaks of beating plowshares into swords and pruning hooks into spears. Perhaps Botticelli had the dual role of Mars in mind when he made it clear that the lower parts of some of the trees near the sword bearing figure had been trimmed by a garden caretaker. If so, he no doubt had Micah 4:3-4 in mind also: "They will beat their swords into plowshares and their spears into pruning hooks. Nation will not take up sword against nation, nor will they train for war anymore. Every man will sit under his own vine and under his own fig tree, and no one will make them afraid, for the LORD Almighty has spoken" (NIV). This famous passage expresses human longing for the Edenic state portrayed so memorably in "Primavera." On the other hand, if the figure in question primarily represents Mercury, as critics have assumed, more commentary about that aspect of the allegory would be welcome.

Like a whimsical afterthought, Cupid floats above Beatrice at the very top center of the picture with his blindfold on and his dangerous unaimed dart ready to fly, as mentioned by Dante in Canto 28.[15] But Cupid was not an afterthought; he represents the central theme of Dante's entire *Comedy*, which is that humans are born to be in love with God and to move ever closer to Him, but their love goes astray when they become so enamored of lesser delights that they don't find out what their deepest yearning is really for. Furthermore, in Canto

---

[15] Some critics claim that Botticelli's Cupid is aiming his arrow at one of the Three Graces; but the fact that he is blindfolded presumably means that he is not aiming his arrow at any specific target.

31 four maidens remind Dante that when he had first looked into the eyes of Beatrice, Cupid had aimed his arrow at Dante. (That symbolic arrow is what eventually led to Dante's salvation.)

Like Dante's poetry, Botticelli's art is extremely lyrical and popular, and also intellectually complex. Why should Botticelli have depicted eight of Dante's Garden of Eden figures as a random assortment of stock figures from classical mythology? This surface ambiguity is an exuberant kind of applique that Botticelli imposed upon his tableau to reflect the fashionable Christian Neoplatonism of the owner of "Primavera" and his like-minded friends; they enjoyed relating elements of Christianity to classical mythology. (In a sense the happy patron got two paintings for the price of one.) This was done in the spirit of Dante, a master of dexterity, double meanings, and extraordinary synthesis.

This tour de force may well have been inspired by Canto 31 of *Purgatory*. There Dante stared into the eyes of Beatrice and was amazed to see a stationary image of Christ somehow change back and forth, back and forth, from human to divine. I suspect that the original purpose of the dual nature of "Primavera" was to create an earthly analogy to that image, in which one painting would have two natures: one human (classical mythology), and the other divine (Christian allegory).

According to Sir Kenneth Clark, Botticelli was obsessed with the study of Dante for at least twenty years, and he was commissioned to illustrate the *Inferno* before he was commissioned to create "Primavera." Until almost 1460, all books were handmade and very expensive, and so the very group of Florentine Neoplatonists connected with the 1478 creation of "Primavera" published a relatively inexpensive edition of *The Divine Comedy* on August 30, 1481. The first volume of this trilogy was illustrated with nineteen Baccio Bandini engravings based upon sketches commonly attributed to Botticelli. Clark claims that Botticelli was working on them early in the 1470s.[16] He also claims that Botticelli studied the leading

---

[16] Kenneth Clark, *The Drawings by Sandro Botticelli for Dante's Divine Comedy: After the Originals in the Berlin Museums and the Vatican* (New York: Harper & Row, 1976) 8-9.

Dante commentary of his day and that one of his friends was a great Dante scholar.[17]

Some fifty years after Botticelli's death, art critic Giorgio Vasari (architect of the Uffizi Gallery) not only claimed that Botticelli produced those designs, but that he also wrote his own commentary on parts of *The Divine Comedy*.[18] Scholars assume that Vasari was in error about the commentary, as he often was about other topics; but Botticelli's brother Simone, who lived with him for many years, owned an unsigned manuscript of a *Divine Comedy* commentary. Could it possibly be by Botticelli? That manuscript reportedly exists to this day in the National Library in Florence. Although critics assume that Botticelli did not write a commentary on Dante, many of them believe he painted the portrait of Dante (circa 1495) that resides in Switzerland.

About fifteen years after commissioning "Primavera," its owner commissioned Botticelli to return to *The Divine Comedy* and illustrate it from beginning to end without any overlay of Greco-Roman mythology. On beautiful white vellum he produced a large illustration for each of the 100 cantos and at least one extra.[19] Most of them were not completely finished, and only a handful were even partially colored. Botticelli's *Divine Comedy* patron was banished from Florence in 1498, which probably accounts for abandonment of the project.

Botticelli's's lavish *Divine Comedy* drawings were much admired; but the sheepskin had been wrongly prepared, and only faint ghosts of the wonderful drawings remained on the vellum. Eight of the 92 surviving pages are in the Vatican, and the rest are in two Berlin museums. None are ordinarily available for public viewing. But in spite of their obscurity, in 1893 Dr. Ludwig Volkmann said in *Iconografia Dantesca*, "no other artist of the Renaissance was so well fitted for the work of illustrating the 'Divine Comedy' as Sandro Botticelli." Bernard Berenson immediately commended Dr. Voltmann's work and called for "an edition of the *Commedia* with

---

[17] By Botticelli's day, many Italian cities had inaugurated professorships for the study of *The Divine Comedy*.

[18] *Lives of the Artists*, 1568

[19] The text of each canto was on the rough side of a sheet of parchment, and its illustration faced it on the smooth side of the next sheet of parchment.

illustration from the finest of fourteenth and fifteenth centuries, and from the best by Signorelli and Botticelli...."[20] Ironically, neither Volkmann nor Berenson realized that "Primavera" was a *Divine Comedy* illustration, and another century was to pass before it would be identified as such in this essay.

The faded illustrations on vellum were finally made available to the general public in Kenneth Clark's large 1976 volume *The Drawings by Sandro Botticelli for Dante's Divine Comedy.* (In 2000-2001, these illustrations were exhibited in Rome, Berlin, and London, resulting in the publication of *Sandro Botticelli: The Drawings for Dante's Divine Comedy* [Royal Academy of Arts, London, 2000].) In "Flights of Angels," Clive James's 1977 review of Clark's book in *New Statesman,* he remarks casually, "Nobody could look at [Botticelli's] Matilda gathering flowers in *Purgatorio* XXVIII[21] without thinking of the 'Primavera'." It seems not to have occurred to James that this was more than an incidental similarity.[22] Twenty more years would pass before the 500-year-old truth was discovered.

I suspect that Dante (1265-1321) would have been greatly pleased with Botticelli's painting. I think Botticelli (1444-1510) would be highly gratified to know that his painting is going to be understood as he intended. And I'm sure that C. S. Lewis (1898-1963), who had a keen sense of humor, would be delighted by the whole affair. If their common conception of the afterlife has proved correct, these three unusual men are no longer separated by centuries; they are together forever where nothing is ever lost or misunderstood.

*Note: Visit www.lindentree.org to see Botticelli's painting in color. Also, thanks to Dan Pater for pointing out the identity of Giovanna (Primavera) in La Vita Nuova.*

---

[20] Bernard Berenson, "Dante's Visual Images and His Early Illustrators" (*The Nation,* 24 December 1893).

[21] James is referring to the illustration on p. 143 of Clark's book.

[22] Clive James, *From the Land of Shadows* (London: Jonathan Cape, 1982) 193.

# 11

# ST. ANNE'S AND ST. ANNE'S: C. S. LEWIS, DOROTHY SAYERS, AND ROSE MACAULAY

*Although C. S. Lewis never tried to impose his religious beliefs on the students he taught at Oxford and Cambridge, he felt called to minister to people in his free time. And this ministry was chiefly to people with intellectual interests.*

Through the years I've occasionally heard readers of *That Hideous Strength* wonder why C. S. Lewis chose to name his protagonists the company of St. Anne's, and I was certainly no help. (In the story a few people are brought together at St. Anne's Manor in a village called St. Anne's on the Hill in order to save England from something dark and hideous.) Forty-five years after I first read *That Hideous Strength*, I suddenly have an answer to that old question.

Barbara Reynolds published her delightful article "Take away the camel, and all is revealed" in the 8 September 2000 issue of *The Church Times,* and she thoughtfully sent me a copy. The paper's lead says "Rose Macaulay's *The Towers of Trebizond* is full of pungent religious debate, and dominated by the forthright High Anglican aunt Dot. Barbara Reynolds thinks she knows who the real aunt Dot was."

Reynolds had edited four volumes of collected letters of her friend Dorothy L. Sayers shortly before she happened to reread *The Towers of Trebizond,* and so she was struck by Sayers's style and rhythm in a letter written by Macaulay's fictional Aunt Dot to a lapsed Anglican. (Rose Macaulay had been a lapsed Anglican herself at one time.) Aunt

Dot's letter seemed to be an excellent pastiche, if not an outright borrowing of a real Sayers letter. In addition to sharing Sayers's epistolary personality, doughty Aunt Dot shared her high Anglican beliefs, her zest and rambunctiousness, her commitment to the equality of women, and even her looks.

After Reynolds unfolded her evidence, I had no doubt that Aunt Dot was Macaulay's playful tribute to Dorothy Sayers. (Macaulay also apparently disguised the well-known Evangelical pastor John Stott as a similar pastor named Scott.) To my surprise, by the time I had finished reading the Reynolds article I realized that Lewis's St. Anne's was his playful tribute to a real one in London that played a part in the lives of both Dorothy Sayers and Rose Macaulay.

"Dorothy Sayers died on 17 December 1957, and her ashes were placed under the floor of the tower of St Anne's, Soho. That ceremony took place in 1958, and only a few people were invited: Dorothy's son Anthony Fleming and his wife, her two Somerville [college] friends Muriel St Clare Byrne and Marjorie Barber; her executor Laurence Harbottle, her friend Fr Patrick McLaughlin, the Vicar of St Anne's, who conducted the ceremony; myself, who had recently become her goddaughter—and Dame (as she had then become) Rose Macaulay." Until she reread *The Towers of Trebizond* Reynolds had always wondered why Macaulay was at the small gathering. She seems to have found the answer in *The Towers of Trebizond* and the history of St. Anne's House.

Late in 1942 two clergymen, Patrick McLaughlin (who would attend Sayers's interment ceremony 15 years later) and Gilbert Shaw, received permission to launch an outreach to people with intellectual interests through discussions and debate in the clergy house at St. Anne's. Religious plays would be produced, and an annual lecture series would begin in the summer of 1943. Dorothy Sayers and two of her friends lectured on aspects of "Christian Faith and Contemporary Culture" that year, along with T. S. Eliot and the director of the Victoria and Albert Museum. Sayers and Eliot remained active in St. Anne's House (later called the Society of St Anne), and at some point Lewis's Oxford friend Austin Farrer, the chaplain of Oxford's Balliol College, lectured there. In 1951 Rose Macaulay was invited also. She had to decline that year because she was too busy, but she greatly enjoyed the theological discussion on St. Anne's Day. She lectured there later, and when she wrote *Towers of Trebizond* she was a member of its Council. In Barbara Reynolds's opinion, some characters and discussions in that novel came directly from Macaulay's observations at St. Anne's.

How does this London church project relate to Lewis? Early in 1941 Lewis started explaining Christianity in a series of wartime BBC Radio broadcasts that revealed what an outstanding communicator and proponent of Christianity he was. At the end of 1941 Stella Aldwinkle founded the Socratic Club at the University of Oxford with C. S. Lewis as its first president and its main drawing card. Its meetings often featured debates between Lewis and prominent spokesmen against Christianity, followed by questions and answers. I suspect that in 1942 the founders of St. Anne's House in London were inspired by the burgeoning Socratic Club in Oxford and read early issues of its publication, *The Socratic Digest*. Both the Socratic Club and St. Anne's House provided a place where cerebral unbelievers might encounter the Christian faith. C. S. Lewis almost surely knew about the unusual project at St. Anne's House when he wrote *That Hideous Strength*. There in St. Anne's Manor cerebral unbeliever Jane Studdock had her dreary life transformed.

No one knows how many student lives were transformed by the Socratic Club, but here is one example. Over fifty years ago, between 1945 and 1948, a Moslem student from the Middle East wrote a B.Litt. thesis under Lewis, on eighteenth century English translations from Arabic. Of his own volition he attended Socratic club meetings and some of Lewis's public addresses about Christianity. As a result, he became a Christian and has remained one ever since.

Similarly, no one knows how many student lives were transformed by Lewis's private discussions with individuals. One example is Sheldon Vanauken, an American graduate student at Oxford who began discussing religion with Lewis late in 1950. On 17 April 1951 Lewis greeted Vanauken's conversion with a letter of advice, ending "Blessings on you and a hundred thousand welcomes. Make use of me in any way you please: and let us pray for each other always." The two remained friends until Lewis died in 1963, and in 1977 Vanauken told the entire story in his popular book *A Severe Mercy*. He remained a staunch Christian until his death in 1996.

I don't think the synchronicities and parallels in the foregoing pattern are coincidental. But I happen to like coincidences for their own sake, the unexpected rhymes in life (both happy ones and sad ones). In 1945, the very year when Lewis published his book about what happened at the fictional St. Anne's in England, I moved to an American St. Anne's about 7,700 miles away—Santa Ana, California. I grew up there, and that is where I discovered Lewis in a Santa Ana Library book in 1954. I gobbled that book down at one sitting and never looked back; from then on, C. S. Lewis was my favorite author and my chief mentor. This encounter with Lewis in Santa Ana was almost as pivotal in my life as Jane Studdock's encounter with Ransom in St. Anne's was in hers.

Until she joined the company at St. Anne's, Jane Studdock was writing a hackneyed thesis on John Donne. (In a 12 September 1945 letter to Cecil and Daphne Harwood, Lewis said "Perhaps I shd have emphasized more the fact that her thesis on Donne was all derivative bilge.") In contrast, within two months of discovering Lewis's work in Santa Ana, I decided to write a thesis about him. It was a wonderful adventure because there were no predecessors to echo or to avoid echoing. I had the thrill of exploring uncharted territory.

I studied Lewis's work independently for a year and a half (first reading *That Hideous Strength* in 1955, when it was ten years old and I was twenty), then had the joy of an hour and a quarter of lighthearted conversation with him in 1956. I didn't know then about the Socratic Club, but back in California I wrote "C. S. Lewis: Modern Christian Writer," to introduce American college students to Lewis. It was published in the January 1957 issue of *His*, the magazine of Inter-Varsity Christian Fellowship. A few months later, I got up my nerve and sent the magazine to Lewis. On 3 June he responded "Thank you for your kind letter enclosing *His* and for the article, which I was vain enough to enjoy...."

In October I sent him my thesis, *The Lion of Judah in Never-Never Land*; and on 29 October he sent me a prize beyond my wildest dreams.[1] But that great good fortune was soon followed by

---

[1] "Your thesis arrived yesterday and I read it at once. You are in the centre of the target everywhere. For one thing, you know my work better than anyone else I've met; certainly better than I do myself.... But secondly, you (alone of the critics I've met) realize the connection, or even the unity, of all the

misfortune; Dorothy Sayers died of of a sudden heart attack on 17 December. Ironically, I didn't hear this bad news at the time; in fact, I doubt that I had ever heard of Sayers at all. (A scant four years earlier I had never heard of C. S. Lewis.)

When the world's leading Dorothy Sayers expert, Barbara Reynolds, read the first draft of this essay and learned that I enjoy coincidences for their own sake, she sent me an extra good one. "You like coincidences, so here is one for you. My birthday is the same as that of Dorothy Sayers: 13 June. I was born on her 21st birthday."

---

books—scholarly, fantastic, theological—and make me appear a single author, not a man who impersonates half a dozen authors, which is what I seem to most. This wins really very high marks indeed."

# 12

## LINKS IN A GOLDEN CHAIN:

## C. S. LEWIS, GEORGE MACDONALD, AND SADHU SUNDAR SINGH

*Sadhu Sundar Singh was a world-famous Christian early in the Twentieth Century, just as Mother Teresa was a world-famous Christian late in the century. Because Sundar Singh somehow lapsed into obscurity, few readers of C. S. Lewis have realized how important he was to Lewis.*

*For so the whole round earth is every way*
*Bound by gold chains about the feet of God*
—Alfred, Lord Tennyson

George MacDonald's spiritual influence upon C. S. Lewis is common knowledge, but until now Sadhu Sundar Singh's influence upon C. S. Lewis has been overlooked.

The earliest hint that Lewis was acquainted with the life of Sundar Singh appears in Book 8, Chapter 2 of *The Pilgrim's Regress*. Lewis told of a Man who descended to help the pilgrim when he was in great need. "I will give you a hand," said the stranger, and pulled him out of a desolate gorge.[1] A few chapters later, the Man helped the pilgrim again. "Then I dreamed that once more a Man came to him

---

[1] C. S. Lewis, *The Pilgrim's Regress: An Allegorical Apology for Christianity Reason and Romanticism* (Grand Rapids, Michigan: William B. Eerdmans Publishing, 1981), Book 8, Chapter 2, 136.

in the darkness." The Man said, "Your life has been saved all this day by crying out to something which you call by many names."[2] According to Lewis's running headline, the Man was Christ.

Lewis seems to have been consciously echoing Sundar Singh's conversion story. Because *Pilgrim's Regress* is made up largely of references to a wide variety of authors, it is not surprising that Lewis referred to someone else's famous conversion experience when telling of his own.

Sundar Singh was born nine years before C. S. Lewis, in 1889. He was the youngest child in an aristocratic Sikh family (all Sikhs are named Singh) in the village of Rampur in Patiala, India. The Sikh faith combines Hinduism and Islam, and so his mother lovingly taught him the Sikh and Hindu scriptures and urged him to become a holy man. When he was seven years old he knew the entire Bhagavad Gita by heart (not a unique feat in India), and he was filled with longing for *santi,* peace of soul.

Sundar Singh eagerly studied holy books, meditated, practiced Yoga, and did good works. When he was fourteen years old, in 1902, his mother and older brother died. (In 1908, C. S. Lewis's mother, uncle, and grandfather died.) Unlike his mother, Sundar Singh's father thought he was overly religious for his age. Once, the boy's Guru said to his father, "Your son will become either a fool or a great man."[3]

Sundar Singh sought God in Sikhism, Hinduism, Buddhism, and Islam. He was exposed to Christianity for a year in a local school provided by American Presbyterian missionaries, but the more he heard of the New Testament, the more he resented it. He quit the school. When he saw missionaries in public he abused them and ordered his father's servants to do the same. He finally burned a New Testament in public to express his outrage.

Later, Sundar Singh saw that his fanatical opposition to Christianity had disguised a secret attraction to it. His father disapproved of his Bible burning as much as his obsession with proper Indian religions and wondered if his son was losing his sanity. Indeed, on December 17, 1904, fifteen-year-old Sundar Singh told his father

---

[2] *Pilgrim's Regress*, Book 8, Chapter 5, 140.

[3] Friedrich Heiler, *The Gospel of Sadhu Sundar Singh*, Abridged Translation by Olive Wyon (Lucknow, India: Lucknow Publishing House, 1970), 31.

good-bye and announced that he would commit suicide before breakfast. He fully planned to lie down on the railroad tracks near his house and be run over by the 5 A.M. express train in order to find God on the other side of death.

At 3 A.M. on December 18, Sundar Singh arose and took a cold bath according to Hindu custom. He begged and begged God to reveal Himself before the train came. Suddenly such a great light appeared in his small room that he looked to make sure the house was not on fire. Then a luminous cloud appeared, and he saw a Man's face in it—radiant with love. The Man spoke in perfect Hindustani, Sundar Singh's mother tongue: "Why do you persecute me? Remember that I gave My life for you upon the Cross."[4]

Sundar Singh wrote later, "What I saw was no imagination of my own. Up to that moment I hated Jesus Christ and did not worship Him. If I were talking of Buddha I might have imagined it, for I was in the habit of worshipping him. It was no dream. When you have just had a cold bath you don't dream! It was reality, the Living Christ!"[5]

Sundar Singh fell down before Jesus and worshipped him. Peace and joy finally flooded his soul. At breakfast he told his bewildered father, "The old Sundar Singh is dead; I am a new being."[6] His conversion was obviously much like that of the apostle Paul, and he told everyone who would listen.

Sundar Singh's Christianity was even less acceptable to his father than the previous enmity to Christianity; he considered his son insane. The family pressured him to abandon his new faith, then finally drove him away. It is said that his last meal at home was poisoned. His friend Gardit Singh, who became a Christian at the same time, actually died from poisoned food. In the local uproar, the mission station had to be closed down and village Christians moved away for safety.

Sundar Singh went to study the Bible at a medical mission station. Because it was unlawful to be baptized until he turned sixteen, he was baptized an Anglican Christian on his birthday, Sunday, September 3, 1905. His teacher advised him to get theological training, but he

---

[4] Heiler, 36.

[5] Heiler, 37.

[6] Heiler, 37.

felt called to preach the gospel as a traditional Indian holy man instead.

Thirty-three days after his baptism, Sundar Singh put on the yellow linen robe of a celibate sadhu and set out with only a Hindustani New Testament and a blanket which he often wrapped around his head as a turban. He used no money, and he never begged; when no one offered him food and shelter, he did without. He also did without the protective dagger that Sikh men always carry. When someone asked him if stones did not cut his bare feet, he answered that his feet were so hard they cut the stones.

As a typical Sikh, Sundar Singh was just over six feet tall, with a full beard and luminous dark eyes. His eyes showed deep inner peace and drew people to him. He stood erect, his body poised. Animals and children were always attracted to him. He loved to play with children, and he had a sense of humor. When Jesus was mentioned, his whole face lit up with a joyful radiance. After his vision on December 18, 1904, he had just one passionate interest—loving and serving Jesus.

Thus he wandered around India and to Afghanistan and Kashmir preaching Christ. He joined Samuel Stokes, an American missionary who had left his wealthy family in order to try to live like Saint Francis of Assisi in India; together the two friends worked in a leper colony and then in the Plague Hospital in Lahore.

In 1909 Sundar Singh took the advice of friends and became a theology student at Saint John's Divinity College in Lahore. He remained an Anglican all his life and preached often in Anglican churches, but as a preacher he refused to be bound to one denomination. To him all Christianity was one. Sundar Singh also respected the religions that had nurtured him as a child, and he saw them fulfilled in Christ. He believed in giving people the living water of God in the cup of their own culture, not in a foreign cup. He felt a special calling to preach to the dangerous, inaccessible land of Tibet, and he made many almost impossible trips there on foot.

In 1912 Sundar Singh's fame began to spread across India, and in 1916 the first of several books about him was published. Wherever he went in India, both Christians and non-Christians thronged to see and hear him. In 1918 he also preached in Ceylon, Burma, Singapore, Japan, and China. In Penang, Malaysia, he was invited to preach the message of Jesus in a Sikh temple. In 1919 Sundar Singh's father received him kindly and said he was ready to become a Christian. They were reconciled at the very time when C. S. Lewis and his father became estranged after World War I. At this time C. S. Lewis was a student at Oxford.

Sundar Singh was told by God to preach in England, and his father offered to pay for the journey. In February 1920 he arrived in England and stayed first at a Quaker center. Then he was a guest of the Anglican Cowley Fathers in Oxford and preached in several colleges and Saint John's Church. It is highly likely that C. S. Lewis heard that Sundar Singh was speaking in Oxford at the time, but it is unlikely that Lewis went to hear him. In the first place, Lewis was especially busy that month. He wrote to his friend Arthur Greeves, "I must work like ten devils this term."[7]

At the age of twenty-one Lewis found Christianity distasteful. Besides that, he had had an upsetting experience early that year after a night talk with a student friend about "shadowy subjects – ghosts and spirits and Gods." His friend told about many supernatural experiences, and Lewis fell into a fit of terror like nightmarish terrors he had suffered in childhood. As a result, he said, he "conceived, for the present, a violent distaste for mysteries and all that kind of business."[8]

From Oxford the Sadhu went to London, where he preached to great crowds in a variety of major churches, including the Baptist Metropolitan Tabernacle. At Church House, Westminster, he addressed a meeting of seven hundred Anglican clergymen, including several bishops and the Archbishop of Canterbury. He also spoke at Trinity College, Cambridge, and crossed to Paris to preach. Then he went to Ireland and on to Scotland, where he preached in leading Presbyterian churches in Glasgow and Edinburgh.

Sundar Singh was not puffed up by international popularity. He pointed out that the ass that bore Christ into Jerusalem would have been very foolish to think that the palms and flowers decking the road

---

7 *They Stand Together: The Letters of C. S. Lewis to Arthur Greeves* (1914-1963), ed. Walter Hooper (New York: Macmillan, 1979), letter dated February 3, 1920, 264.

8 *They Stand Together*, letter dated February 3, 1920, 265.

were in its own honor. Likewise, it would be foolish for those who carry Christ to people today to take credit for the response.

In May the Sadhu crossed the Atlantic and spent three months preaching in American cities from New York to San Francisco. Next he preached in Honolulu, then in several places in Australia. In contrast to other traveling speakers from India in those days, Sundar Singh did not seek to explain and praise Indian wisdom; he came to preach only Jesus. Finally, at the end of September, he returned to India, grieved about the greedy materialism he had seen in the West. In the East many people worship idols, he observed, but in the West people worship themselves.

In 1921 Sundar Singh ministered in Tibet again. Then in early 1922 an old dream of his came true; he toured Palestine, tracing the steps of Jesus. From there he went to preach in Egypt; then in France; and then in Switzerland, where he spoke in the hall used by the League of Nations. In Germany he spoke in Martin Luther's own church in Wittenberg. Then he spoke in Sweden, Norway, Denmark, and Holland. He arrived back in England very tired, and spoke only at the Keswick conference in Wales. That year he turned down pressing invitations to speak in Finland, Russia, Greece, Romania, Serbia, Italy, Portugal, the United States, and New Zealand.

In spite of the fame and adulation heaped upon him, Sundar Singh reportedly remained unassuming and humble. He said he came not to preach (the world has plenty of sermons), but to witness to the saving power of Jesus. His one interest was to come nearer and nearer to Jesus, to grow more and more like Him, and to wear out in His service. Indeed, people everywhere were struck by what they perceived as his resemblance to Jesus. Some people were interested in the Sadhu chiefly because of the miracles and marvels in his life, but when he realized this, he quit telling much about them. What he wanted to emphasize most was prayer. He attributed all he knew and did and experienced to prayer. "Prayer, prayer, and again prayer" was his motto.[9]

In April 1929, he set off on his dangerous trek to Tibet again in spite of heart trouble and blindness in one eye. After he set off, no one ever heard from him again. Although friends went searching for information about him, no clues were ever found; he had simply

---

[9] Heiler, 88.

disappeared. When the government of India announced four years later that he was officially given up for dead, some suspected that he had withdrawn from civilization in order to meditate and pray in the Himalayas. But most likely he died shortly after he set out on his final missionary journey. For years he had been eager to leave this life in order to get to heaven to be closer to God.

It was almost surely in April or May 1929 that Sundar Singh ended his Christian vocation on this earth. And, oddly enough, that is when C. S. Lewis knelt down in his room in Oxford and reluctantly admitted that God is God and began his own journey in Christian ministry.

There can be no question that C. S. Lewis was aware of Sadhu Sundar Singh. In May 1943 Dorothy Sayers' radio play *The Man Born To Be King: A Play-Cycle on the Life of Our Lord and Savior Jesus Christ* was first published, and C. S. Lewis promptly read it. He wrote later, "For my own part, I have reread it every Holy Week since it first appeared, and never re-read it without being deeply moved."[10] He quoted from its preface. In that preface Dorothy Sayers included a footnote quoting from *The Sadhu* by B. H. Streeter and A. J. Appasamy: "The Sadhu's mind is an overflowing reservoir of anecdote, illustration, epigram, and parable, but he never makes the slightest effort to avoid repetition; in fact he appears to delight in it. 'We do not,' he says, 'refuse to give bread to hungry people because we have already given bread to others.' Hence we have constantly found the same material occurring in more than one of the written or printed authorities we have used. 'My mouth,' he says, 'has no copyright.'"[11]

Seven months after first reading the tribute to Sundar Singh quoted by Sayers, C. S. Lewis wrote his preface for *That Hideous Strength*. In it he advised readers that his new book was not history but "a modern fairy tale for grown-ups."[12] In the story itself, evident-

---

[10] C. S. Lewis, "A Panegyric for Dorothy L. Sayers," *"On Stories" and Other Essays on Literature*, ed. by Walter Hooper, (New York: A Harvest HBJ Book, 1982), 93.

[11] Dorothy Sayers, *The Man Born to Be King: A Play-Cycle on the Life of Our Lord and Savior Jesus Christ* (London: Victor Gollanez Ltd., 1969) 32-33.

[12] C. S. Lewis, *That Hideous Strength* (New York: Macmillan Company, 1946) subtitle and preface, vii.

ly written in 1943, protagonist Elwin Ransom takes on a strange assignment that has come to him indirectly from a man in India, "the great native Christian mystic whom you may have heard of—the Sura," as one character explained to another in chapter five.[13] This fictional Sura foresaw a great danger to the human race coming to a head in England, and he left prophetic word that a group of committed people would gather around Ransom to combat the evil. After giving this message the Sura disappeared, and no one knew if he was alive or dead. It has seemed to some alert readers that Lewis expected readers to be familiar with such a figure.

What did Lewis mean by the term Sura? In Sanscrit the word means god. In the Hindu pantheon, a sura is a good angel or genie. In Arabic a sura is one of the 114 chapters of the Koran. Lewis must have known all this when he chose the word. I believe that Lewis used the word sura because he was hinting at the word *sadhu,* which means a holy man in India. (As an adjective in Sanscrit, *sadhu* means straight.) If Lewis had actually called his Christian mystic the Sadhu, some readers might have believed that his tale was a true account about the famous Sadhu Sundar Singh.

When Lewis wrote *That Hideous Strength,* Sundar Singh had been missing only fifteen years and would have been fifty-four years old if still alive. He was the Mother Teresa figure of his day. On October 24, 1949, Queen Wilhelmina of Holland wrote, "I never met him. I know him only from his books and books about him. I belong to those who are deeply impressed by his life and teaching and I am sure the way he manifested his radiant love for Christ and His peace, and in general his teaching, was a real help to me in the worst episodes of the terrible catastrophe that was the last war."[14]

To check my conviction that C. S. Lewis's Sura was really meant to represent Sadhu Sundar Singh, in 1987 I contacted Lewis's Oxford pupil and lifetime friend Dom Bede Griffiths, since 1955 a Benedictine monk in India. I explained my theory and asked him what he thought. (Griffiths, like Sundar Singh, wore the traditional robe of an Indian holy man.)

---

[13] Lewis, *That Hideous Strength*, 125-6.

[14] A. J. Appasamy, *Sundar Singh: A Biography* (Madras, India: C. L. S., 1966), 7.

"As regards Sadhu Sundar Singh," Griffiths wrote on June 12, 1987, "I know his life well and have always admired him. Lewis would have admired him especially for his nondenominational or 'mere' Christianity. I don't recall C. S. Lewis ever mentioning him, but I think it is almost certain that the reference in *That Hideous Strength is* to him."[15]

"I don't suppose that anyone has made the link between Lewis and Sundar Singh before," Bede Griffiths continued in another letter on July 27, 1987. "On reflection I feel that it is very likely that Lewis heard of him through the Cowley Fathers with whom he was very close. In any case, Sundar Singh needs to be more widely known."[16] (The Cowley Fathers were the devout Anglicans who had hosted Sundar Singh during his 1920 visit to Oxford.)

Sundar Singh may have influenced C. S. Lewis in several ways. For example, the name Singh comes from the Sanskrit word for lion. Because Sundar Singh was popularly perceived as the most Christlike man in Lewis's day, it is possible that Sundar Singh was in the back of Lewis's mind when Aslan the lion came bounding into Lewis's first story of Narnia. (Aslan is the Turkish word for lion.)

C. S. Lewis and Sundar Singh happened to express the same idea about the relationship between wishes and truth. Sundar Singh taught that every desire we have is given for a special purpose, and we would have no desire to believe in God unless he exists. "The capacity for religion is...rather like thirst....Just as thirst has been created to make men use water, so the religious thirst has been created to make men come to God."[17] In comparison, Lewis wrote: "But what does the existence of the wish [for God] suggest? At one time I was much impressed by Arnold's line 'Nor does the being hungry prove that we have bread.' But surely, tho' it doesn't prove that one particular man will *get* food, it *does* prove that there is such a thing as food! i.e. if we

---

[15] Dom Bede Griffiths, letter to Kathryn Lindskoog (unpublished), June 12, 1987.

[16] Dom Bede Griffiths, letter to Kathryn Lindskoog (unpublished), July 27, 1987.

[17] B. H. Streeter, *The Message of Sundar Singh* (New York: Macmillan, 1921) 68.

were a species that didn't normally eat, weren't designed to eat, would we feel hungry?"[18]

It seems that George MacDonald, C. S. Lewis, and Sadhu Sundar Singh all converged in the pages of *The Great Divorce*. (On July 20, 1956, when I told Lewis how much I loved that book, his eyes lit up; he said that it was his Cinderella—much better than *The Screwtape Letters,* in his opinion, but far less popular.) *The Great Divorce* is the story of a busload of disgruntled residents of hell who travel to the outskirts of heaven, where they are welcomed in vain. Most of them prefer to get back on the bus and return to hell.

In Chapter 9, C. S. Lewis (like Dante encountering Virgil in *The Divine Comedy*) encounters the wise, holy figure of George MacDonald on the outskirts of heaven. MacDonald explains to Lewis that "the damned have holidays—excursions, ye understand."[19] Most of them take trips to earth, but some take trips to heaven and refuse to stay. "Milton was right. The choice of every lost soul can be expressed in the words 'Better to reign in Hell than serve in Heaven.'....Ye see it easily enough in a spoiled child that would sooner miss its play and its supper than say it was sorry and be friends."[20] "All that are in Hell, choose it."[21]

When he put those words into the mouth of his mentor George MacDonald in *The Great Divorce,* Lewis might have been thinking of the following words of Sundar Singh: "Men were not created for Hell and therefore do not enjoy it, and, when there, desire to escape into Heaven. They do so, but they find Heaven even more uncongenial than Hell, so they return."[22] These words appeared in 1921 in *The Message of Sundar Singh* by B. H. Streeter, an Oxford professor impressed by Sundar Singh's visit the year before.

In Lewis's invented plot in *That Hideous Strength,* the Sura in India passed on a spiritual assignment to Ransom in England, whom he had never met. Is it possible (I wonder) that in real life the Sadhu

---

[18] C. S. Lewis letter to Sheldon Vanauken, December 23, 1950, quoted from Sheldon Vanauken, *A Severe Mercy* (New York: Bantam Books, 1981) 89-90.

[19] C. S. Lewis, *The Great Divorce* (New York: Macmillan Company, 1946) 62.

[20] *The Great Divorce*, 66.

[21] *The Great Divorce*, 69.

[22] B. H. Streeter, *The Message*, 101.

in India unknowingly passed on a spiritual assignment to C. S. Lewis in England? Such synchronicity would be in keeping with the Sadhu's strange and marvelous life. (The Bible speaks of such a transfer in the story of Elijah and Elisha in 2 Kings 2.)

George MacDonald died on September 18, 1905. Just then the young Sundar Singh decided to become a wandering Sadhu, and less than three weeks after MacDonald's death he set out on his twenty-four-year ministry. When Sundar Singh died in the spring of 1929, C. S. Lewis dedicated his life to God and gradually began his own remarkable ministry. All three of these men ministered by public speaking, by writing, and by deep and constant prayer.

Perhaps the chronological links between the prayer and teaching ministries of George MacDonald, Sundar Singh, and C. S. Lewis were only a coincidence. Life is full of coincidences, and George MacDonald believed that we don't even notice most of them. But he believed that they are all significant.

C. S. Lewis no doubt failed to notice the chronological coincidence that linked his ministry to the ministries of Sundar Singh and George MacDonald. But in 1948, just three years after publishing his fictional tribute to Sundar Singh in *That Hideous Strength*, Lewis published his little book titled *George MacDonald: An Anthology*. One of the insightful passages he decided to include was from MacDonald's novel *Annals of a Quiet Neighborhood*: "And if we believe that God is everywhere, why should we not think Him present even in the coincidences that sometimes seem so strange? For if He be in the things that coincide, He must be in the coincidence of those things."[23]

*A Short Bibliography of Sundar Singh:*

Andrews, C. F. *Sadhu Sundar Singh: A Personal Memoir*. Hodder & Stoughton, London, 1934.

Appasamy, A. J. *Sundar Singh: A Biography*. Published by Lutterworth Press in London, 1958. First Indian edition, 1966.

---

[23] C. S. Lewis, editor, *George MacDonald: 365 Readings*, #278, 115.

Heiler, Friedrich. *The Gospel of Sadhu Sundar Singh.* First published in German in 1924, then published in English in 1927. First Indian edition published by the Lucknow Publishing House in Lucknow, India, 1970. Abridged English translation by Olive Wyon.

Parker, Rebeccah. *Sadhu Sundar Singh, Called of God.* Published by the Christian Literature Society in Madras and the S. C. M. Press in London, 1920.

Singh, Sundar. *The Complete Works of Sundar Singh,* including *At the Master 's Feet* (1922), *Reality and Religion* (1923), *Search After Reality* (1924), *Spiritual Life* (1925), *Spiritual World* (1926), *Real Life* (1927), *With and Without Christ* (1928), and *Life in Abundance* (first published in 1980). Published by the Christian Literature Society in Madras, 1986.

Singh, Sundar. *Visions of Sadhu Sundar Singh of India.* Foreword by Bishop LaFroy of Lahore, India. First published by Anker G. Dahle in 1926. Now published (no date) by Osterhus Publishing Company of Minneapolis, Minnesota.

Singh, Sundar. *With and Without Christ.* Introduction by the Lord Bishop of Winchester. Harper & Brothers, New York, 1929.

Streeter, B. H. and Appasamy, A. J. *The Message of Sadhu Sundar Singh.* New York: Macmillan, 1921.

# 13

# THE WOOLWORTH CONNECTION: SINCLAIR LEWIS, C. S. LEWIS, AND JOHN UPDIKE

*What do C. S. Lewis's* Pilgrim's Regress *(1933) and John Updike's* Rabbit Is Rich *(1981) have in common? They both drew upon Sinclair Lewis's novel* Babbitt *(1922). And what did Sinclair Lewis secretly draw upon? Read on...*

A hidden chain of events links three early twentieth-century cultural landmarks: one building and two books. First came the "cathedral" that was the loftiest building in the world; second came a down-to-earth international bestseller that mocked the famous evangelist Billy Sunday (calling him Mike Monday); and third came the story of C. S. Lewis's personal pilgrimage.

The scenario begins in 1879, when Frank Winfield Woolworth opened his first store. In just thirty years, his small business had exploded into a chain of five-and-ten-cent stores that became the largest retail business in the world. Mr. Woolworth was now an extremely wealthy man, and in 1910 he decided to erect a magnificent office building in New York City for five million dollars. As construction proceeded, Woolworth's plans expanded; and in the end he erected the tallest building in the world at a cost of thirteen and a half million dollars, fully paid for from his personal fortune.

The result was a modern skyscraper clad in fifteenth-century gothic splendor. An admirer from England declared, "The Woolworth Building does not scrape the sky; it greets the sky." In addition to its elaborate tower, observation gallery, lace-like tracery, Italian marble, graceful arches, splendid mosaics, vaulted ceilings, grand arcade and opulent balconies, the building boasted gargoyle portraits of its engineer, rental agent, and bank president. In 1913, one year after the sinking of the Titanic, President Wilson pressed a button in the White House that switched on 80,000 lights in the Woolworth Building for its grand opening.

When that spectacular event occurred, twenty-eight-year-old Sinclair Lewis was an aspiring writer from Minnesota who had been working at a New York publishing house for fifteen dollars a week. So far, his only book was a story for boys published under the penname Tom Graham. In 1914, however, he launched a series of minor novels. His wildest dreams came true in 1920, when he published *Main Street*; it sold a million copies and became an international sensation. In 1922 he published *Babbitt*, and it was another spectacular success, especially in Europe; in fact, he considered it the book that would guarantee his lasting reputation. In 1925 he published *Arrowsmith*, and in 1930 he became the first American to win the Nobel Prize for literature. (By this time C. S. Lewis was a young professor at Oxford, and his first two books had fizzled.)

*Babbitt* opens with a reference to some towers "delicate as silver rods. They were neither citadels nor churches, but frankly and beautifully office-buildings." The fictitious city of Zenith is a caricature of Minneapolis. (Ironically, Sinclair Lewis was living in London when he wrote this American novel.) In my opinion Zenith's Second National Tower is an allusion to what was then the nation's first tower, the celebrated Woolworth Building.

At the end of the first chapter, George Babbitt contemplated the Second National Tower from his bedroom window. "Its shining walls rose against April sky to a simple cornice like a streak of white fire. Integrity was in the tower, and decision. It bore its strength lightly as a tall soldier. As Babbitt stared, the nervousness was soothed from his face, his slack chin lifted in reverence... He beheld the tower as a temple-spire of the religion of business, a faith passionate, exalted, surpassing common men..." Inspired, Babbitt turned away and whistled a popular song as if it were a noble hymn.

Where did Sinclair Lewis get the idea of people worshipping business and of great office buildings serving as temples of this new religion? Four years before Sinclair Lewis published *Babbitt*, Edwin A.

Cochran and S. Parkes Cadman, D.D., S.T.D., wrote an elegant 31-page promotional booklet called *The Cathedral of Commerce*. It was expensively produced and lavishly illustrated. Dr. Cadman rhapsodized, "Brute material has been robbed of its density and flung into the sky to challenge its loveliness. Just as religion monopolized art and architecture during the Medieval epoch, so commerce has engrossed the United States since 1865."

> Here, on the Island of Manhattan, and at its southern extremity, stands a succession of buildings without precedent or peer. The vision of their grandiose effect from the Brooklyn Bridge at dusk, when the gathering darkness softens their bold outlines, and every one of the numberless windows coruscates with radiance, is beyond the brush of Turner to paint or the eloquence of Ruskin to describe. It outvies the imagination in its most fertile moments. Of these buildings the Woolworth is Queen, acknowledged as premier by all lovers of the city and the commonwealth, by critics from near and far, by those who aspire toward perfection, and by those who use visible things to attain it. When seen at nightfall bathed in electric light as with a garment, or in the lucid air of a summer morning, piercing space like a battlement of the paradise of God which St. John beheld, it inspires feelings too deep even for tears. The writer looked upon it and at once cried out, "The Cathedral of Commerce"—the chosen habitation of that spirit in man, which, through means of change and barter, binds alien people into unity and peace, and reduces the hazards of war and bloodshed.

In the end the booklet devotes at least eight pages to descriptions of the awesome engineering and mechanical feats required to create and sustain the Cathedral of Commerce, including the highest-rise elevators in the world and "four mighty engines and dynamos, operating days and nights."

What *The Cathedral of Commerce* would have inspired in a social critic like Sinclair Lewis is not Cadman's "feelings too deep even for tears," but satire. In *Babbitt* he ironically mocks not only the romanticized veneration of commerce, but also the romanticized awe of technology. George Babbitt reveled in the modern attachments on his alarm-clock, including its cathedral-chime. "Babbitt was proud of being awakened by such a rich device. Socially it was almost as creditable as buying expensive cord tires."

> The standard advertised wares—toothpaste, socks, tires, cameras, instantaneous hot water-heaters—were his symbols of excellence; at first the signs, then the substitutes for joy and passion and wisdom." He felt enhanced by his new water-cooler: "And it was the very best of water-coolers, up-to-date, scientific, and right-thinking. It had cost a great deal of money (in itself a virtue).

> He had enormous and poetic admiration, though very little understanding, of mechanical devices. They were his symbols of truth and beauty. Regarding each new intricate mechanism—metal lathe, two-jet carburetor, machine gun, oxyacetylene welder—he learned one good realistic-sounding phrase, and used it over and over, with a delightful feeling of being technical and initiated.

Babbitt was a "pious motorist," and "his motor car was poetry and tragedy, love and heroism." "Epochal as starting the car was the drama of parking it... It was a virile adventure masterfully executed." Filling its gasoline-tank was a familiar rite, and when he paused in traffic by the Second National Tower his car and others were to him "a line of polished steel restless as cavalry."

When asked if he knew who Dante was, one of Babbitt's friends was insulted: "Certainly I know who he was! The Wop poet." Another one volunteered, "I suppose that Dante showed a lot of speed for an old-timer— not that I've actually read him, of course—but to come right down to hard facts, he wouldn't stand one-two-three if he had to buckle down to practical literature..."

C. S. Lewis was an eclectic reader, and in *The Pilgrim's Regress* he made playful allusions to dozens of famous books. In my opinion *Babbitt* is one of them. In *Regress* a brash, slangy American named Gus Halfways (evidently halfway between artistic Romanticism and hard-boiled cynicism) showed the pilgrim his car and soon began to speak in a changed and reverent voice.

> She is a poem. She is the daughter of the spirit of the age. What was the speed of Atlanta to her speed? The beauty of Apollo to her beauty?

Our fathers made images of what they called gods and goddesses... All self-deception and phallic sentiment. But here you have real art...

Sheer power, eh? Speed, ruthlessness, austerity, form, eh? Also (and here he dropped his voice) very expensive indeed.

Gus Halfways and George Babbitt are two of a kind. Both Sinclair Lewis and C. S. Lewis were satirizing the materialistic substitution of commerce for religion (as in *The Cathedral of Commerce*), and the substitution of technology for mythology and Romanticism. But Sinclair Lewis wrote his heavily ironic book in the form of straightforward popular fiction, and C. S. Lewis wrote his heavily ironic book as elaborate intellectual allegory. An even greater difference between *Babbitt* and *Pilgrim's Regress*, however, is that Sinclair Lewis (the son of a doctor) was a diagnostician but not a healer. In the first book that C. S. Lewis wrote as a Christian, he set out to be both.

Today, far below the Woolworth Building's 30-story base and tapered 30-story tower, cars are still starting and stopping like Babbitt's 1922 "line of polished steel restless as cavalry." But most other things have changed. According to John Updike's 1962 opinion in the *New Yorker*, the jagged old skyline was airier than the new one. Unlike new skyscrapers, the old ones seemed to have more silhouette than mass. "At the point of exhaustion, where the old skyscrapers used to taper, gather their dwindling energy, and lunge upward with a heart-stopping spire, [today's] glass boxes suffer the architectural embarrassment" of having to house bulky air-conditioning apparatus at the top.

Dr. Cadman's ebullient claim "Woolworth is Queen" proved true for less than twenty years; in 1930, when Sinclair Lewis won the Nobel Prize, the Empire State Building went up. But almost seventy years after being deposed, the dowager Cathedral still stands firm and strong. (It has its own web page now: http://www. commkey.net/daniel/wool.htm.) In contrast, the mighty Woolworth company itself became so structurally unsound that in 1997 it collapsed. In 1998 the Woolworth Building was purchased by a syndicate.

And what of Sinclair Lewis? His boyhood home in Sauk Centre, Minnesota, has been preserved in his honor. In fact, the Sinclair Lewis Society held a conference in Sauk Centre in 1997 to celebrate the seventy-fifth anniversary of the publication of *Babbitt*. Sinclair Lewis scholars from far and wide presented papers there about aspects of his life and works, but none of them mentioned that a prospectus for the Woolworth Building had inspired *Babbitt*. Until now, apparently, no one knew.

One last note. Because I am a C. S. Lewis scholar, not a Sinclair Lewis scholar, one might ask how I made such an esoteric double discovery about *Babbitt*. On one level C. S. Lewis's 1957 observation that I "realize the connection" is a partial answer. (That brings to mind E. M. Forster's epigram about cognition, "Only connect!") But on another level the answer is simply coincidence. When my reclusive bachelor uncle died in Escondido, California, I found a copy of *The Cathedral of Commerce* tucked away in a kitchen cupboard by the woodburning stove in the bookless family farmhouse. How it got there is a mystery. The weatherbeaten old house was soon destroyed to make way for a massive freeway, but I saved both the stove and *The Cathedral of Commerce*.

It has often been said that novelists should avoid coincidence in their stories because although minor coincidence is common in life, it usually seems too far-fetched in fiction. I've noticed a real-life coincidence in the seventh chapter of *Babbitt*. There Sinclair Lewis introduced a minor character named Horace Updike, who had just attended a lecture by an eminent novelist. Exactly ten years after the manifestation of this fictional Updike, a real Updike was born who was destined to *be* an eminent novelist in the last half of the twentieth century, as Sinclair Lewis was in the first half.

John Updike was born in Pennsylvania in 1932, the year when the pilgrim named John was born in Puritania in C. S. Lewis's mind. When Updike was thirteen years old he got to visit New York City for a few hours one afternoon. He leaned out of his uncle's hotel window to survey the city, and his father pointed out the graceful Chrysler Building. Then he added, "The one deep in back from this window is the Woolworth Building. For years it was the tallest building in the world."

Down at ground level later, John looked up in wonder. "Shimmering buildings arrowed upward and glinted through the treetops. This was New York, I told myself, the silver town. Towers of ambition rose crystalline within me." Then the boy had to board the train for home. Twenty-three years later he would be living in New York and describing the city in the "Talk of the Town" column in *The New Yorker*.

There is a bit more coincidence. John Updike would eventually publish a series of four novels about Harry Angstrom, a businessman known as Rabbit. The four novels are *Rabbit, Run* (1960), *Rabbit Redux* (1971), *Rabbit Is Rich* (1981), and *Rabbit at Rest* (1990). The last two won Pulitzer prizes. When I wrote to Updike and asked him if the name Rabbit was an allusion to Babbitt, he answered "No—not until the 3rd book, *Rabbit Is Rich*, did I think of Babbitt." That book has two epigraphs: one from Wallace Stevens and the other from George Babbitt.

I also asked Updike if he has ever read C. S. Lewis's *Pilgrim's Regress*. He answered, "No, but I did read a number of other volumes with pleasure and gratitude."

# 14

# PLAN FOR THE CURING:
# GEORGE MACDONALD AND MODERN
# CHILD-TRAINING METHODS

*Few who read George MacDonald's beloved fantasy story "The Wise Woman" realize that it was a century ahead of its time as advice for parents.*

> "If the wise woman had but pinched her, she would
> have shown herself an abject little coward.... Nothing
> such, however, was the wise woman's plan for the
> curing of her."
> "The Wise Woman," *The Gifts of the Child Christ,*
> Vol. I, p. 235.

George MacDonald's story "The Wise Woman" which he also called "The Lost Princess—A Double Story," was one of C. S. Lewis's favorites. In this story MacDonald, successful father of thirteen (two of them adopted), clearly anticipated the child-training rules that would be developed and taught by behavioral scientists a century later.

"Each year thousands of parents seek professional advice on how to handle problems with their children." So began the book *Living with Children: New Methods for Parents and Teachers* (by Gerald Patterson and M. Elizabeth Gullion, 1972). The authors of this book and others like them seek to show parents how to encourage desirable behavior in their children and gradually eliminate undesirable behavior. Their method is based on the "social learning" approach. The rules are simple, but few people follow them.

In MacDonald's story a distraught king and queen sought professional advice about their terrible daughter. Not from a behavioral scientist in an air-conditioned office, but from a famous witch who lived in the heart of a forest. She was not an evil witch, but a strange, good, wild, and wise woman.

The princess was lost indeed when the wise woman came to the rescue. In fact, this woman came to two families whose girls had both become unbearable, and in both cases she soon perceived that the parents would not cooperate in the cure she envisioned. In both cases she snatched the girl up in her large black cloak and carried her off before anyone suspected what had happened. In today's terms, it was clearly a case of illegal deprogramming.

Both girls were only children born to doting parents—one in a palace and the other in a distant shepherd's hut. Both were taught from infancy by everyone they met that they were "Somebodies." They were awash in parental affection, but they were both totally selfish and unloving. Their parents wanted them to be happy, but for some reason they were both rather miserable; and so was everyone who had to be around them.

As the wise woman put it to the frustrated parents, "You are sufficiently punished by the work of your own hands. Instead of making your daughter obey you, you left her to be a slave to herself; you coaxed when you ought to have compelled; you praised when you ought to have been silent; you fondled when you ought to hove punished; you threatened when you ought to have inflicted — and there she stands, the full-grown result of your foolishness. She is your crime and your punishment."

According to today's behavior modification experts, futile coaxing, inappropriate praise and fondling, and empty threats actually reinforce undesirable behaviors. As Gerald Patterson says in *Families: Applications of Learning to Family Life* (1971), "It isn't too much love that spoils a child; it is being reinforced for the wrong behaviors."

Permissive parents like to let a child's natural impulses unfold freely. But according to John Krumboltz in *Changing Children's Behavior* (1972), there is a deceptive appeal in the idea that children should be allowed to do whatever they want whenever they want. If the adult withdraws from the child's environment, the child is not then automatically "free." When parents decrease their influence, other forces increase theirs.

The wise woman knew the only thing that could save the princess from her hatefulness was that she should be made to mind somebody else than her own miserable Somebody.

Krumboltz meets head-on the question "Isn't it harmful to a child's happiness to frustrate her by not letting her do as she wishes?" He claims that the goal of keeping a child happy will keep her from being happy. In contrast, he quotes the current folk-authority Dear Abby: "If you raise your children to be dependable, industrious, honest and considerate of others, they will make themselves happy."

We are taught now that the first five or six years of a child's life are the most formative. Some parents feel that if they fail during those years, all is lost; but behavior modification experts disagree. Learning continues throughout life, they say, and their principles apply throughout life. Past events predict present behavior, but present behavior changes for better or for worse. Krumboltz says "What shall we do now? What kind of environment can we arrange for the child now that will encourage desirable behavior and diminish undesireable behavior? We can take action that will make a difference."

The two girls the wise woman undertook to help were well past five or six. Significantly, she never scolded or spanked either one. Instead, she provided an effective new learning environment immediately. The princess was grasped under a cloak and borne away against her will. Later in the journey when Princess Rosamond rammed her head into the woman to hurt her, the woman did not raise her hand or her voice; the cloak could be hard as brass at such times, and Rosamond bruised her head on it. Natural consequences like that punished her repeatedly during her curing.

When Rosamond became so angry that she refused to travel on, the woman never said a word or looked around. Instead, she left Rosamond behind four different times on that journey. After the fourth time Rosamond made her first weak effort to follow the kind woman's advice. What happened after that is far too much to describe here; MacDonald's ideas for new learning environments were literally fantastic.

There are four alternative principles that Krumboltz offers for stopping inappropriate behavior, and the wise woman used all four during her course of treatment.

1.  Satiation principle: Allow the child to continue (or insist that she continue) performing the undesired act until she tires of it.
2.  Extinction principle: Arrange conditions so that the child receives no rewards following the undesired act.
3.  Incompatible alternative principle: Reward an alternative action that cannot be performed at the same time as the undesired act.
4.  Negative reinforcement principle: Arrange an unpleasant situation which the child can terminate immediately by improving her behavior.

According to Patterson, the most powerful reinforcers for a child or an adult are social reinforcers: the close attention of another person, a touch, words of approval, a smile, a glance, or a kiss. In some cases the yelling of "Shut up" serves as an unintentional reinforcer. When all social reinforcers and other reinforcers are removed for a time, that is called Time Out.

Time Out is an ingenious replacement for spankings, a most effective means of producing rapid decreases in the occurrence of problem behaviors; if a parent uses Time Out consistently, the effect is usually noticeable in three or four days. Time Out means removing the child from the situation where all of the reinforcers for inappropriate behavior are located; "she is placed In a new situation where there are few, if any. Patterson reports that five minutes alone in the bathroom is the best form of Time Out for a child in most families. (He tells why and discusses both medicine cabinets and flooding.)

The wise woman apparently had no bathroom in her home in the forest, but she used several kinds of Time Out. By far the most severe was placing the shepherdess girl Agnes into a spherical blue isolation chamber, magic and invisible, where she was left alone with her obnoxious self for five days. (At night, while Agnes was asleep, she lay in the loving woman's arms all night long and drank her wonderful milk without knowing it.) The treatment worked, but it was only the beginning of retraining for Agnes. As the wise woman told her kindly after rewarding her for her first good behavior, "Agnes, you must not imagine that you are cured...."

Other key ideas of Patterson that the wise woman exemplified a century earlier are:

Begin where the child is.
Reinforce desired behavior immediately and often.
To be consistent, set up a program including a specific goal, specific steps, small steps.
Be sure the child is reinforced from the very beginning.
Be specific.
Make use of natural consequences that occur every day.
Do not nag or scold. Wait for the prosocial behavior to come and then reinforce it.

The wise woman, being perfect, could do all of this without lapsing into outbursts, forgetting her goals, or having to fight her own bad habits. Krumboltz assures ordinary mortals that they are to be congratulated if they are putting behavior modification principles to use at all, that children are resilient enough to tolerate some parental failings, and that there are practical ways to gain self-control and improve skill in this art.

Behavior modification principles are so effective that they even help to train autistic children. Like any other art, this one con be used for good or evil ends. If the wise woman had been an evil witch she could have used the same methods to turn the two girls into evil witches. Behavioral scientists tell adults how they can change children's behavior, not what behavior they ought to change.

Fortunately, few adults would purposely teach their children wicked or sick behavior; but great are the numbers who do it accidentally. When George MacDonald was writing the story of the lost princess he may hove been thinking of his monarch, Queen Victoria, and the heartache that her own beloved young son was turning out to be. Her child-rearing techniques were extremely defective, and his character turned out to be defective.

It was the inner person, not outer pleasantness, that MacDonald was really concerned about. He said of the conceited shepherdess, "if she were not made humble, her growing would be a mass of distorted shapes all huddled together; so that, although the body she now showed might grow up straight and well-shaped and comely to behold, the new body that was growing inside of it, and would come out of It when she died, would be ugly, and crooked...."

The wise woman summed up her rules of behavior for Rosamond by saying, "It just comes to this, that you must not do what is wrong, however much you are inclined to do it, and you must do what is right, however much you are disinclined to do it." The purpose was to get rid of her weary shadowy self and to find her strong, true self.

When Rosamond's behavior had been well modified, she asked the wise woman if she could forgive her for all the trouble she had caused.

> "If I had not forgiven you, I would never have taken the trouble to punish you. If I had not loved you, do you think I would have carried you away in my cloak?"

> "How could you love such an ugly, ill-tempered, rude, hateful little wretch?"

> "I saw, through it all, what you were going to be," said the wise woman, kissing her. "But remember you have yet only begun to be what I saw."

Rosamond is sent home and given the job of serving her blind parents (now doubly blind) as the wise woman has served her, and bringing them to the wise woman eventually. As Patterson says, "Children change their parents, just as the parents contribute to the changes in their children."

George MacDonald never intended this 79-page fantasy to be a tract on child-training, and a prophetic one at that. But he knew very well that it was a mysterious, powerful story with at least two meanings. Although it is usually called "The Wise Woman," he also called it "The Lost Princess—A Double Story." Here is the way he ended it:

And that is all my double story. How double it is, if you are to know, you must find out. If you think it is not finished — I never knew a story that was. I could tell you a great deal more concerning them all, but I have already told more than is good for those who read but with their foreheads, and enough for those whom it has made look a little solemn, and sigh as they close the book.

One can read the story with one's forehead to glean MacDonald's insights about child training, and that is good. But he has been known to use a great feminine figure as his symbol for God, and he has been known to state that every child on earth is both the child of a king and the child of a shepherd.

MacDonald's double story is about everyone, because he believed that everyone is part of God's ultimate plan for the curing.

# 15

## CARVED IN STONE:
## WHAT THE BIRD DID NOT SAY
## EARLY IN THE YEAR

by Kathryn Lindskoog
with Gracia Fay Ellwood and Joe R. Christopher

ddison's Walk was a familiar haunt of C. S. Lewis, but his poem on the 1998 memorial stone there might not seem familiar to him at all.

"I must say that I am surprised that any editor would present so many changed texts to the public without saying where he got them."[1] That was Richard Wilbur's informal response to the news that under Walter Hooper's editorship more than half the poems published in Lewis's lifetime (forty-five of approximately seventy-five) appear posthumously only in revised versions.[2] Twenty-six of the seventy-five have been published since Lewis's death with altered titles.[3]

---

[1] A letter to Kathryn Lindskoog dated 19 June 1995 from Richard Wilbur in Cummington, Massachusetts.

[2] *Poems* (London: Geoffrey Bles, 1964; New York: Harcourt, Brace & World, Inc., 1964) contains over a hundred poems written throughout Lewis's life, edited by Walter Hooper. *The Collected Poems of C.S. Lewis* (London: Collins Fount, 1994) is a compilation of *Spirits in Bondage* and *Poems* with seventeen additional poems, edited by Walter Hooper.

[3] Some of the title alterations are radical. For example, "Break Sun my Crusted Earth" became "A Pageant Played in Vain." "The Shortest Way Home" became "'Man Is a Lumpe Where All Beasts Kneaded Be'." "The World Is Round" became "Poem for Psychoanalysts and/or Theologians."

Richard Wilbur claims no particular expertise in Lewis studies.[4] But until 1995 even those with expertise in Lewis studies were unaware of the momentous changes that first occurred in texts of Lewis's published poetry a few months after his death. And even after 1995 this information has not spread fast.[5]

Lewis's posthumous editor Walter Hooper writes in his "Preface" to *Poems*, "It was not always easy to determine his final version of a poem, especially if there were slightly different versions or if the poem had already appeared in print."[6] All one can say to this is if all the changes in Lewis's poems were the result simply of choices between drafts, Mr. Hooper has the distinction of being an editor who almost invariably chooses the poorer reading when he has a choice of more than one.[7]

In 1996 one of the lesser-known Lewis poems suddenly began its ascent from almost sixty years of obscurity into prominence. Michael Ward, Centenary Secretary of the Oxford C. S. Lewis Society, made the following announcement in *Seven, An Anglo-American Literary Review* under the title "Addison's Walk."[8]

As part of the celebrations of the centenary of Lewis's birth in 1998, the Oxford University C.S. Lewis Society will be erecting at Magdalen College a free-standing stone[9] bearing Lewis's poem, "What the Bird Said Early in the Year"....

---

[4] Richard Wilbur is the second United States Poet Laureate, winner of two Pulitzer Prizes for poetry, and winner of both the National Book Award and the Bollingen Prize.

[5] A series of revelations about some of the poetry revisions first appeared in the quarterly newsletter *The Lewis Legacy* in the winter 1995 issue. Information about Lewis's *Pilgrim's Regress* poems first appeared that year in *Finding the Landlord: A Guidebook to C. S. Lewis's Pilgrim's Regress* by Kathryn Lindskoog (Chicago: Cornerstone Press Chicago, 1995).

[6] *Poems*, p. vii; *Collected Poems*, p. 5.

[7] When Lewis died in 1963 he left a treasured sheaf of poems that he had intended to include in a book. Walter Hooper says that in 1964 he found multiple versions of Lewis's poems here and there, and—alone in a locked room—incorporated them into Lewis's collection. He has never said where he found them, where he keeps them, or why he does not reveal their contents to researchers and scholars.

[8] *Seven, An Anglo-American Literary Review*, Volume 13, 1996, pp. 7-8.

[9] In fact, the stone was designed to be mounted on the old wall.

The poem is about Addison's Walk, a mile-long. circuit round the deer park at Magdalen, which Lewis traversed frequently with pupils and friends. It was in Addison's Walk in 1931 that Lewis had the famous midnight conversation about myth with Tolkien and Dyson that led to his conversion to Christianity.

It's a short poem, suitable for inscription on stone, and, dealing as it does with the fruition of desire, is typically Lewisian. The President of Magdalen, Anthony Smith, has kindly given permission for the stone to be put up, and a site in Addison's Walk has been agreed upon.

The stonemason, Alec Peever, who has created original commemorative works in Westminster Abbey, St. Paul's and Canterbury Cathedrals, has been commissioned to design the stone and the estimated cost will be in the region of five thousand pounds sterling.

If *Seven* readers would like to contribute to the cost of this stone, which will become an enduring part of the Oxford landscape, they should make cheques payable to "The C.S. Lewis Centenary Stone" and send them to Mr. Peter Cousin, The Treasurer, The Oxford University C. S. Lewis Society, c/o Pusey House, St Giles, Oxford, OXl 3LZ. For further information about the stone or about the Society, please write to Mr. Michael Ward, Centenary Secretary, at the same address.

### What the Bird Said Early in the Year

I heard in Addison's Walk a bird sing clear:
This year the summer will come true. This year. This year.
Winds will not strip the blossom from the apple trees
This year, nor want of rain destroy the peas.
This year time's nature will no more defeat you,
Nor all the promised moments in their passing cheat you.
This time they will not lead you round and back
To autumn, one year older, by the well-worn track.
This year, this year, as all these flowers foretell,
We shall escape the circle and undo the spell.

Often deceived, yet open once again your heart,
Quick, quick, quick, quick!—the gates are drawn apart.

C. S. Lewis, 1898-1963

The monument thus described by Michael Ward might make
"What the Bird Said Early in the Year" Lewis's most famous poem.
Mr. Ward did not mention the fact that this 12-line version of Lewis's
14-line poem was never published until after Lewis's death. Lewis
titled his original poem "Chanson D'Aventure" and published it in
*The Oxford Magazine* on 10 February 1938. (Line numbers are added
below.)

Chanson D'Aventure

1. I heard in Addison's Walk a bird sing clear
2. 'This year the summer will come true. This year. This year.
3. 'Winds will not strip the blossom from the apple trees
4. This year, nor want of rain destroy the peas.
5. 'This year time's nature will no more defeat you,
6. Nor all the promised moments in their passing cheat you.
7. 'This summer will not lead you round and back
8. To autumn, one year older, by the well-worn track.
9. 'Often deceived, yet open once again your heart,
10. The gates of good adventure swing apart.
11. 'This time, this time, as all these flowers foretell,
12. We shall escape the circle and undo the spell.'
13. I said, 'This might prove truer than a bird can know;
14. And yet your singing will not make it so.'

"Chanson D'Aventure" is not the most memorable of Lewis's poems, but it is a skillful lyric and uniquely appropriate for his memorial
stone at Magdalen College. It not only hints at his fondness for
Addison's Walk, but subtly expresses what lies at the heart of his life
and all his writing. Couplets and brevity are especially appropriate in
a poem using the imagery of birdsong, and especially practical on a
memorial stone.

The poem is Lewis's intellectual response to spring. It is essentially about his longing for Joy and, ultimately, all human longing for heaven. It is about our natural desire to escape from human mortality and futility, from the cycle of life and death, and from the mutability of all earthly joys. It is about the endless summer that can exist only outside nature as we know it, if at all. And it is also about epistemology.

Lewis's title "Chanson D'Aventure" refers to the medieval tradition of a noble quest or adventure undertaken in the spring in a spirit of valor and optimism. In medieval thought, two kinds of adventure focusing on the Ultimate were (in literature) the knightly quest for the Holy Grail, and (in life) pilgrimage to the shrine of a saint. The Grail is the source of Christ's blood, the wine of Eternal Life; at the shrine, the pilgrim stands between earth and heaven, potentially participating in the death and divine life of the Saint. In both quests, the journeyer risked his or her life in hopes of attaining the ultimate divine gift. Thus the poem is about a birdsong encouraging a veteran traveller who has been disappointed in all his or her previous quests. (Lewis was repeatedly disappointed in his early searches for Joy, just as John was repeatedly disappointed in his search for the Western Island in *The Pilgrim's Regress*.) Lewis's choice of title shows the importance of line 10, "The gates of good adventure swing apart."[10]

Line 1: Lewis begins and ends this poem in the first person, reporting the narrator's experience to the reader. The birdsong he hears in line 1 turns out to symbolize the hopeful spirit that comes unbidden in the spring.

Line 2: "Summer will come true" means that the pleasantest season won't be transitory, but will give ultimate fulfillment. Repetition of "this year" not only suggests the repetitious phrasing of

---

[10] In this way and others, "Chanson D'Aventure" is related to the Narnian Chronicles. In Narnia Aslan breaks the witch's spell that makes it always winter. But in spite of the miracle of spring, summer never lasts in Narnia. Life remains locked in its circle of mutability, and the whole world is eventually destroyed. As Lucy says tearfully near the end of *The Last Battle*, "I did hope it might go on forever." Then in the last chapter she learns that the true Narnia does go on forever. Narnia will come true.

birdsong, but perhaps suggests also the contrast between time and eternity.[11]

Lines 3-4: Time destroys whatever is beautiful and life-enhancing, suggested by blossoms, potential fruits (apples) and vegetables (peas). Within the first four lines, Lewis has used "this year" four times.

Line 5: "This year" is used for the fifth time. The bird (natural instinctive hope) claims that the nature of time will not continue to prevail.

Line 6: The (false) promise of spring is for lasting joy, not the fleeting joy that always disappoints.

Lines 7-8: This is the central couplet of the poem, and summer is the central season of the year. Here Lewis likens his treks around the year to his treks around (circular) Addison's Walk. In both cases he ends back where he started, with less time left to live. In diction, the general "this year" gives way to the more immediate "this summer" of the year's cycle (in contrast to autumn).

Line 9: Hope urges the narrator to believe again in an incipient fullness of Joy in spite of the fact that so far he has always ended up back where he started. This part of the poem portrays what Lewis called "the dialect of desire" that led him through the adventures he portrayed allegorically in *The Pilgrim's Regress*. By contrast, one who chooses self-protective cynicism keeps his heart shut.[12]

Line 10: This key line likens the open heart to open gates through which a pilgrim or knight ventures out to seek the elusive *sunum bonum*.[13] (Perhaps Lewis had in mind the large, handsome gates through which one leaves Addison's Walk.)

---

[11] In retrospect, the publication of this poem early in 1938, the year of Munich and Kristallnacht, adds special poignancy to the bird's false promise.

[12] In chapter 13 of *The Last Battle*, a group of dwarfs showed cunning rather than belief. Aslan explained that they were in prison in their own minds, so afraid of being taken in that they could not be taken out.

[13] Lewis did not have the inborn temperament of such an ebullient adventurer. "I was also, as you may remember, one whose negatives demands were more violent than his positive, far more eager to escape pain than to achieve happiness, and feeling it something of an outrage that I had been created without my own permission. To such a craven the materialist's universe had the enormous attraction that it offered you limited liability." *Surprised by Joy* (London: Geoffrey Bles, 1955) 162.

Line 11: Here Lewis switches from "this year" and "this summer" to "this time." "All these flowers" shows that the setting of the poem is full spring.

Line 12: Spring's promise to an open heart is that the spell of mutability will be broken and that we can escape earth's endless circle of life and destruction. (Spring blossoms were the occasion of Lewis's first longing for Joy, described in the first chapter of *Surprised by Joy*.)[14] The images of escaping a circle and undoing a spell are those of magic–with the hidden suggestion that it will take real magic–God's own magic–to escape the cycle of nature. This prepares the reader for the final couplet.

Line 13: The poem concludes with the narrator's response to the bird's message. He admits that nature's portents about eternity may happen to be true, but nature itself is within the circle of time and cannot comprehend eternity.

Line 14: The possible truth of nature's occasional portents about the coming of eternal Joy (summer) does not mean that nature is an authority. Nature is a secondary cause, part of the created (and fallen) order. Nature only "will come true" outside itself, in the realm of the Supernature. (Exactly six years after publication of "Chanson D'Aventure," Lewis declared in a BBC radio talk: ". . .vague religion – all about feeling God in nature and so on – is so attractive. . . .But. . .you will not get eternal life by just feeling the presence of God in flowers or music."[15]) It could be argued that Lewis's final couplet is

---

The symbolic spiritual door that Lewis once chose to open on a busride up Headington Hill, described in the last chapter of *Surprised by Joy*, is another matter. Choosing to open that door was Lewis's response to the realization that he had been shutting something out of his life.

[14] In his diary on 21 March 1967 Warren Lewis spoke of the annual childhood thrill of spring currant blossoms, a thrill like homesickness for heaven. That passage can be read in *Brothers and Friends: the Diaries of Major Warren Hamilton Lewis* (San Francisco: Harper & Row, 1982) 272.

[15] This statement was published on p. 216 of the 24 February 1944 issue of *The Listener* under the heading "The Map and the Ocean; The first of a series of talks by C. S. Lewis entitled 'Beyond Personality: The Christian View of God.'" ("Beyond Personalty" was published later in 1944 as a small book, and in 1952 it was published as the last section of *Mere Christianity*.) In the 2 March 1944 issue a reader named W. R. Childe responded vehemently, "'Just feeling' is good! If I tell Mr. Lewis that 'feeling the presence of God in flowers and music' is Eternal Life, he may prepare his faggots for the usual heresy hunt in which Christian

also a comment on his own philosophical poetry ("singing"); thus the dialog between the narrator and the bird is Lewis's playful depiction of the dialog between aspects of his own mind.[16]

In contrast to posthumous versions of some of Lewis's other poems, this one incorporates few changes. But these few changes create significant problems. For one thing, the new title sets the poem "early in the year" (presumably January, February or March) rather than in the flowering of spring (traditionally May). More importantly, the new title omits all reference to medieval pilgrimage or chivalric quest.

Lines 7 and 8 were the heart of the original poem. But in the edited version the word summer, intentionally linked here to autumn, is inexplicably replaced by the phrase "time they."

The removal of the fifth couplet is puzzling. Line 9 is shifted to the sixth couplet, and line 10 is completely deleted.

Because the subject of this poem is the contrast between time in general (mutability and loss) and eternity, removal of the key phrase "this time, this time" in line 11 is also puzzling. Repetition of "this year, this year" from line 2 adds nothing.

Omission of Lewis's final couplet does away with the first-person brackets that shaped the entire poem; thus the substitute ending is apt to strike many readers as the weakest part of the posthumous version. The reason for the bird to urge the narrator "Quick, quick, quick, quick!" is not at all clear. (The song of a British thrush reportedly includes a note that can be transcribed as "quick.") "[T]he gates are drawn apart" seems more ambiguous and less felicitous than Lewis's "The gates of good adventure swing apart."[17] And, finally,

---

dogmatists have in the past so often liberated their own suppressed intellects and passions...." On 9 March Lewis responded to Childe: "I agree with Mr. W. R. Childe that it is no use to say 'Lord, Lord', if we do not do what Christ tells us: that, indeed, is one of the reasons why I think an aesthetic religion of 'flowers and music' insufficient."

[16] See Lewis's poem "Reason and Imagination" (mistitled "Reason"), *Poems*, 81.

[17] "The gates are drawn apart" suggests that an agent is briefly offering the narrator entrance or exit from a private area. In contrast, Lewis's line "The gates of good adventure swing apart" refers to traditional and instinctive spring zest for hopeful adventure.

the narrator's conclusion in "Chanson D'Aventure" was that the feeling of transcendence sometimes provided by nature (and celebrated by poets) is insufficient as a way to find eternal life; for some readers "Chanson D'Aventure" has been eviscerated by its removal.

In conclusion, "What the Bird Said Early in the Year" lacks cogency compared to Lewis's original version. We propose that "Chanson D'Aventure" would be a far more fitting inscription on Lewis's memorial stone.

# 16

# ROOTS AND FRUITS OF THE SECRET GARDEN: GEORGE MACDONALD, FRANCES HODGSON BURNETT, WILLA CATHER, AND D. H. LAWRENCE

*Relatively few George MacDonald readers know his 1871 story "The Carasoyn," and those who have read it are unaware of its connection to three famous novels. This connection is an amusing bit of literary history that would have interested MacDonald.*

Until now, no one has noticed the surprising links between "The Carasoyn" (1871), *The Secret Garden* (1911), *My Antonia* (1918), and *Lady Chatterley's Lover* (1928). The first is a Christian fairy tale; the second, a heartwarming story for children and their elders; the third, a great American novel; and the fourth, a book so sexually explicit that it was banned for decades in the British Isles and America.

"The Carasoyn" is a twelve-chapter tale about a motherless boy named Colin who has magical adventures. Colin, the son of a shepherd, discovers a human child named Fairy who has been held captive for seven years by a band of fairies who won't permit her to escape or to grow up. An old woman in a humble cottage out on a desolate Scottish moor tells Colin how to rescue Fairy, and he succeeds. Fairy grows up and marries Colin, but eventually the fairies find his little family in England. When Colin's children are playing in their apple orchard one day, the fairies steal the littlest one, a three-year-old boy. This time Colin finds the old woman's cottage on an English moor, and once again her directions enable him to rescue the missing child. It takes him seven years, and once again the rescued child has failed to mature any during his captivity but will do so when restored to human company.

In 1872 George MacDonald crossed the Atlantic on a Cunard oceanliner and arrived in Boston with his wife Louisa and oldest son Greville, for a triumphant United States lecture tour. He was the popular author of over twenty books by this time, and he could hold an audience of two or three thousand spellbound without any loudspeakers. Before he went home in 1873 he had met Emerson, Longfellow, Whittier, Stowe, and other prominent American authors—plus a prolific young writer named Frances Hodgson Burnett.

Forty years after MacDonald published "The Carasoyn," Burnett published her 1911 book *The Secret Garden*, the wonderful story of a motherless boy named Colin and the two children who work a change in him. Colin, his rich father, and his new friend Mary—the heroine of the book—all burst through from darkness and grief to light and joy, with the help of the secret garden and Dickon, a boy who lives on the moors close to nature. First Dickon rescues Mary, a stereotypical poor little rich girl. She is a case of arrested development because of parental neglect, a thin, pale, ignorant, unpleasant orphan. Next, the two of them rescue Colin, a bright but miserable boy who is a bedfast invalid imprisoned by fear and loneliness. And finally the three of them rescue Colin's father, a prisoner of depression and despair. The story has delicious mystery and enchants its readers. When its copyright expired in 1985, several new editions appeared at once from different publishers, with a variety of illustrations and a wide range of prices.

Needless to say, Burnett could have written a magical story about a motherless boy named Colin without knowing MacDonald's magical story about a motherless boy named Colin. But we know that she made the effort to go to meet MacDonald in 1872-73, and he was still important to her forty-four years later. According to Phyllis Bixler's essay "Frances Hodgson Burnett" (in volume 42 of *Dictionary of Literary Biography*), Burnett's *In the Closed Room* (1904) invites comparison to MacDonald's *At the Back of the North Wind*. Moreover,

Burnett's *The White People* (1917) contains what is apparently a fictional tribute to MacDonald himself. This story is set in Scotland and features MacDonald's trademark, an ancient library. Much of the story depicts the narrator's growing friendship with a writer she had long admired. Like MacDonald, the writer is a world-renowned Scotchman who writes essays, poems, and marvelous stories.... In the final scene the writer dies, and the narrator says she has frequently seen him since, smiling at her." MacDonald died twelve years before *The White People* was published.

(The story of Frances Hodgson Burnett's writing career is a happy one. Her widowed mother moved the family from England to Tennessee when Frances was sixteen. She started to write stories in a cold little attic room, and her stories eventually made her rich and famous. She published over fifty books, but the most beloved are *Little Lord Fauntleroy* [1886], *A Little Princess* [1905], and *The Secret Garden* [1911]. She said of herself, "With the best that was in me, I have tried to write more happiness into the world." In the Conservatory Garden of New York City's Central Park, there is a fountain honoring Burnett for her children's classics—a particularly fitting tribute to the woman who gave us an enchanted story garden. Children's literature is like a secret garden for many adults. They don't know how welcome they are to enter and how pleasant it is to linger there with or without a child.)

While Dickon, Mary, and Colin are singing the Doxology, a pivotal minor character enters the garden; she is Dickon's mother, Susan Sowerby, a wonderfully wise and nurturing woman who lives in a humble cottage on the moor. (Note the word *sower* in her name.) She is the Earth Mother *par excellence*. (In "The Carasoyn" the old woman who helps Colin perform his rescues lives in a little cottage on a moor.)

There is such a striking resemblance between Susan Sowerby and a character invented a bit later by Willa Cather that in my opinion Willa Cather must have read *The Secret Garden* shortly after it came out in 1911. In 1918 Cather published her finest novel, *My Antonia,* to wide popular acclaim, including H. L. Mencken's declaration, "No romantic novel ever written in America, by man or woman, is one half so beautiful."

In the first part of the fifth section, "Cuzak's Boys," the narrator describes his visit to middle-aged Antonia Cuzak and her big crowd of healthy, happy children at their humble but thriving home on the Nebraska plains (reminiscent of the Sowerby home on the Yorkshire moors). They take a walk in an enclosed apple orchard set off from the outside world and sit there talking and drinking in the beauty.

"The orchard seemed full of sun, like a cup, and we could smell the ripe apples on the trees. The crabs hung on the branches as thick as beads on a string, purple-red, with a thin silvery glaze over them...." This flowery, vine-draped orchard seems as much a bower of bliss as Burnett's Secret Garden.

Of all her fine children, Antonia frankly finds special joy in her son Leo, as Susan finds special joy in her son Dickon. Great peace radiates from both women; they both exude generosity, energy, and accomplishment. "She had only to stand in the orchard, to put her hand on a little crab tree and look up at the apples, to make you feel the goodness of planting and tending and harvesting at last," the narrator reflects. "It was no wonder that her sons stood tall and straight. She was a rich mine of life, like the founders of early races." In reality it is Cather herself who makes you feel the goodness of planting and tending and harvesting — as Burnett did before her. It is hard to imagine other novels so full of earthy fecundity as *The Secret Garden* and *My Antonia,* or other heroines so rich with lifegiving as Susan Sowerby and Antonia Cuzak. Drawn to Susan Sowerby's power and goodness, Colin asks, "Do you believe in Magic?"

"That I do, lad," she answers. She says she never called it that, but that the name doesn't matter. It is what sets the seed to swelling and the sun to shining and made Colin well, and it is the Good Thing. Colin should never stop believing in the Good Thing and knowing the world is full of it, whatever he calls it. He and his friends were singing to it when they sang the Doxology. It was the joy that mattered in their singing, she continued. They were singing for the Joy Maker. (This is what William James called healthy-minded religion.)

Barbara Reynolds is managing editor of the Anglo-American journal *Seven,* and one of the seven authors it covers is George MacDonald. When I told her about my idea that Burnett had borrowed MacDonald's Colin, she responded immediately. "Here is another Colin for you. Years ago, when I was reading *The Secret Garden* aloud to my daughter (she was about seven) I came to the part where Colin in his wheelchair is being pushed by Dickon, with Mary walking alongside. Suddenly I had a revelation and stopped reading. My daughter said, "Go on, Mummy, go on", but I couldn't for a few moments. I had suddenly seen the characters in *Lady Chatterley's Lover*—the husband in the wheelchair, Lady Chatterley alongside and Mellors pushing and lifting it when it got stuck. There they were: Colin, Dickon and Mary, only adult and transformed by Lawrence. Dickon is surrounded by animals and lives on the Yorkshire Moors. Mellors is a gamekeeper and lives among animals in the countryside based on Lawrence's own county, Nottinghamshire. There is also the transformation of Susan Sowerby into Mrs Bolton. I suspect that *The Secret Garden* was a book which Lawrence's mother had and that he had read it when he was a boy. These echoes and scattered ingredients were probably unconscious memories as far as Lawrence was concerned."

It's a far cry from George MacDonald's Colin to D. H. Lawrence's, and MacDonald would not have been pleased by the connection; I assume that Burnett and Cather would have disliked it also. (However, as Barbara Reynolds points out, they might have recognized the tender descriptions of growing things, of the budding leaves in Spring, of the primroses and violets.) Burnett's temporary invalid Colin has transmogrified into the permanently paralyzed and impotent Sir Clifford Chatterley. Mary has transmogrified into his frustrated wife Connie. And Dickon has transmogrified into her virile servant-class rescuer Mellors, who transforms Connie with the healing, life-giving magic of passionate carnal love. In addition to being intensely erotic and written in language bound to shock most potential readers for years to come, Lawrence's novel intentionally makes a religion of sexuality. It teaches that all that is meaningful is embodied in physical love.

In contrast, MacDonald would have been pleased with Agnes Sanford's little book *Let's Believe* (1954). (Unfortunately, Harper & Row eventually had to let it go out of print, and it has not yet been reissued.) Although I can't prove it, in my opinion Sanford must have read *The Secret Garden*. (She was twelve years old when it was published.) She ardently believed and taught Burnett's gospel that was vividly expressed by Susan and Dickon Sowerby—the transcendent beauty, joy, glory, and healing power of nature. The goodness at the heart of things. But for Sanford all this was part of the traditional, biblical Christian faith. Her autobiography, *Sealed Orders* (1972), makes that clear, and all her books illustrate it. That was the basis of her remarkable healing and teaching ministry. (Sanford was the daughter of Presbyterian missionaries in China, where she spent her childhood, and the wife of an Episcopal priest. There is a little garden prayer chapel in the sanctuary of St. Luke's Episcopal Church in Monrovia, California, in memory of her teaching ministry, on the same wall as the stained glass window in memory of C. S. Lewis's teaching ministry.) *Let's Believe* is simple, straightforward, practical teaching. Sanford said, "It is primarily for parents and teachers to use in imparting to children a knowledge of the ways of prayer. Children ask continually 'Mother, where is God?' 'Daddy, what is God?' *Let's Believe* was written to answer that question and to teach children how to pray to him."

# 17

# THE SALTY AND THE SWEET: MARK TWAIN, GEORGE MACDONALD, AND C. S. LEWIS

*Few readers of C. S. Lewis know what he thought of* Huckleberry Finn. *More importantly, few readers of Mark Twain and George MacDonald know what part they played in each other's lives and how MacDonald contributed to* Huckleberry Finn.

The connection between Mark Twain and George MacDonald evidently began in 1870, the year when 35-year-old Twain married the woman he adored, Olivia Langdon. The newlyweds were soon reading MacDonald's latest novel, *Robert Falconer:* and Twain reacted with great gusto and disgust. In a letter to their friend Mary Mason Fairbanks, who had probably recommended the book or given it to them, he spoke his mind on September 2, 1870.

"My! but the first half of it is superb! We just kept our pencils going, marking brilliant & beautiful things—but there was nothing to mark, after the middle. Up to the middle of the book we did so admire & like Robert—& after that we began to dislike & finally ended by despising him for a self-righteous humbug, devoured with egotism.

[Robert was a young Scot with a heart of gold—a forerunner of Gibbie, who would be invented later.]

"I guess we hated his grandmother from the first. The author was always telling of us her goodness, but seldom letting us see any of it.

[At this point Livy added a note: "I did not. I liked her all the time, her heart was all right, and what was wrong came of her education."]

"Shargar was the only character in the book who was *always* welcome, & of him the author gave us just as little as possible, & filled his empty pages with the added emptiness of that tiresome Ericson & his dismal 'poetry'—hogwash, *I* call it.

"Oh, yes, & there was Dooble Sanny, an imperial character—but of *course* he had to die in order to give Robert a chance to air some of his piety, & talk like a blessed Sunday-school book with a marbled cover to it.—

[Livy inserted "thats not correct."]

"But what on earth the author lugged in that inanity, Miss Lindsay, for, goes clear beyond my comprehension. Page after page, & page after page about that ineffable doughnut, & not even the poor satisfaction that Lord Rothie ruined her, after all. Hang such a character!

[Livy added a note: "how dreadful."]

"And Miss St. John—well there never was any interest about *her*, from the first. And when she concluded that the man she first loved was small potatoes & that that big booby of an Ericson was the man that completely filled her idea of masculine perfection I just wanted to send her a dose of salts [to purge her] with my compliments.

"Mind you, we are not through yet—two or three chapters still to read—& that idiot is still hunting for his father. I hoped that as he grew to years of discretion he would eventually appreciate that efforts of a wise Providence to get the old man out of the way (seeing that he wasn't very eligible property, take him how you would,)—but no, nothing would do for him, clear from juvenile stupidity up to mature imbecility but tag around after that old bummer.

[Livy added one word: "scandalous."]

"I do just wonder what he is going to make of him now that he is about to find him. A missionary, likely, along with Rev. De Fleuri, & trot him around peddling sentiment to London guttersnipes while he continues his special mission upon earth of reclaiming venerable strumpets and exhibiting his little wonders at midnight for the astonishment & admiration of chance strangers like the applauding Gordon."

[At this point Livy took her turn: "I would make erasures in this letter but it is a hopeless undertaking, I should have to erase the last three pages of it—However I know that he is rather ashamed of it because he said that he had left plenty of room for me to say something pleasant—

"The last part of the book we have not enjoyed as much as the first part, but the first we did enjoy intensely— Lovingly yours, Livy—"][1]

Mark Twain was ten years younger than George MacDonald and had waited ten years longer to get married; so it was that when he and Livy were newlyweds reading *Robert Falconer,* the MacDonalds had already been married twenty years. Two years later these colorful couples would meet each other.

In the fall of 1872 George MacDonald crossed the Atlantic on a Cunard oceanliner and arrived in Boston with his wife Louisa and oldest son Greville, for a triumphant United States lecture tour. He was the popular author of over twenty books by this time, and he could hold an audience of two or three thousand spellbound without any loudspeakers. He soon met Emerson, Longfellow, Whittier, Stowe, and other prominent American authors, plus the prolific young writer Frances Hodgson Burnett. The tour was plagued with occasional illnesses and travel problems; therefore, the MacDonalds greatly appreciated a five-day pre-Christmas rest "in *lapsury's luck*" at the Elmira, New York, home of "the Mother-in-law of Mark Twain," as MacDonald wrote on December 22 to his children back in England.[2]

It was only seven years after the end of the Civil War. On January 17, 1873, the MacDonalds went for the second time to hear the Jubilee Singers, a group of freed slaves sponsored by Fisk University. The first time that they heard these singers, George MacDonald sat with tears rolling down his cheeks and Louisa MacDonald was choked with a combination of tears and laughter. On January 17, the MacDonalds stayed after the performance to talk with the singers and to persuade them to sing in England. When the auditorium lights

---

[1]Mark Twain, *Mark Twain to Mrs. Fairbanks*, ed. Dixon Wecter (San Marino, Huntington Library: 1949) 134-137.
[2]Greville MacDonald, *George MacDonald and His Wife* (London: George Allen & Unwin, 1924) 432.

went out, one of the singers called out in the dark, "All the same color now!"[3]

On January 27, 1873, ten days after attending their second Jubilee Singers concert, the MacDonalds visited with Livy (and possibly Mark Twain) again.[4] Because the two couples shared an admiration for the Jubilee Singers, it seems likely that one of their topics of conversation was that group.[5]

On May 19, 1873, Mark Twain sat on the platform with other famous American writers at a farewell benefit for George MacDonald before he returned to England.[6]

Two months later, the Clemenses were in England. On July 10, 1873, Louisa MacDonald wrote to Livy that her garden party on the following Wednesday afternoon, July 16, would feature a MacDonald family play called *July Jumble*. Guests would include some poor and needy people, prominent London professionals, the Twains, and the Jubilee Singers, who were now in England on a concert tour.[7] At this time the large MacDonald family lived at a home they called The Retreat on the banks of the Thames in Hammersmith.[8]

Although the MacDonalds were often in financial distress, this fine old home had a garden of nearly an acre, a roadway bordered by ancient elms, and a tulip-tree said to be the second largest in England. The family had a portable stage that they used to set up on the lawn for performances. On Oxford and Cambridge boat-race days friends and relatives gathered from near and far to watch the race

[3]MacDonald, 442.

[4]MacDonald, 443.

[5]Almost eighteen years later, on November 16, 1890, Mark Twain attended a concert given by the Jubilee Singers in Asylum Hill Congregational Church in Hartford. He recorded the song titles in his journal, and they are listed in Mark Twain's *Notebooks & Journals*, Volume III, ed. Frederick Anderson (Berkeley: University of California Press, 1979) 593-594.

[6]MacDonald, 459.

[7]Mark Twain's *Notebooks and Journals*, Volume I, ed. Frederick Anderson (Berkeley: University of California Press, 1979) 564.

[8]The MacDonalds were visited by several of their new acquaintances from the United States. Greville MacDonald tells of a visitor who "avowed devotion to the negro cause, brought an uneducated coloured wife with him, and, in return for unbounded hospitality and money, as well as literary help, swindled and insulted my father." This account appears on page 466 of Greville's *George MacDonald and His Wife*.

from the water's edge. Alfred, Lord Tennyson attended once.[9] (After the MacDonald family gave up The Retreat, William Morris moved in and renamed it Kelmscott.)

Twain's daughter Susy briefly described her parents' 1873 visit to England, although she was too young to understand any of it at the time. She spoke of her father meeting such men as Thomas Hardy, Robert Browning, and Anthony Trollope. Then she added, "and mamma and papa were quite well acquainted with Dr. Macdonald and family."[10] Mark Twain quoted that passage from Susy in his autobiography and mentioned in passing that George MacDonald was a lively talker.[11]

Greville MacDonald, who had accompanied his parents on their tour in the United States, agreed with Susy about the friendship. "The two writers were very intimate and had discussed co-operation in a novel together, so as to secure copyright on both sides of the Atlantic. But there were many difficulties in the way, not chiefly [sic] those of motive and style."[12] Is it possible that the two men conceived of a story about a white orphan boy whose friend was a good-hearted black man? Within thirteen years they both happened to write and publish such a story.

Mark Twain had been working on *Tom Sawyer* in 1873 and had put it aside. In 1875 he took the pages out of their pigeonhole in his desk and finished the book without any trouble. He published *Tom Sawyer* in 1876.

George MacDonald was publishing one to three books every year at that time. In 1876 he published *Thomas Wingfold, Curate*, a 666-page novel, and Mark Twain owned a copy that cost $1.25.[13]

Twain started *Huckleberry Finn* in 1876; but it bogged down, and he took seven years to finish the first draft. He put it aside and returned to it three or four times between 1876 and the complete first draft in 1883. Years later, he described his creative process:

---

[9]Macdonald, 380.

[10]Mark Twain, *Mark Twain's Autobiography*, Volume II (New York: Harper & Brothers, 1924), 231. George MacDonald received an honorary doctorate from his alma mater, King's College in Aberdeen.

[11]*Mark Twain's Autobiography*, 232.

[12]MacDonald, 457.

[13] Alan Gribben, *Mark Twain's Library: A Reconstruction* (Boston: G.K. Hall & Co., 1980), 442.

As long as a book would write itself I was a faithful and interested amanuensis and my industry did not flag; but the minute the book tried to shift to *my* head the labor of contriving its situations, inventing its adventures, and conducting its conversations I put it away and dropped it out of my mind.... It was by accident that I found out that a book is pretty sure to get tired along about the middle and refuse to go on with its work until its powers and its interest should have been refreshed by a rest and its depleted stock of raw material reinforced by lapse of time.

It was when I had reached the middle of *Tom Sawyer* that I made this invaluable find. At page 400 of my manuscript the story made a sudden and detemined halt and refused to proceed another step. Day after day it still refused. I was disappointed, distressed and immeasurably astonished, for I knew quite well that the tale was not finished and I could not understand why I was not able to go on with it. The reason was very simple—my tank had run dry; it was empty; the stock of materials in it was exhausted; the story could not go on without material; it could not be wrought out of nothing.

When the manuscript had lain in the pigeon hole two years I took it out one day and read the last chapter that I had written. It was then that I made the great discovery that when the tank runs dry you've only to leave it alone and it will fill up again in time, while you are asleep—also while you are at work on other things and are quite unaware that this unconscious and profitable cerebration is going on. There was plenty of material now, and the book went on and finished itself without any trouble.[14]

On May 10, 1880, Mark Twain bought a new book from the J. R. Barlow bookstore in his home city of Hartford, Connecticut: *Sir Gibbie*, by his British friend George MacDonald.[15] It was in a paperback Seaside Library Edition, and it cost twenty cents.[16] In July

---

[14]*Autobiography of Mark Twain*, ed. Charles Neider (New York: Harper & Row, 1959) 288-289. This passage in chapter 53 is dated August 30, 1906.

[15]Gribben, 442.

[16]Abridged versions of *Sir Gibbie* have been made available in four editions. The latest is an abridged version by Kathryn Lindskoog, the only one to retain all sixty-two chapters and all their content; it is illustrated by Patrick Wynne and was first released in 1992. An adaptation for young readers by Michael Phillips, titled *Wee Sir Gibbie of the Highlands*, was released by Bethany House in 1990. An abridged version by Elizabeth Yates, which omits parts of the story, was re-

Twain received a bill for the book. On July 5, 1880, he paid the twenty cents. And that long-forgotten twenty-cent purchase apparently contributed significantly to *Huckleberry Finn.*

In 1881 Twain had his publisher send a copy of *The Prince and the Pauper* to MacDonald as a gift.[17] In August 1882 MacDonald recommended his literary agent A. P. Watt to Mark Twain. On September 19, 1882, Twain answered that he didn't need an agent because he had turned his literary business over to Osgood in Boston (later known as Houghton, Mifflin & Co.) and Chatto in London. "A book of mine used to pay me nothing in England—pays me two or three thousand pounds now. Osgood sells my occasional magazine rubbish at figures which make me blush, they are so atrocious. I perceive, after all these wasted years, that an author ought always to be connected with a highwayman."[18]

Twain had begun this letter by saying, "I'll send you the book [*Life on the Mississippi* ] with names in it, sure, as soon as it issues from the press... Since I may choose, I will take the *Back of the North Wind* in return, for our children's sake; they have read and re-read their own copy so many times that it looks as if it had been through the wars." (*At the Back of the North Wind* was first published in 1871.)

On February 16, 1883, George MacDonald wrote to Mark Twain to suggest a scheme for protection against pirating. If Twain would write brief sections of MacDonald's forthcoming sequel to *Sir Gibbie,* titled *Donal Grant,* both authors' names could appear on it and it would be copyrighted in both countries. On March 9 Twain politely declined. He said that if it were not for the pressure of his own work and his doubtfulness about the success of collaborative efforts, he would enjoy writing "the Great Scottish-American novel" with MacDonald, "each doing his full half." He promised again to send MacDonald a copy of *Life on the Mississippi.*[19]

In the same letter, Twain thanked MacDonald "in advance for the North Wind which is coming," and added a postscript: "The North

---

released by Schocken in 1987. An abridged version by Michael Phillips titled *The Baronet's Song* was released by Bethany House in 1983.

[17]Gribben, 440.

[18]MacDonald, 458.

[19]Twain, *Notebooks and Journals*, Volume III, 11.

Wind has arrived; & Susy lost not a moment, but went to work & ravenously devoured the whole of it once more, at a single sitting."[20]

*At the Back of the North Wind* remained important to Twain. Susy died in 1896. In a 1899 letter to William Dean Howells, Twain reflected upon his successful career and then added, "All these things might move and interest one. But how desperately more I have been moved to-night by the thought of a little old copy in the nursery of *At the Back of the North Wind*. Oh, what happy days they were when that little book was read, and how Susy loved it!"[21]

According to Alan Gribben, author of *Mark Twain's Library: A Reconstruction,* this book had been such a favorite in the Twain household that his children sometimes prevailed upon him to invent new stories about its hero, the motherless boy called little Diamond. The benevolent North Wind gave little Diamond a series of adventures and carried him up among the stars. She "eventually imparts the greatest favor of all—swift and painless death." Little Diamond's final journey was to "the country at the back of the North Wind."[22]

Similarly, in Twain's fairytale "The Five Boons of Life" a good fairy bestowed the valuable gift of death upon an innocent little child, after that gift had been spurned by a man who foolishly put his trust in pleasure, love, fame, and riches. "[The child] was ignorant," the fairy explained, "but trusted me, asking me to choose for it."[23] There is at least a superficial resemblance between the role of Twain's good fairy and MacDonald's North Wind.

Coleman O. Parsons suggested that *At the Back of the North Wind* provided the mode of airborne conveyance employed by Mark Twain's Satan in "The Chronicle of Young Satan." Gribben notes Parsons' idea and claims far more: that *At the Back of the North Wind* was an important inspirational source for *No. 44, The Mysterious Stranger*. According to Gribben, Mark Twain's Satan is a bitter and perverse transmogrification of MacDonald's kind North Wind.[24] If

---

[20]Gribben, 441.

[21]Albert Bigelow Paine, *Mark Twain, A Biography*, Volume II (New York: Harper & Brothers, 1912) 1074.

[22]Gribben, 440-441.

[23] First published in *Harper's Weekly*, July 5, 1902.

[24]Gribben, 441-442.

*The Mysterious Stranger* was influenced by *North Wind,* perhaps *Huckleberry Finn* was influenced by *Sir Gibbie.* When Mark Twain declined George MacDonald's 1883 invitation to co-author a sequel to *Sir Gibbie,* perhaps he was already responding to *Sir Gibbie* quite differently as he wrote *Huckleberry Finn.*

MacDonald's story is about a mute, barefoot, illiterate child of the streets in a city in northeastern Scotland; his mother is dead and his father is a miserable alcoholic. After his father dies, Gibbie is befriended and cared for by a kind black sailor; but the sailor is brutally murdered in Gibbie's presence. Gibbie flees the city and wanders away, living off the land and eventually becoming a secret helper at a farm. He is especially vulnerable because he is physically incapable of speech. After he is almost killed by a cruel buffoon, he is informally adopted by a kind old shepherd couple in a remote mountain cottage. He befriends the buffoon's spunky daughter by rescuing her when she is lost on the mountainside. Later he performs magnificently during a great flood, saving animals and people.

When Gibbie is found to be a lost baronet and heir to a fortune, he is taken back to the city and trained to be a gentleman. Among his many good deeds, he runs a secret lodging place for homeless people and goes to great lengths to rescue an alcoholic friend. He graduates from college, becomes an extraordinary philanthropist, and finally marries the girl he loves in spite of her cruel father.

Both *Sir Gibbie* and *Huckleberry Finn* explore questions of ethics and truth through the life of an unusually bright and unusually unfortunate boy. Both are set in the colorful region where the author spent his boyhood. Both were written for children as well as adults. And they have at least twenty plot elements in common.

1. *Parents:* The hero is a motherless, ignorant, but good-hearted boy who has lived with an alcoholic and criminally negligent father. He is occasionally helped by kind women, one of whom thinks of him as a lost lamb.

2. *Talents:* The boy enjoys extraordinary health, resilience, and courage. He is a strong swimmer. Although he is illiterate when the book opens, he learns to read once he gets the opportunity.

3. *Black Man:* The boy finds a kind of foster-father in a tender-hearted black man. The relationship changes the boy's life.

4. *Runaway*: The boy has little sense about money, but much practical sense about survival skills. He becomes a runaway who lives off the land.

5. *Flood*: The boy is thrilled by a dramatic storm that causes a severe river flood. Surprising objects float down the river in the flood. The flood causes wild rabbits to perch in trees, where they can be easily caught by boys.

6. *Raft*: Someone takes a remarkable journey down river on a raft.

7. *Silent Child*: An adult beats a child for refusing to respond, only to discover later that the child was physically unable to do so.

8. *Sign Language*: Someone in the novel communicates regularly by means of sign language.

9. *False Piety*: There is much artificial Christianity and some false sermonizing in the story.

10. *Pilgrim's Progress*: The boy reads repeatedly in John Bunyan's *Pilgrim's Progress*.

11. *Inheritance*: The boy meets and loves a fine girl who is being cheated out of her inheritance. With great effort, he restores it to her.

12. *Title Fraud*: An outrageously immoral and rather humorous character wrongly appropriates a hereditary title and demands and receives special courtesies as a result.

13. *Missing Child*: The boy is futilely sought by his townspeople as the supposed victim after a break-in by (real or imagined) murderers.

14. *Forgiveness*: The boy demonstrates a surprisingly tolerant spirit toward people who have harmed him.

15. *Wounded Boy*: An adult shoots a boy in the calf of his leg.

16. *A Trust*. A boy who has usually worn rags owns money that is held in trust for him by a stuffy professional man.

17. *Murder and alcohol*: Grisly murder and chronic alcoholism of are important plot elements.

18. *Superstition*: The novel describes eccentric local superstitions that some of the characters believe in.

19. *Dialect*: The novel makes heavy use of colorful dialect that is appropriate to its locale, but far from standard English.

20. *Kind Couple*: The boy finds an ideal home with a friend's relatives, a white-haired country couple with small means and large hearts. Though a bit vague mentally, the elderly gentleman in this

home displays admirable piety and leads devotions in a muddled but kindly way.

Literary cross-pollination is a fact of life, and some similarities are to be expected in the popular fiction of an era. Common story elements do not in themselves constitute proof of direct influence. Frances Hodgson Burnett's *Little Lord Fauntleroy* (1886) and *Sara Crew* (1888) have elements in common with *Sir Gibbie* also.[25] Similarly, in my opinion Willa Cather's *My Antonia* (1918) has a scene reminiscent of a scene in Burnett's *Secret Garden* (1911). According to John Docherty of the George MacDonald Society, MacDonald alludes to *A Connecticut Yankee in King Arthur's Court* in both the drafts and the final version of *Lilith*.[26] At the very least, tracing these apparent links between authors is a pleasant pastime, and it gives readers new occasions to talk and write about the books they care about. Twain scholar Walter Blair has shown that there are many sources for *Huckleberry Finn*,[27] and fresh claims of sources are occasionally set forth.[28]

The similarities between *Sir Gibbie* and *Huckleberry Finn* have no doubt been obscured by the books' great differences. *Sir Gibbie* is longer and traces the life of Gibbie (Gilbert Galbraith) from the age

---

[25] According to Phyllis Bixler's essay "Frances Hodgson Burnett" in *American Writers for Children Before 1900*, Volume 42 in *Dictionary of Literary Biography* (Detroit: Gale Research, 1985), Burnett met MacDonald when he visited New York in 1873. Burnett's *In the Closed Room* (1904) invites comparison to MacDonald's *At the Back of the North Wind*, and Burnett's *The White People* (1917) contains what may be a fictional tribute to MacDonald. This story is set in Scotland and features MacDonald's trademark, an ancient library. "Much of the story depicts the narrator's growing friendship with a writer she had long admired. Like MacDonald, the writer is a world-renowned Scotchman who writes essays, poems, and marvelous stories…. In the final scene the writer dies, and the narrator says she has frequently seen him since, smiling at her. " (MacDonald died twelve years before *The White People* was published.)

[26] John Docherty's book *The Literary Products of the Lewis Carroll—George MacDonald Friendship* (New York: Mellon, 1995) explores George MacDonald's and Charles Dodgson's literary allusions to each other.

[27] *Mark Twain and Huck Finn*, (Berkeley: University of Californis Press) 1960.

[28] In *Was Huck Finn Black? Mark Twain and African-American Voices* (New York: Oxford UP, 1993), Shelley Fisher Fishkin contends that the germ of Huck Finn was a 1874 newspaper sketch in which Twain explored the possibilities of using a young boy (in this case black, and younger than Huck) as narrator.

of eight to adult success and happy marriage. In contrast, Huck Finn is about fourteen years of age throughout his book, which fits Twain's dictum at the end of *Tom Sawyer:*

> It being strictly a history of a boy, it must stop here; the story could not go much further without becoming the history of a man. When one writes a novel about grown people, he knows exactly where to stop— that is, with a marrage; but when he writes of juveniles, he must stop where best he can.

In the twentieth century *Huckleberry Finn* has won world acclaim and *Sir Gibbie* has been consigned to near oblivion. The two factors most responsible for *Sir Gibbie'* s eclipse were MacDonald's sometimes preachy, long-winded style, and a northern Scots dialect which has become unreadable.

Although George MacDonald's immense popularity faded after his death in 1905, some of the fifty-seven books published in his lifetime are still beloved today. Early copies of his books sometimes sell for hundreds of dollars. More significantly, in 1992 there were ninety-five current American editions of books by George MacDonald listed in *Books in Print.* Three of them are illustrated by Maurice Sendak, and one bears an afterword by W. H. Auden. The most highly esteemed of all George MacDonald's books are probably *At the Back of the North Wind, The Golden Key, The Light Princess, Lilith, Phantastes, The Princess and Curdie, The Princess and the Goblin,* and *The Wise Woman.*

No one claims that George MacDonald was a consistently excellent writer, but such luminaries as G. K. Chesterton, W. H. Auden, Roger Lancelyn Green, and C. S. Lewis have lavished praise on his mythopoeic imagination. According to Chesterton, MacDonald was the most original thinker of his time. According to Auden, he was the Kafka of his century. According to Green, his strange gift set him among the very greatest story-tellers. According to C. S. Lewis, he was a rare mythopoeic genius like Kafka or Novalis and the greatest of them all. "I have never concealed the fact that I regarded him as my master; indeed I fancy I have never written a book in which I did not quote from him."[29]

---

[29]*George MacDonald: An Anthology*, ed. C.S. Lewis (New York: Macmillan, 1947), 20.

C. S. Lewis readily admitted that MacDonald's more realistic novels were inferior. "Necessity made MacDonald a novelist, but few of his novels are good and none is very good. They are best when they depart most from the canons of novel writing... Sometimes they depart in order to come nearer to fantasy, as in the whole character of the hero in *Sir Gibbie*..."[30]

C. S. Lewis buffs are well aware of his enthusiasm for George MacDonald, but few know of his enthusiasm for what he called "the divine *Huckleberry*." On 6 December 1950 C.S. Lewis wrote to an American correspondent, "I have been regaling myself on *Tom Sawyer* and *Huckleberry Finn*. I wonder why that man never wrote anything else on the same level. The scene in which Huck decides to be 'good' by betraying Jim, and then finds he can't and concludes that he is a reprobate, is unparalleled in humor, pathos, and tenderness. And it goes down to the very depth of all moral problems."[31]

> It was awful thoughts, and awful words, but they was said. And I let them stay said; and never thought no more about reforming. I shoved the whole thing right out of my head; and said I would take up wickedness again, which was in my line, being brung up to it, and the other waren't.

Twain's Huck Finn combines keen moral intuition with a dearth of independent religious imagination. In contrast, MacDonald's Gibbie is not only a moral prodigy, but also a Mozart of religious sensibility. Both *Huckleberry Finn* and *Sir Gibbie* include humor, horror, irony, and sorrow; but *Sir Gibbie* is permeated by the sweetness of George MacDonald's profound trust in the goodness of a God with whom Mark Twain was often at war.

What might unflappable George MacDonald, an ordained Congregational preacher, have said about Mark Twain's profound distrust in the goodness of God? MacDonald happened to publish

---

[30]*George MacDonald: An Anthology*, 17.

[31]From a letter to Warfield Firor of Baltimore, Maryland. William Griffin, *C. S. Lewis: A Dramatic Life* (San Francisco: Harper, 1986), 314. A year later, on 8 January 1952, he wrote in an unpublished letter to Ruth Pitter, "I can't bear the least suggestion (however sportive) of love affairs between different species or even between children. That is one of the many things which for me sinks *Tom Sawyer* so immeasurably below the divine *Huckleberry* ."

this line just one year after Twain published *Huckleberry Finn*: "Complaint against God is far nearer to God than indifference about him."[32] I challenge Mark Twain lovers to locate Twain's most appropriate quotation for a salty reply. [33]

*With thanks to Thomas Tenney, editor of The Mark Twain Journal, for his help.*

*Key Dates in the Twain-MacDonald Relationship*
1870 Samuel Clemens married Olivia Langdon.
　　　The couple read George MacDonald's *Robert Falconer*.
　　　Twain objected to too much sweetness and piety.
1872 George MacDonald visited the United States and met Twain.
1873 Mark Twain visited the MacDonalds in England.
1876-1883 The two authors sometimes exchanged books.
1880 Mark Twain bought MacDonald's new novel *Sir Gibbie*.
1883 MacDonald invited Twain to co-author the sequel to *Sir Gibbie*.
　　　Twain declined; appreciated *At the Back of the North Wind*.
1885 Mark Twain published *Huckleberry Finn*.
1899 Mark Twain was deeply moved by memory of *North Wind*.

---

[32]*George MacDonald: An Anthology*, 126. This quotation is from chapter 39 of What's Mine's Mine.

[33] A contender is found in the third Benares chapter of *Following the Equator* (1897), as from Pudd'head Wilson's New Calendar: "True irreverence is disrespect for another man's god."

# 18

# UNGIT AND ORUAL:
## FACTS, MYSTERIES, AND EPIPHANIES

*C. S. Lewis had the basic idea for* Till We Have Faces *brewing at the back of his mind for over thirty years before he wrote it. When he did, it flowed out of him very quickly and was immediately his favorite of all his books. But it is a mysterious book, with layers of meaning that puzzle many readers. The key to some of that meaning resides in a poem by C. S. Lewis that has been accidentally hidden from the public for sixty years.*

The Narnian Chronicles are the best known of all C. S. Lewis's fiction, but the meanings of the key names Aslan and Tash are not widely known. (Aslan is the Turkish word for lion, and Tash is the Turkish word for stone.) Readers interested in Lewis's mind and creative processes are glad to learn about the etymology and associations of these and other names in the Chronicles—Emeth, Tisroc, Tashbaan, and Clodsley Shovel, for example.

Shortly after completing the Narnian Chronicles, Lewis wrote his favorite of all his own books, *Till We Have Faces*. Again, it is possible to value and enjoy his fiction without being aware of the implications of the names Lewis chose. But this is Lewis's most subtle book, and a little understanding of certain names and archetypes will make us more aware of the depth, texture, and psycho-spiritual meaning of the story.

*Ungit*

Ungit is Glome's Babylonian-style fertility goddess, equivalent to the Greek goddess Aphrodite. She is a dreadful but holy black stone that is anointed with sacrificial blood. According to tradition, this stone once pushed its way up out of the earth; yet, according to Arnon the priest, Ungit "signifies the earth, which is the womb and mother of all living things." Ungit is the great mother and the great devourer, and her cult is one of darkness.

Surprisingly, Ungit's name is not related to stone or darkness; instead, it is derived from the Latin *ungo* or *unguo*, meaning to smear or anoint with any fatty substance. *Ungo* came to Latin from the Sanskrit word *anjana*, meaning ointment, and the word *anj*, meaning to rub or besmear. (The Irish word *ongain* and the new Irish word *ungadh* both mean ointment.)

English words closely related to Ungit refer to oil. An unguent is an ointment; unguentous means smeared with oil; unctuous means oily; and unction is the act of anointing a person in a religious ceremony or healing ritual to indicate and perhaps bring about a divine spiritual anointing. (Two of the ancient uses of oil are for healing and for light.)

The Old Testament makes much mention of oil, holiness, stones, and anointing. For example:

> Genesis 28:18: And Jacob rose up early in the morning, and took the stone that he had put for his pillows, and set it up for a pillar, and poured oil upon the top of it.

> Exodus 29:21: And thou shalt take of the blood that is upon the altar, and of the anointing oil, and sprinkle it upon Aaron, and upon his garments, and upon his sons, and upon the garments of his sons with him: and he shall be hallowed...

> Job 29:6: ...the rock poured me out rivers of oil...

In his undated poem "Reason and Imagination" (mistitled "Reason" after his death), C. S. Lewis likened Greek mythology's Demeter to human imagination,

> ...But how dark, imagining,
> Warm, dark, obscure and infinite, daughter of Night:
> Dark is her brow, the beauty of her eyes with sleep

Is loaded, and her pains are long, and her delight.
...Wound not in her fertile pains
Demeter, nor rebel against her mother-right.
...mother
... depth
... imagination's dim exploring touch

## Orual

It is Queen Orual's name, not Ungit's, that refers to stone. (Orual
was a human being, but she had a stony heart.) The Greek word
ορυκσισ means a digging (excavation, ditch, tunnel, or mine), and
the word ορυσσο means to dig up or dig through, especially in mines
or quarries. Accordingly, Orual uses a pickaxe and descends into the
psycho-spiritual underworld late in *Till We Have Faces* (part 2,
chapter 2). She goes down, against her will, to find dark, hidden
meanings and truths.

One of Orual's major accomplishments as queen of Glome was the
success of her silver mines. In the world Lewis lived in, the world in
which we read his books, Russia's Ural Mountains are a natural
boundary between Europe and Asia. They are rich with ore, and the
mid to central section is called the Ore Urals. (There is a Ural
language group or family [linguists disagree] named after the
mountains.) Similarly, the western Bolivian state of Oruro is primarily
known for its tin mining. I don't think the connection of Orual's
name to mineral deposits and mining can be coincidental.

Orual's devotion to Psyche resembles Dante's devotion to
Beatrice. Her descent into the earth is reminiscent of Dante's descent
in the *Inferno,* and her finding Psyche alive on a mountain top—"the
real Mountain"—resembles Dante finding Beatrice alive in the
Garden of Eden on top of Mount Purgatory. Orual and Dante had to
cross a little stream to join Psyche and Beatrice on the other side.
(See *Till We Have Faces,* chapters 9-10, and *Purgatory,* cantos 30-31.)

Orual's teacher from Greece called her Crethis; in Greek the
closest word to Crethis is ξρεο, meaning need, desire, or longing. In
the Cupid and Psyche myth, the older sister becomes a destroyer
because she is jealous about love Psyche receives from Eros; and in
*Till We Have Faces* she[ becomes a destroyer because she is jealous

about love Eros receives from Psyche. At one point in Orual's story she hears herself admitting that, figuratively speaking, she has devoured those she loved: "I am Ungit." As her teacher used to tell her, "We're all limbs and parts of one Whole. Hence of each other. Men, and gods, flow in and out and mingle." In this book that is true.

## Mysteries and Ephiphanies

Ungit is an example of the earth-womb archetype. Lewis wrote about the earth as a womb in his little-known three-stanza poem "Break Sun, My Crusted Earth," published in 1940 in the anthology *Fear No More* and, unfortunately, omitted from Lewis's posthumous poetry collections.

Break, sun, my crusted earth,
Pierce, needle of light, within,
Where blind, immortal metals have their birth
And crystals firm begin.

To limbs and loins and heart
Search with thy chemic beam,
Strike where the self I know not lives apart
Beneath the surface dream.

For life in secret goes
About his work. In gloom,
The mother helping not nor hindering, grows
The man inside the womb.

(In my opinion the six-stanza poem "A Pageant Played in Vain" that Walter Hooper published in 1964 cannot possibly be Lewis's revision of "Break Sun, My Crusted Earth" as claimed. To begin with, it is not about the same subject; secondly, it is an inferior poem.)

The main key to "Break Sun, My Crusted Earth" can be found in part two of Lewis's superb essay "Imagination and Thought in the Middle Ages," a lecture he gave on July 17-18, 1956. It was first published in *Studies in Medieval and Renaissance Literature* (Cambridge: Cambridge University Press, 1966):

Medieval man looked up at a sky not only melodious, sunlit, and splendidly inhabited, but also incessantly active: he looked at agents to which he, and the whole earth, were patients.... First, on the physical side, the beams of each planet (which penetrate through the Earth's crust) find the appropriate soil and turn it into the appropriate metal; Saturn thus producing lead, Mars iron, the Moon silver. and so forth. The moon's connection with silver, and the Sun's with gold, may be real survivals (at many removes) of pre-logical, pictorial, thinking. Venus is, perhaps, a maker of copper because she was, centuries earlier, Kupris, the lady of Cyprus, and that accursed island produced copper in ancient times. Why Saturn made lead, or Jove tin, I do not know.

In "Break Sun, My Crusted Earth" Lewis is using this medieval cosmology (unfamiliar to most readers today) as allegory or symbol for spiritual and psychological realities. In the strictly spiritual sense, this poem seems to me to express the receptiveness of the Virgin Mary at the Annunciation; Renaissance paintings sometimes portray the conception of Jesus with beams of golden light from heaven striking Mary. (In Florence see Lorenzo Monaco's *Annunciation*, c. 1425, in the Salumbeni Chapel, Santa Trinita; Alesso Baldovinetti's *Annunciation*, 1457, in the Galleria degli Uffizi; and Mariotti Albertinelli's *Annunciation with God the Father*, 1510, in the Gallaria dell' Accademia.)

In asking the sun to pierce his own crusted earth, Lewis is asking God to create spiritual gold in his deep inner self. I may be wrong, but I suspect that he is simultaneously asking God to create within him what Paul called a "new man" (Ephesians 2 and 4; Colossians 3).

Sixteen years after Lewis wrote "Break Sun, My Crusted Earth," hints of the same haunting imagery appeared (with or without Lewis's conscious awareness) in his strange story about Orual, the virgin queen of Glome. I think the third stanza of "Break Sun, My Crusted Earth" can relate to Orual:

> For life in secret goes
> About his work. In gloom,
> The mother helping not nor hindering, grows

The man inside the womb.

The similarity of the name Glome to the word gloom is obvious to many readers of *Till We Have Faces* who have never heard of "Break Sun, My Crusted Earth." In naming Orual's kingdom Glome, Lewis may have had in mind the word gloaming, which means twilight or dusk. (Gloaming is derived from the Teutonic root glûm.)

Although Orual was biologically barren, life (spiritual life) was secretly growing inside her. (The person "inside the womb" for Orual reminds me of the person described by the Apostle Paul in Colossians 3:10-11 "...the new man, which is renewed in knowledge after the image of him that created him: Where there is neither Greek nor Jew, circumcision nor uncircumcision, Barbarian, Scythian, bond nor free: but Christ is all, and in all.")

There is no overt reference to Christ in *Till We Have Faces*; in fact, there is not even any reference to Hebrew monotheism. But there is a clear reference to Eros, the "Brute" bridegroom of Psyche. (In Christian tradition, the divine bridegroom is Christ: "...as the bridegroom rejoiceth over the bride, so shall thy God rejoice over thee," Isaiah 62.5.) Just before Orual's transfiguration, she heard voices say "He is coming. The god is coming to his house. The god comes to judge Orual."

Suddenly "The air was growing brighter and brighter about us; as if something had set it on fire. Each breath I drew let into me new terror, joy, overpowering sweetness. I was pierced through by the arrows of it." "The only dread and beauty there is was coming, was coming." This echoes Dante's experience at the end of *Paradise*: "So my mind hung in abeyance, staring fixedly, immovable. intent, its ardor increasingly enflamed by the sight. Anyone who sees that Light becomes a person who would not possibly consent to turn away to any other sight; for the good that is the object of all desires is ingathered there in its fullness, and elsewhere it falls short of its perfection."

Midway between "Break Sun, My Crusted Earth" and *Till We Have Faces*, Lewis published another favorite book of his, *The Great Divorce* (1946). In this story Lewis left a twilight city (a predecessor of Glome) and travelled to the foothills of "the real Mountain." In the last chapter, Lewis sees a great assembly of motionless figures standing forever around a silver table, watching the actvities of little figures that resembled chessmen. "And these chessmen are men and women as they appear to themselves and to one another in this world. And the silver table is Time. And those who stand and watch are the immortal souls of these same men and women." In a sense, the beautiful Orual figure at the end of *Till We Have Faces* is the queen's immortal soul. Orual's transformation is like a fulfillment of 1 John 3:2: "... we know that when He appears we shall be like Him, for we shall see Him as He is."

The sunrise ending of *The Great Divorce* is strikingly similar to the ending of *Till We Have Faces*. In *The Great Divorce* Lewis heard spirits sing, "It comes! It comes! Sleepers awake! It comes, it comes, it comes." Then " ...the rim of the sunrise that shoots Time dead with golden arrows and puts to flight all phantasmal shapes." Like Orual after her encounter with God, Lewis awakened on earth after his near encounter with God. Dante, too, had awakened back in this world after the crescendo of light that climaxed with his finally seeing God. In each of these three books, *Paradise, The Great Divorce,* and *Till We Have Faces*, reawakening into life on the little silver table was the protagonist's temporary withdrawal from the real awakening.

In *The Great Divorce* Lewis had George MacDonald say 'The picture is a symbol: but it's truer than any philososphophical theorem (or, perhaps, than any mystic's vision) that claims to go behind it." Lewis's poem "Reason and Imagination" is about the inadequacy of either reason (the Fox: philosophical theorems) or imagination (Ungit: mystic vision) to show us reality.

Oh who will reconcile in me both maid and mother,
Who make in me a concord of the depth and height?
Who make the imagination's dim exploring touch
Even report the same as intellectual sight?
Then could I truly say, and not deceive,
Then wholly, say, that I BELIEVE.

For Orual (and C. S. Lewis), the answer is an encounter with divinity himself. At the end of her adventures, Orual realizes that before the face of God all questions die away and even all words die away. But we who are readers of *Till We Have Faces* are not yet at the end of our adventures and questions. Until we finally meet the gods face to face for ourselves, we continue to mine Lewis's deep words for wisdom.

# SAGE OBSERVATIONS

# 19

# C. S. LEWIS AND THE HOLY SPIRIT

*Although C. S. Lewis was not a Pentecostal or a Charismatic Christian, he thought deeply about how spiritual reality is manifest in our material world.*

C. S. Lewis was embarrassed by the phenomenon of speaking in tongues; but he once preached an entire sermon about the subject. According to the 2 June 1944 issue of *The Daily Telegraph,* "in the middle of the sermon Mr. Lewis, under stress of emotion, stopped, saying 'I'm sorry,' and left the pulpit.... After a hymn was sung, Mr. Lewis returned and finished his sermon ... on a deeply moving note." That sermon exists to this day as the essay "Transposition" in *They Asked for a Paper* and *The Weight of Glory.*

C. S. Lewis believed in angels and demons and a thoroughly supernatural reality. He believed in mystical experience. I suspect that if he had lived ten years longer he might have welcomed the Charismatic movement that was coming to the Anglican Church.

So it was that on Sunday, 28 May 1944, Lewis found himself preaching his memorable Pentecost Sunday sermon at Mansfield College Chapel in Oxford. He admitted at the start that *glossolalia,* speaking in tongues, was a subject that was a problem to him. (It would have been a problem for his listeners also.) But since it is part of the story of Pentecost, and since St. Paul said he spoke with tongues more than anyone else, Lewis felt he should deal with the subject.

To begin with, Lewis assumed that some cases of speaking in unknown tongues are just expressions of nervous excitement. But that doesn't mean that tongues can't ever be the work of the Holy Spirit.

If some cases of speaking in tongues are this-worldly, Lewis insisted, it does not follow that other cases aren't genuinely spiritual.

The English that some saints use to talk about God sounds much like the expressions that human lovers use, but that does not mean that the saints are only fooling themselves about spiritual love. All spiritual things as we know them resemble parts of ordinary physical life. In fact, real human love would look like some kind of lust to humans who have never felt any love. Things can be far above the things that they resemble.

Furthermore, some of our physical sensations serve for two or more kinds of events. Lewis himself noticed that gorgeous music and bad news both caused the same odd feeling in his chest. He loved the feeling when it was part of his pleasure and hated it when it was part of his misery. The fact is that we have far more emotions than the physical responses to go with them. So our physical responses are multi-purpose. (Readers can think of their own examples. A person may weep with sorrow or with joy or from peeling onions; laugh with anger or with delight or from being tickled; tremble with terror or with ecstasy or from a chilly breeze.)

Our spiritual life manifests itself through our physical life. Speaking in tongues as a holy activity might sound just like meaningless gibberish to an outsider, but those on the inside know the difference. Spiritual things must be spiritually understood. There will always be people who say that religion is nothing but psychological need, justice nothing but self-protection, love nothing but lust, and thought nothing but twitching of the grey matter in the brain. (Since Lewis's time this reductionism has been labelled "nothing-buttery.") People who think this way are like a dog that looks at the pointing finger instead of at what the finger is pointing at. They miss the meaning of everything.

At the end of his sermon, Lewis looked ahead to the resurrection of the body. Perhaps when the Holy Spirit causes Christians to speak in tongues, that is a tiny sample of what lies ahead for us. Lewis supposed that in our resurrected bodies there will be far fuller experiences of God himself. We probably won't have new senses, but our present senses will be flooded by God in ways we cannot now imagine.

Lewis not only believed in the supernatural gifts of tongues, but he also believed in the reality of miracles; he twice preached sermons in London on that topic. Eventually he wrote an entire book called *Miracles*, ending with an afterthought: if we were heroic missionaries, apostles, or martyrs, we would be apt to see miracles. Miracles and martyrdoms, he warned, tend to cluster in certain dangerous areas of history.

Later, Lewis witnessed the apparently miraculous healing of his wife's cancer after he called in a friend to pray for her when she was on her deathbed early in 1957. Their brief marriage after her healing was the happiest part of both their lives. Then she died in 1960.

Lewis published one of his last books, *The Four Loves*, in 1960. At the end of the book he spoke of bereavement. It is no good seeking earthly comfort for our losses, he said. In the long run there is no earthly comfort. But heaven offers us heavenly comfort. What we loved in people here, we will find in Him. "By loving Him more than them, we shall love them more than we do now." In the meantime, we must try to believe what we cannot feel in our bereavement, that God is our true Beloved.

But God sometimes awakens in man, towards Himself, a supernatural Love. (Is this not a gift of the Holy Spirit?) Of all gifts, this one is the most to be desired; here is the center of all human and angelic life. Lewis thought that he had tasted this heavenly love for God, but just a little. "For news of this fully waking world, you must go to my betters," he said. Three years later he went to the fully waking world himself. There, no doubt, he is flooded by God in ways we cannot now imagine.

# 20

# BRIGHT SHOOTS OF EVERLASTINGNESS: C. S. LEWIS'S SEARCH FOR JOY

C S. Lewis's life was basically a quest for joy, and the central theme of his writing was the story of that quest.

The following quotations are from the writings of C. S. Lewis and Karl Marx. One of these quotations mentions joy a great deal, and the other does not touch upon it at all. They both bear careful attention.

1. "Union with Christ imparts an inner elevation, comfort in affliction, tranquil reliance, and a heart which opens itself to everything noble and great not for the sake of ambition or desire for fame, but for the sake of Christ. Union with Christ produces a joy which the Epicurean seeks in vain in his shallow philosophy, which the deeper thinker vainly pursues in the most hidden depths of knowledge. It is a joy known only to the simple and childlike heart, united with Christ and through Him with God, a joy which elevates life and makes it more beautiful."

2. "You know, I think, that I believe in no religion. There is absolutely no proof for any of them, and from a philosophical standpoint Christianity is not even the best. All religions, that is, all mythologies to give them their proper name, are merely man's invention—Christ as much as Loki. Primitive man found himself surrounded by all sorts of terrible things he didn't understand... Thus religion, that is to say mythology grew up. Often too, great men were regarded as gods after their death—such as Heracles or Odin: thus after the death of a Hebrew philosopher Yeshua (whose name we have corrupted into Jesus) he became regarded as a god, a cult sprang up, which was afterwards connected with the ancient Hebrew Jahweh-worship, and so Christianity came into being—one mythology among

many... Of course, mind you, I am not laying down as a certainty that there *is* nothing outside the material world; considering the discoveries that are always being made, this would be foolish. Anything MAY exist."

In fact, these two statements were made when Lewis and Marx were still very young and not really so settled in their beliefs as they sound here. The first one was by Marx,[1] and the second was by C. S. Lewis.[2]

C. S. Lewis wrote the words of the second paragraph to his friend Arthur Greeves when he was seventeen years old. (Greeves was a Christian and Lewis was not.) Seventeen years later Lewis was a recent convert to Christianity and had just published a book telling how he journeyed from atheism to faith in Christ. That strange little book, *The Pilgrim's Regress,* is the oldest book by Lewis that has always stayed in print. It is a fanciful retelling of Lewis's intellectual and spiritual journey from early childhood through the atheism that he described at seventeen and on to the mid-point of his life when he came to Christ.

Lewis wrote *The Pilgrim's Regress* in 1932, the same year when his Christian friend J.R.R. Tolkien wrote *The Hobbit.* Of all places, Lewis wrote *The Pilgrim's Regress* at the home of his old friend Arthur Greeves during a two-week visit with him. In a letter to a reader twenty years later Lewis said, "I don't wonder that you got fogged in *Pilgrim's Regress.* It was my first religious book and I didn't then know how to make things easy. I was not even trying to much, because in those days I never dreamed I would become a 'popular' author and hoped for no readers outside a small 'highbrow' circle." But he loved the book and wanted people would read it.

This story is set in an allegorical dream in which the hero leaves home to search for the beautiful Western Island he has glimpsed a few times with intense longing, beginning in his childhood. His trip is full of detours, each one representing some intellectual error that Lewis had encountered as he was searching for whatever he was searching

---

[1] Karl Marx as a schoolboy, from Marx-Engels Gesamtausgabe, quoted from "The Baptism of Karl Marx" in *The Hibbert Journal.*

[2] Young Lewis's condemnation of Christianity is found in a letter he wrote to his friend Arthur Greeves on October 12, 1916 (as published in *They Stand Together,* p. 135).

for. He didn't know what it was. Lewis knew that one thing he *didn't* want was orthodox Christianity. Since the age of thirteen when he rejected religion, he had no interest in the atoning work of Christ or in heaven. There are delicious ironies in Lewis's life.

Finally in 1955 Lewis published his autobiography *Surprised by Joy,* in which the story of *The Pilgrim's Regress* is told in a factual and detailed way. This autobiography is largely interior; and it only covers what turned out to be the first half of Lewis's life, up to his conversion to Christ at the age of thirty-two.

When Lewis was a very little boy indeed, his brother once created a toy garden with stems and leaves in the lid of a tin cookie box. Countless miniature gardens like this have been made by children in boxes and pie pans, but this particular toy garden became famous. It made the child Lewis aware of the beauty of nature for the first time—nature that was cool, dewy, fresh and exuberant. (Because these children lived in Northern Ireland, nature really *was* cool, dewy, fresh, and exuberant.)

The next incident is the key to Lewis's life story. When he was perhaps five years old, he stood beside a flowering currant bush on a summer day. Suddenly the memory of his brother's toy garden arose as if from centuries ago. The child Lewis was overwhelmed with an enormous bliss beyond description. It was a kind of desire, but before he could know what he desired, the sensation was gone. One might think that he desired the beauty of nature or the little garden of long ago, but that was not it. In a sense all his previous short life was insignificant after that moment, it seemed. The currant bush, or what had come through the currant bush, had marked him for life.

A second experience like the first one came to him through the Beatrix Potter book *Squirrel Nutkin.* It shocked and troubled him because it caused him to somehow fall in love with autumn. There was a sense of immeasurable importance about this sensation that came over him. It was different from any other pleasure in life; it seemed to be what other people might call "in another dimension."

The third experience of this emotion for Lewis came from a brief passage of poetry about the Norse god Balder. When Lewis read those few lines of poetry, they created in him a desire of almost sickening intensity.

At this point in the autobiography Lewis warns anyone who is bored by those childhood incidents—his unusual response to the bush, the book, and the poetry—to quit reading the autobiography; because in a sense the central story of his life is about nothing else. It is unsatisfied desire which is better than any satisfaction. The Joy that Lewis talks about is distinct from all other pleasures. It has the stab and pang of longing.

When he was a young teenager, Lewis thought naturally enough that this Joy was pointing him toward sex; but he learned that sex had nothing to do with it. They are completely separate things. He also learned that the lure of magic and the occult had nothing to do with it. There can be a lust for the occult, but that is entirely different.

For a few years Lewis had no experience of the Joy and even forgot it. Then he came across *Siegfried and the Twilight of the Gods* illustrated by Arthur Rackham. It flooded him with an unendurable sense of desire and loss, and that became his lost Joy anew. He knew then that this experience of his was the supreme and only important object of desire for him. "I was sick with desire," he wrote later, "that sickness better than health." Obviously, it was a bit like being in love.

It is important to note that Lewis was never much of a pleasure-seeker in the ordinary sense. In all his life he never asked to be amused; he only demanded not to be interrupted. He preferred monotony to disturbance. He would have preferred nonexistence to unhappiness. (He had a fair amount of unhappiness and pain in his life, beginning with toothaches and viruses in his childhood and the loss of his mother to cancer when he was nine, then contending with an extremely difficult father and some dreadful boarding schools as he grew up, and plenty of adult trials.) Lewis had no lust for life. He liked fun, but he was not a greedy person for fun and pleasure.

When Lewis was sixteen he met Arthur Greeves, a teenage neighbor boy outside Belfast, and to their amazement they learned that they shared their passion for Norse mythology. Arthur too knew the stab of Joy. Their reaction to each other was "You too?!" Now Lewis had someone to consult and to confide in. They shared their love of natural beauty and art and literature.

As time went on and Lewis became an expert about Norse mythology, the thrill disappeared from it. Then once when Lewis was remembering a particularly vivid moment of his lost Joy and was longing for it, he was stabbed by Joy again. Not Joy in Norse mythology, but Joy in his own past Joy in Norse mythology. "Thus the very moment when I longed to be so stabbed again, was itself such a stabbing," he observed.

But when his attention was on his inner feelings, the Joy never came. When Northerness no longer produced the Joy in him, he should have realized that the object of his desire was further away and more outside himself than Norse mythology. He did not realize that for a long time. He kept seeking special sensations in every walk he took, in every poem he read.

He had learned by now not to look for it in sex. He said, "Joy is not a substitute for sex; sex is very often a substitute for Joy. I sometimes wonder whether all pleasures are not substitutes for Joy."

Then Lewis came across the book *Phantastes* by George MacDonald, and although Lewis did not realize it until later, Joy started to take on a holy quality for him. As he put it later, his imagination was baptized. Not that he got on the right track very soon. That came more than ten years later. In the meantime, he decided for a while that his experience of Joy had all along been simply a keen appreciation of beauty, and he talked about its value a great deal and experienced it very little.

But eventually he learned that even love of beauty was not the real Joy. Joy seemed to say to him, "It is not I. I am only a reminder. Look! Look! What do I remind you of?" And it said, "You want... something other, outside, not you or any state of you." That meant that a state of thrill was not his goal. He asked himself... what is it? What was he longing for? And finally an answer came to him in his current philosophy which had replaced his atheism.

As a young philosophy professor at Oxford, Lewis was forced by his intellectual honesty into a belief called Absolute Idealism. In this system of belief the Absolute was a spirit a lot like God; but there was nothing to fear and nothing to obey. It was safely impersonal. Nevertheless, there was some wisdom in this pseudo-religion, and Lewis was on the right track. What he really wanted in his moments of clearest consciousness, he decided, was to merge with the Absolute. That gave him his best understanding yet of his longing Joy.

One day on a bus ride up Headington Hill, where he lived, Lewis became aware that he was in some sense holding a door shut and that he could open it if he chose. He chose to open it, for whatever that meant. From that moment on, his philosophical defenses against the existence of a personal God began to crumble. Here is part of his famous account of his eventual conversion in his own words:

> You must picture me in that room at Magdalen, night after night, feeling, whenever my mind lifted even for a second from my work, the steady, unrelenting approach of Him whom I so earnestly desired not to meet. That which I greatly feared had at last come upon me. In the Trinity Term of 1929 I gave in, and admitted that God was God, and knelt and prayed: perhaps, that night, the most dejected and reluctant convert in all England...

At the end of *Surprised by Joy* and in his biographies one can read how Lewis took about two years to move on from this belief in God and surrender to God to a definite belief in Christ—in the incarnation, crucifixion, resurrection, and our redemption. And from that time forward Lewis often experienced stabs of Joy, but he never took such interest in the subject again. He felt that the delights of his early days were given to help to lure him into the world of the Spirit.

Joy had certainly not been a physical appetite. Furthermore, it had not been an emotional and psychological appetite as some would claim. It had been a spiritual hunger that spilled over into Lewis's consciousness. Lewis finally saw Joy as what some call our mortal homesickness for heaven, and he knew he was well on his way home.

Although Joy had served its major purpose for Lewis himself in the first half of his life, it shines to us through the books he wrote in the second half of his life. I tend to think of Lewis as a latter-day Moses, in that God first called him when he saw a bush aflame with flowers (although he didn't recognize the call for many years), and then God used him to lead many people out of the slavery of our culture's materialistic world view, toward the ultimate Promised Land. Like Moses, Lewis didn't want that job at all. He had no desire to become a popular Christian teacher who set ordinary people to longing for heaven. But evidently that is what he was called and equipped to do.

*Following are some of C. S. Lewis's words to us about our deepest yearning, in chronological order, as he published them.*

In 1940 Lewis published his first book of Christian apologetics, *The Problem of Pain*. In the last chapter he says:

> There have been times when I think we do not desire heaven; but far more often I find myself wondering whether, in our heart of hearts, we have every desired anything else.... that something which you were born desiring and which, beneath the flux of other desires and in all the momentary silences between the louder passions, night and day, year by year, from childhood to old age, you are looking for, watching for, listening for? You have never had it. All the things that have ever deeply possessed your soul have been but hints of it—tantalizing glimpses, promises never quite fulfilled, echoes that died away just as they caught your ear. But if it should ever really become manifest—if there ever came an echo that did not die away but swelled into the sound itself—you would know it. Beyond all possibility of doubt you would say "Here at last is the thing I was made for"... All your life an unattainable ecstasy has hovered just beyond the grasp of your consciousness. The day is coming when you will wake to find, beyond all hope, that you have attained it, or else, that it was within your reach and you have lost it forever.

Two years later, in 1942, Lewis preached his most famous sermon, *The Weight of Glory*. He said:

> At present we are on the outside of the world, the wrong side of the door. We discern the freshness and purity of morning, but they do not make us fresh and pure. We cannot mingle with the splendours we see. But all the leaves of the New Testament are rustling with the rumor that it will not always be so. Some day, God willing, we shall get IN.... The faint, far-off results of those energies which God's creative rapture implanted in matter when He made the worlds are what we now call physical pleasures; and even thus filtered, they are too much for our present management. What would it be to taste at the fountain-head that stream of which even these lower reaches prove so intoxicating? Yet that, I believe, is what lies before us. The whole man is to drink joy from the fountain of joy.

Two years later, in 1944, in *Beyond Personality* (which was later incorporated into *Mere Christianity*), Lewis said:

> If you want to get warm you must stand by the fire: if you want to be wet you must get into the water. If you want joy, power, peace, eternal life, you must get close to, or even into, the thing that has them. They are not a sort of prize which God could, if He chose, just hand out to anyone. They are a great fountain of energy and beauty spurting up at the very centre of reality.... Look for yourself, and you will find in the long run only hatred, loneliness, despair, rage, ruin, and decay. But look for Christ and you will find Him, and with Him everything else thrown in.

One year later, in *The Great Divorce*, Lewis said of an ordinary Christian woman named Sarah Smith who had died:

> Who knows where it will end? Redeemed humanity is still young. But already there is joy enough in the little finger of a great saint such as yonder lady to waken all the dead things of the universe into life...

Four years later, in a 1949 issue of the British humor magazine *Punch*, Lewis published a serious poem about a day of unexpected ecstasy. He asks whether this Joy was caused by something physical (an elf in the blood), something mental (a bird in the brain), or something spiritual (an angel's presence)—and he obviously believes the latter.

### The Day with a White Mark

> All day I have been tossed and whirled in a preposterous happiness...
> Reason kept telling me all day my mood was out of season...
> Yet I—I could have kissed the very scullery taps. The colour of
> My day was like a peacock's chest....
> ...I doubt if the angel himself
> Is free to choose when sudden heaven in man begins or ends.

The next year after his poem "The Day with a White Mark," Lewis published his first book for children, *The Lion, the Witch and the Wardrobe*.

Lewis's first, loftiest ambition had been to write narrative and even epic poetry. The greatest epic poetry, Homer's *Iliad* and *Odyssey* were written in Greek at about the time the Olympics began, near 800 B.C. The next great epic was Virgil's *Aeneid*, written about 20 B.C. in Latin. Virgil was trying to continue the epic tradition with echoes of Homer. The first Christian epic was Dante's *Divine Comedy*, written in Italian in about 1300. Milton wrote the great Christian epic of the English language, *Paradise Lost*, in about 1660. These epics are works of genius that have been cherished by multitudes through the centuries.

During the entire 2,500 years when our five greatest epics were produced, there was no such thing as children's literature. There was no such thing as a children's writer. People told stories to children, but no one wrote a storybook for them to enjoy. That never happened until 250 years ago. Books for children are a new phenomenon in world history. It is interesting to see how C. S. Lewis incorporated elements of the great epics into his Narnian books for children: grand themes, voyages or struggles with profound consequences, and immensities of cosmic history.

In *The Lion, the Witch and the Wardrobe* Lewis described the feelings of the children when they first heard the name of Aslan, before they knew who he was. They all had powerful feelings, like the strange feeling in a dream, "the dream so beautiful that you remember it all your life and are always wishing you could get into that dream again." The stories of Narnia are full of this yearning and Joy.

In 1954 Lewis finally published his exhaustive study *English Literature in the Sixteenth Century, Excluding Drama* as part of the Oxford History of English Literature series. There he touches upon a special kind of Protestant joy:

> The experience is that of catastrophic conversion. The man who has passed through it feels like one who has waked from nightmare into ecstasy. Like an accepted lover, he feels that he has done nothing, and never could have done anything, to deserve such astonishing happiness...

His own puny and ridiculous efforts would be as helpless to retain the joy as they would have been to attain it in the first place. Fortunately, they need not. Bliss is not for sale, cannot be earned.... From this buoyant humility... Protestant doctrines originally sprang. For it must be clearly understood that they were at first doctrines not of terror but of joy and hope; indeed, more than hope, fruition, for as Tyndale says, the converted man is already tasting eternal life.

In 1956 Lewis published his strange and wonderful novel *Till We Have Faces.* In it the woman named Psyche says:

I have always—at least, ever since I can remember—had a kind of longing for death.... It was when I was happiest that I longed most. It was on happy days when we were up there on the hills... with the wind and the sunshine... Do you remember? ...And because it was so beautiful, it set me longing, always longing.

Two years later, in 1958, in *Reflections on the Psalms,* Lewis spoke of the Psalmist's "appetite" for God. He mentions that there is a tragic depth in our worship which Judaism lacked. Our joy has to be the sort which can coexist with tragedy. Lewis felt that one of the greatest lyric poems in the world is Psalm 19. One can read this psalm with the knowledge that it was one of Lewis's favorite pieces of literature and, no doubt, one which he very frequently used in his personal devotional life. It expresses *joy in nature, joy in goodness,* and then *personal commitment to God.*

PSALM 19
> *Joy in Nature*

The heavens are telling the glory of God;
    and the firmament proclaims his handiwork.
Day to day pours forth speech,
    and night to night declares knowledge.
There is no speech, nor are there words;
    their voice is not heard;
yet their voice goes out through all the earth,
    and their words to the end of the world.

In them he has set a tent for the sun,
>    which comes forth like a bridegroom from his chamber,
>    and like a strong man runs its course with joy.
Its rising is from the end of the heavens,
>    and its circuit to the end of them;
>    and there is nothing hid from its heat.

### Joy in Goodness

The law of the Lord is perfect, reviving the soul;
>    the testimony of the Lord is sure, making wise the simple;
>    the precepts of the Lord are right, rejoicing the heart;
>    the commandment of the Lord is pure, enlightening the eyes;
>    the fear of the Lord is clean, enduring forever;
>    the ordinances of the Lord are true, and righteous altogether.
More to be desired are they than gold, even much fine gold;
>    sweeter also than honey and drippings of the honeycomb.
Moreover, in keeping them is thy servant warned;
>    in keeping them there is great reward,

### Commitment to God

But who can discern his errors?
>    Clear thou me from hidden faults.
Keep back thy servant also from presumptuous sins;
>    let them not have dominion over me!
Then I shall be blameless,
>    and innocent of great transgression.
Let the words of my mouth and the meditations of my heart
>    be acceptable in thy sight,
>    O Lord, my rock and my redeemer.

Two years later, in 1960, in *The Four Loves,* Lewis said:

He [God] can awake in man towards Himself, a supernatural Appreciative Love. This is of all gifts the most to be desired. Here, not in our natural loves, nor even in ethics, lies the true centre of all human and angelic life. ... even the imagining has made all other objects of desire—

yes, even peace, even to have no more fears—look like broken toys and faded flowers.

Three years later, Lewis ended the last book he ever wrote with the same affirmation that he made twenty-three years earlier in *The Problem of Pain.* This last book was *Letters to Malcolm, Chiefly on Prayer,* and Lewis died before it was published. Here is what he said at the end of his life, or, as he might have put it, just before the beginning:

> Even in Heaven, some perpetual increase in beatitude, reached by a continually more ecstatic self-surrender...
>
> But... if that other world is once admitted, how can it, except by sensual or bustling preoccupation, be kept in the background of our minds? How can the "rest of Christianity"—what is this "rest?"—be disentangled from it? How can we untwine this idea, if once admitted, from our present experience in which, even before we believed, so many things at least looked like "bright shoots of everlastingness"?...
>
> Then the new earth and sky, the same yet not the same as these, will rise in us as we have risen in Christ. And once again, after who knows what aeons of the silence and the dark, the birds will sing and the waters flow, and lights and shadows move across the hills, and the faces of our friends laugh upon us with amazed recognition.
>
> Guesses, of course, only guesses. If they are not true, something better will be. For "we know that we shall be made like Him, for we shall see Him as He is."

"You know, I think, that I believe in no religion," Lewis boasted when he was seventeen. Ironically, a few equally misleading words from young Karl Marx sum up Lewis's ultimate life message: "Union with Christ produces a joy which the Epicurean seeks in vain in his shallow philosophy, which the deeper thinker vainly pursues in the most hidden depths of knowledge. It is a joy known only to the simple and childlike heart..." C. S. Lewis acquired that simple and childlike heart.

# 21

# C. S. LEWIS:
# THE NATURAL LAW
# IN LITERATURE AND LIFE

by Kathryn Lindskoog and Gracia Fay Ellwood

*C. S. Lewis's first teaching appointment at Oxford was in philosophy, and he was at heart a moralist. It is no wonder that he was a lover of what is called the Natural Law.*

The human race is haunted by the idea of doing what is right. In the first five chapters of *Mere Christianity*, C.S. Lewis discusses the fact that people are always referring to some standard of behavior that they expect other people to know about. People are always defending themselves by arguing that what they have been doing does not really go against that standard, or that they have some special excuse for violating it.

What they have in mind is a law of fair play or a rule of decent behavior. Different people use different labels for this law—traditional morality or the Moral Law, the knowledge of right and wrong, or Virtue, or the Way. We choose to call it the Natural Law. This law is an obvious principle that is not made up by humans but is for humans to observe. Lewis claims that all over the earth humans know about this law, and all over the earth they break it; he further claims that there is Something or Somebody behind this Natural Law.

## A Law Hard as Nails

According to Lewis, we find out more about God from Natural Law than from the universe in general, just as we find out more about a person by listening to his conversation than by looking at a house he built. We can tell from Natural Law that the Being behind the universe is intensely interested in fair play, unselfishness, courage, good faith, honesty and truthfulness. However, the Natural Law does not give us any grounds for assuming that God is soft or indulgent. Natural Law obliges us to do the straight thing no matter how painful or dangerous or difficult it is to do. Natural Law is hard: "It is as hard as nails" *(Mere Christianity* 23).

This last sentence also appears as the central thought in Lewis's moving poem "Love." In the first stanza he tells us how love is as warm as tears; in the second, how it is as fierce as fire; in the third, how it is as fresh as spring. And in the final stanza he tells us how love is as hard as nails.

> Love's as hard as nails,
> Love is nails;
> Blunt, thick, hammered through
> The medial nerve of One
> Who, having made us, knew
> The thing He had done,
> Seeing (with all that is)
> Our cross, and His. (*Poems* 123)

In Lewis's first chronicle of Narnia, *The Lion, The Witch and The Wardrobe,* this hardness of the love of God was predicted by the lion Aslan when he promised to save Edmund from the results of treachery. He said "All shall be done. But it may be harder than you think" (104). When he and the White Witch discussed her claim on Edmund's life, she referred to the law of that universe as the Deep Magic. Aslan would not consider going against the Deep Magic; instead, he gave himself to die in Edmund's place, and the next morning came back to life. He explained to Susan that though the

Witch knew the Deep Magic, there is a far deeper magic that she did not know. This deeper magic says that when a willing victim is killed in place of a traitor, death itself would start working backwards. The deepest magic worked toward life and goodness.

In Narnia, and in this world as well, if the universe is not governed by an absolute goodness all our efforts and hopes are doomed. But at the beginning of "Right and Wrong as a Clue to the Meaning of the Universe," the first section of *Mere Christianity*, Lewis explains that if the universe *is* ruled by perfect goodness, we are falling short of that goodness all the time; we are not good enough to consider ourselves allies of perfect goodness In Narnia Edmund fell so far short of goodness that he finally realized with a shock of despair that he needed forgiveness.

At the end of the end of "Right and Wrong as a Clue to the Meaning of the Universe" Lewis claimed that until people repent and want forgiveness, Christianity won't make sense. Christianity explains how God can be the impersonal mind behind the Natural Law and yet also be a Person. It tells us how, since we cannot meet the demands of the law, God Himself became a human being to save us from our failure.

Lewis was of course aware that the presence of natural and moral evil in the world makes the governance of the world by absolute goodness seem questionable, to say the least. He understood Housman in his bitter complaint against "whatever brute and blackguard made the world." But Lewis asks by what standard the creator is judged a blackguard. The very lament for Moral law or rejection of Moral Law itself implies a Moral Law.

## Natural Law Lost

Lewis was deeply concerned about the fact that many people in this century are losing their belief in Natural Law. He spoke about this in the Riddell Memorial Lectures given at the University of Durham in 1943 and published as *The Abolition of Man*.

In *Abolition* he used "the Tao" as a shorthand term for the Natural Law or First Principle. A clarification may be helpful. The term "Tao" in the West is most often associated with Chinese Taoism. According to the *Tao Te Ching*, the Tao (though ineffable) can best be described with words such as "the Flow," "the way things change," "the Life," "the Source." Its locus is first of all in nature. To follow the Tao is indeed to live morally, for it requires respect for the lowly and avoidance of oppression or pride. However, the Tao is ultimately a way of accepting what is, whether tending toward life or death. Confucianists see the locus of the Tao as first of all in human society, expressed primarily in the respect of inferiors for patriarchal superiors, the responsibility of superiors for inferiors, and the subordination of the individual to the welfare of the group. Neither of these uses quite corresponds to what Lewis seems to intend in *Abolition*. Perhaps the Chinese concept that comes closest to Lewis' apparent intent would be "The Way of Heaven."

Lewis claimed in *Abolition* that until quite recent times everyone believed that objects could merit our approval or disapproval, our reverence or our contempt. It was assumed that some emotional reactions were more appropriate than others.

This conception is vividly represented in *The Lion, The Witch and the Wardrobe;* Edmund had inappropriate emotional responses from the very beginning. His brother and sisters imagined pleasant creatures they would like to meet in the woods, and Edmund hoped for foxes; but Lewis changed Edmund's choice to snakes for readers of the Macmillan version in the United States. In both versions, when the children met the wise old professor, Edmund laughed at his looks. When Edmund met the White Witch, his initial fear quickly turned to trust; and when she gave him a choice of foods, he stuffed himself with Turkish Delight candy. His attitude toward his sister Lucy was resentful and superior; he was even suspicious of the good Robin and Beaver who came to guide the children to safety. Instead of noticing the Beaver's house, he noticed the location of the Witch's castle in the distance. When the name Aslan was first spoken to the four children, they all had wonderful feelings except Edmund; he had a sensation of mysterious horror. Later events would educate Edmund to respond as the others did.

Lewis pointed out that according to Aristotle the aim of education, the foundation of ethics, was to make a pupil like and dislike what he ought. According to Plato, we need to learn to feel pleasure at pleasant things, liking for likeable things, disgust for disgusting things, and hatred for hateful things. In early Hindu teaching righteousness and correctness corresponded to knowing truth and reality. Psalm 119 says the law is "true." The Hebrew word for truth here is "emeth," meaning intrinsic validity, rock-bottom reality, and a firmness and dependability as solid as nature.

This meaning is reflected in the final book of Narnia, *The Last Battle,* where Lewis introduced a young man named Emeth who had grown up in an oppressive country where people worship the evil deity Tash. In spite of his upbringing, Emeth was a man of honor and honesty who sought what was good. He died worshipping Tash and found himself in the presence of Aslan instead. He responded with reverence and delight. All that he thought he was doing for Tash could be counted as service to Aslan instead. He was one of Aslan's friends long before he knew it because he liked what was likeable and hated what was hateful.

## Innovation in Values

Lewis was alarmed by all the people in our day who deny that some things are inherently likeable, debunking traditional morality and the Natural Law, thinking that there can be innovation in values. Some of them try to substitute necessity, progress or efficiency for goodness. But in fact necessity, progress or efficiency have to be related to a standard outside themselves to have any meaning. In many cases that standard will be, in the last analysis, the preservation of the person who thinks of himself as a moral innovator, or the preservation of the society of his choice. Such people direct their scepticism toward any values but their own, disparaging other values as "sentimental" (*Abolition* 19).

But Lewis's analysis shows that if Natural Law is sentimental, *all* value is sentimental. No factual propositions such as "our society is in danger of extinction" can give any basis for a system of values; no observations of instinct such as "I want to prolong my life" give any basis for a system of values. Why is our society valuable? Why is my life worth preserving? Only the Natural Law, asserting that human life is of value, gives us a basis for a coherent system of values.

"If nothing is self evident, nothing can be proved," Lewis claimed. "If nothing is obligatory for its own sake, nothing is obligatory at all" (27). He means that if we do not accept Natural Law as self-evident and obligatory for its own sake, then all a person's conceptions of value fall away. There are no values that are not derived from Natural

Law. Anything that is judged good is such because of values in the Natural Law. The concept of goodness springs from no other source.

Thus, modern innovations in ethics are just shreds of the old Natural Law, sometimes isolated and exaggerated. If any values at all are retained, the Natural Law is retained. According to Lewis, there never has been and never will be a radically new value or value system. The human mind has no more power of inventing a new value than of inventing a new primary color.

Admittedly, there are imperfections and contradictions in historical manifestation and interpretations of Natural Law. Some reformers help us to improve our perceptions of value. But only those who live by the Law know its spirit well enough to interpret it successfully. People who live outside the Natural Law have no grounds for criticizing Natural Law or anything else. A few who reject it intend to take the logical next step as well: they intend to live without any values at all, disbelieving all values and choosing to live their lives according to their whims and fancies.

Lewis's poem "The Country of the Blind," published in *Punch* in 1951, presents an image of people who have come to this. He describes what it would be like to live as a misfit with eyes in a country of eyeless people who no longer believe that vision ever existed.

This poem tells of "hard" light shining on a whole nation of eyeless men who were unaware of their handicap. Blindness had come on gradually through many centuries. At some transitional stage a few citizens remained who still had eyes and vision after most people were blind. The blind were normal and up-to-date. They used the same words that their ancestors had used, but no longer knew their meaning. They spoke of *light* still, meaning an abstract thought. If one who could see tried to describe the grey dawn or the stars or the green-sloped sea waves or the color of a lady's cheek, the blind majority insisted that they understood the feeling the sighted one expressed in metaphor. There was no way he could explain the facts to them. The blind ridiculed such a person who took figures of speech literally and concocted a myth about a kind of sense perception that no one has ever really had.

*Beyond the Natural Law*

If one thinks this is a far-fetched picture, Lewis concluded, one need only go to famous men today and try to talk to them about the truths of Natural Law which used to stand huge, awesome, and clear to the inner eye. One of those famous men is B. F. Skinner, who answered in his book *Beyond Freedom and Dignity* that the abolition of the inner man and traditional morality is necessary so that science can prevent the abolition of the human race. Lewis had already exclaimed in *Abolition*, "The preservation of the species?—But why should the species be preserved?" (40) Skinner does not provide an answer, but welcomes Lewis's scientific "Controllers" who aim to change and dehumanize the human race in order more efficiently to fulfill their purposes.

Lewis satirized this kind of progress in his poem "Evolutionary Hymn," which appeared in *The Cambridge Review* in 1957. Using Longfellow's popular hymn stanza form from "Psalm of Life," Lewis exclaimed: What do we care about wrong or justice, joy or sorrow, so long as our posterity survives? The old norms of good and evil are outmoded. It matters not if our posterity turns out to be hairy, squashy, or crustacean, tusked or toothless, mild or ruthless. "Goodness is what comes next." His conclusion is that our progeny may be far from pleasant by present standards; but that matters not, if they survive.

Lewis has often been carelessly accused of being against science. In fact, he gives us an admirable scientist in Bill Hingest in *That Hideous Strength*. Significantly, Hingest was murdered by order of the supposed scientists who directed the NICE. The enemy is not true science, which is fueled by a love of truth, but that applied science whose practitioners are motivated by a love of power. In Lewis's opinion the technological developments that are called steps in Man's Conquest of Nature in fact give certain men power over others. Discarding Natural Law will always increase the dangers of having some people control others. Only Natural Law provides human standards which over-arch rulers and ruled alike. Lewis went so far as to claim, "A dogmatic belief in objective value is necessary to the very idea of a rule which is not tyranny or an obedience which is not slavery." *(Abolition 46)*

*The Magician's Nephew,* the tale of the creation of Narnia, gives us two characters who exemplify the Controllers—Jadis and Uncle Andrew Ketterley. Both claimed to be above Natural Law; they had "a high and lonely destiny." Jadis was a monarch and Uncle Andrew was a magician, but both were strongly suggestive of modern science gone wrong. They both held that common rules are fine for common people, but that singular great people must be free—to experiment without limits in search of knowledge, to seize power and wealth. The result was cruelty and destruction. In contrast, the wise men of old had sought to conform the soul to reality, and the result had been knowledge, self-discipline, and virtue.

Two examples from Lewis's verse illustrate this traditional wisdom. The 1956 poem "After Aristotle" praises virtue, stating that in Greece men gladly toiled in search of virtue as their most valuable treasure. Men would willingly die or live in hard labor for the beauty of virtue. Virtue powerfully touched the heart and gave unfading fruit; virtue made those who love her strong.

A second example is "On a Theme from Nicolas of Cusa," published in the *Times Literary Supplement* in 1955. In the first stanza Lewis notes how physical foods are transformed by our bodies when we assimilate them; in the second, he points out that when we assimilate goodness and truth they are not transformed, but we are.

At the end of *Abolition* Lewis implores his readers to pause before considering Natural Law only one more accident of human history in a wholly material universe. To "explain away" this transcendent reality is perhaps to explain away all explanations. To "see through" the Natural Law is the same as not to see at all.

## Lewis's Literary Criticism

The idea that some things are inherently good and others are not is also the basis for Lewis's approach to literature in *An Experiment in Criticism.* His thesis is that the work of art, and particularly the literary work, is to be *received* for its own sake, not *used* for other purposes. Each detail is to be savored and, if good, enjoyed. We are to look *at* the work, not to use it as a mirror to reflect ourselves and our own fantasies or as a lens through which we look at the world.

This principle is a particular application of the Natural Law. We approach a work of literature, as we might a person or flower, with the assumption that here is something good for its own sake, something worth attending to. After we have looked at it attentively, objectively, either our efforts will have been rewarded or we may decide it is not of much value after all; but in any case we will have given it a fair try, done it justice.

In *Experiment* Lewis contrasts the principle of the inherent value of works of literature with the habits of people who use literature (and thus misuse it), who prostitute the work to some other purpose.

The unliterary read a work only for the excitement they can get from the plot (as in an adventure story), for the provocation and satisfaction of their curiosity (as in a detective story), or for vicarious emotional fulfillment (as in a love story). Such readers use literature much as a child uses a toy, or a worshipper a crucifix: as a starting point for a journey inward or beyond. Unlike the child or the worshipper, who cherish their object and use it many times over, the unliterary usually use a story only once; then it is used up, discarded.

There are also users among the literary. There are the status seekers, who read the academically fashionable literature in order to impress themselves and others. There are the self-improvers—whose concern with their mental enrichment takes the place of a focus on the work itself.

And there are the wisdom-seekers, who value a work for the Statement about Life that it presents. But, says Lewis, works of art do not give us adequate world views. Too much selection is involved. In life, suffering is not often grand and noble and attributable to Tragic Flaws; matters do not end at points of satisfying finality, but go drizzling on. Works of literature may in fact make us wiser, but that is really incidental to their true function; and the wisdom we think came from a particular Great Work may in fact have come largely from within ourselves. Wisdom seeking is carried to absurdity in a particularly keen group he calls the Vigilants (he is surely referring to F.R. Leavis and friends) who will place their stamp of approval only on those few works that express their own conception of how life should be lived. They form a kind of Committee of Public Safety, lopping a new head every month.

By contrast with the users, the receivers surrender to a work of literature, getting themselves out of the way, attending closely to each part and its relationship to other parts, for the time being taking the author's viewpoint as their own. Their refusal of a subjective reading enables them to enlarge the narrow prison of the self and see with others' eyes. The temporary annihilation of the self that takes place actually serves to heal the loneliness of the self. Lewis overtly compares the process to what happens in the pursuit of knowledge, or of justice, or the experience of love: we temporarily reject the facts as they are for us in favor of the facts as they are. In the work of literature we are experiencing the (morally) good or evil data, the (aesthetically) good or poor data, that really are out there and really possess the qualities we perceived. Lewis does not deny that our perception and judgment are sometimes flawed. But good and bad are real.

Lewis's aesthetic provides a necessary and refreshing corrective to rigorously dutiful approaches that have ruined the enjoyment of literature for many from student days onward. For those Christians to whom literary pleasures have seemed frivolous or dangerous temptations that might lead away from the Straight Path, Lewis affirms their goodness. He also exposes the sort of single-issue criticism that darkens counsel by words without knowledge. Unless we can put ourselves to one side for a time and see what is actually in the text, we ought not to say anything about a work; and in many instances we might be better off not reading it at all.

## Minor Reservations

Having gratefully accepted Lewis's basic aesthetic enterprise, we must express a few reservations. Of course it is true that any work of imaginative literature is too selective to present an adequate philosophy of life. But much the same could be said of any essay or multi-volumed work in discursive prose. Any time we want to speak of the whole, of universals (or the absence thereof), we must be selective. Most formal treatises on Being, Becoming or Causality leave out the terror and the joy of the world. The supposedly universal human experience of Reality discussed in nearly all of theology turns out to be a truncated view of reality. Humans are limited; we may intend the universal, but any reflection upon Reality is bound to be limited.

The need for selectivity does not prohibit a work of literature from being intended, or taken, as a dramatized world view. This is particularly evident when a work gives support to oppressive social structures. For example, a story whose few Jewish characters are rapacious schemers or (if admirable) get baptized, may well give generous minds such as Lewis's the enlarging experience of finding out what it is like to be antisemitic. Unfortunately, it will also cause certain readers to come away with sharpened convictions that the Jewish Conspiracy is the fountainhead of the world's evil. Likewise, a work whose achieving and admirable characters are all male, with its females frothy, manipulative, passive, victimized, and/or marginal, is saying something about the relative value of male and female.

Lewis in fact acknowledges, in an exchange of letters in *Theology* (1939-1940), that there are (morally) bad books that corrupt people by making false values attractive *(Christian Reflections* 30-35). He does not refer specifically to fiction, nor does he exclude it. Surely, then a (morally) bad work of literature can be bad because it presents a dangerously false view of life, quite possibly by its selections. In contrast, a (morally) good work of literature can present true values. There is no reason why we cannot receive such a work with diligent and delighted care, and also use it as a parable. Surely what is objectionable is, in Kant's language, to make the work a means only and not an end also. It is ironic that Lewis should have rejected the concept of the literary work as a parable, in view of the fact that his own novels (especially the Narnian tales) are parables of such enormous power and wisdom.

This, of course, is not to say that every work of literature offers a world view. The comedy is not necessarily saying that life is finally a joke, nor is the whodunit perforce telling us that the ills of the world have a neat and gratifying solution right at hand, if we could only be perceptive enough to see. Even Freud realized that sometimes a cigar is just a good cigar.

## Life's Intrinsic Value

We have affirmed, with minor reservations, Lewis's reasoning that a work of literature possesses value in itself. Now we turn back to his thesis of intrinsic value as applied to all of life, his corrective to a totally relativistic value (or rather nonvalue) system. Sensitive persons who have felt their meaning-world collapse around them know how dehumanizing felt meaninglessness is. Lewis knew whereof he spoke.

(People who experience this collapse without pain are even more dehumanized.) As to the end result of consistent subjectivism, the world of the Controllers, Lewis's portraits of Jadis and the directors of the NICE tell us more vividly than his discursive prose just how nightmarish such a world would be.

Within the context of a basic agreement, once more we offer a qualifier. Consistent and total subjectivism we certainly do not want, and we know why. But within limits subjectivism and relativism have value; they can be freeing. People with a sharp and absolute vision are not often as broad in mental sympathies and as rich in charity as Lewis; they tend more towards psychological imperialism. Many of us, Lewis included, would rather live among people who hold firmly that "Love thy neighbor as thyself" is the only universally binding principle in personal morality than among people who know in detail God's will for other private lives as well as their own and are busy trying to bring about theocracy. Theocracy is one of our oldest banes, and one that Lewis particularly detested.

In conclusion, Lewis's teaching about Natural Law has acquired unique urgency since his day. In 1933 Lewis published the allegorical *Pilgrim's Regress*, in which he warned that savage dwarfs called "the Cruels" were then multiplying; communists, fascists, organized crime syndicates, and many other sub-species that value violence and a perverse kind of heroism. (It seems reasonable to assume that he would have included contemporary perpetrators of genocide and terrorist groups of all kinds as sub-species of the Cruels.) He published *Abolition* in 1943; since then there have been radical shifts in the locus and imminence of threat to the world.

Lewis sensed, by 1955, the increasing power of modern death technology. In *The Magician's Nephew* Jadis decided to use the Deplorable Word, a weapon she had paid a terrible price to obtain. A moment later every living thing in the world of Charn was dead. She did this in outright defiance of Natural Law. There was not enough of a nuclear arsenal in 1955 to destroy all life on earth; only part of the public foresaw the cancer-like proliferation of nuclear weapons that would soon threaten to destroy human life (and our libraries and literary heritage), and to cause a nuclear winter. (This scenario sounds like the end of the world as foretold in the Norse mythology that Lewis found so compelling.)          .

Since the fall of the Soviet Union, the threat of worldwide destruction caused by weaponry is far more diffuse. Biological and nuclear tools of modern death technology (as well as possible new alternatives) are sought by power-hungry men with many motives.

In *The Last Battle,* published in 1956, the land of Narnia dies away more gradually than the land of Charn, ending in darkness and ice. "I *did* hope," said Jill, "That it might go on forever. I knew our world couldn't" (160). Lewis knew that our earth had to die eventually, but he would be intensely grieved by today's accelerated destruction of the environment caused not by acts of war, but by reckless plundering and pollution in defiance of the Natural Law. (Obvious examples are depletion of the ozone layer, burning of the rain forests, accumulation of nuclear waste, and contamination of the oceans.)

In Aslan's beautiful everlasting country Peter found that Lucy was crying because of the death of Narnia, and he tried to stop her. But Lucy appealed to the law in all our hearts and said she was sure it was not wrong to mourn the death of the world they dearly loved. And Tirian, last king of Narnia, affirmed her. "It were no virtue, but grave discourtesy, if we did not mourn" (160).

The Natural Law teaches us to fight to save our world from death, and, should it die, to mourn its destruction. But C. S. Lewis predicted that the Natural Law itself will outlast all worlds. And he promises us a new life that will be the Great Story which goes on for ever, in which every chapter is better than the one before. (184). And all who live that story will be receivers.

## Works Cited

Lewis, C.S. *The Abolition of Man*. New York: Macmillan, 1947. *Christian Reflections*. Grand Rapids: Eerdmans, 1967. *The Last Battle*. London: The Bodley Head, 1956. *The Lion, the Witch and the Wardrobe*. New York: Macmillan, 1950. *Mere Christianity*. New York: Macmillan, 1953. *Poems*. New York: Harcourt, 1964.

# 22

# C. S. Lewis's Free Advice to Hopeful Writers

*Few people realize that throughout his life C. S. Lewis took time to be a generous advisor to other writers, adults as well as children.*

Your manuscript is both good and original;
but the part that is good is not original,
and the part that is original is not good.
—Samuel Johnson[1]

C. S. Lewis was so fond of crusty old Samuel Johnson's writing that he thought of him as a member of his family and said he looked forward to meeting him in heaven. He never tired of reading Johnson.

I think every writer should have a beloved author to admire and feel close to that way, a chosen mentor. My own favorite author was C. S. Lewis himself, and I didn't have to wait to meet him in heaven. Thanks to what felt like a miracle at the time, I managed to meet him in Oxford.

---

[1]Samuel Johnson (1709-1784) was a prominent London author and wit, the foremost conversationalist of his age. He was most celebrated for his monumental *Dictionary of the English Language* (1755).

I was an English major at the University of Redlands in California when I first sampled a book by C. S. Lewis one summer and was caught for life. When I was invited to do an honors project in the field of English, I chose Lewis for my subject and plunged in. I read everything by and about him that was available in the Los Angeles Public Library and wrote a thesis showing that all of Lewis's major beliefs were present in his brand new series of Narnian fantasies for children.

I worked part-time in the cafeteria for seventy-five cents an hour in those days and had no hopes of getting to England. Then in the spring of my senior year I happened to see an announcement about scholarships for a summer course at the University of London, and I applied. As soon as I got word that I had won a scholarship, I wrote to C. S. Lewis for the first time—telling him that I had been studying his work for a year and a half and asking if I could hear him lecture or meet him while I was in England.

Lewis said that I should write again when I got to England and that I could come to meet him in Oxford. My dream was coming true. I graduated from college; crossed the United States by train; and crossed the Atlantic—economy class on an old ocean liner, seasick all the way. I got to England on July 7 and wrote to C. S.Lewis immediately.

On July 20, 1956, I finished my London classes for the week and caught an afternoon train to Oxford. Lewis was meeting me in the lobby of the Royal Oxford Hotel for 4 o'clock tea, and I had a panic attack as I approached the place. If I had been given free choice of all the famous people who ever lived, Lewis was the one I would have chosen to meet. I was a penniless California student who looked only sixteen and felt like an ignoramus, getting a personal visit with my favorite author. My awe for Lewis's mind was so great that when I finally sat on the hotel sofa by him, I had to fight for a minute not to faint and fall on the floor.

He was so entertaining that we chatted and laughed without pause for well over an hour. I have never met anyone more enjoyable before or since. I knew at the time that this little afternoon tea was bound to be a high point of my entire life, and that has proved true. But it is what Lewis's books have been giving me ever since that has enriched me far more, and they are available to everyone. I don't think I could possibly have chosen a better mentor to help me to grow in understanding of what I want to understand about life.

I didn't try to strike up a regular correspondence with Lewis after our meeting, because I didn't want to take up too much of his precious time; and that was a proper decision. But in 1957 I mailed him my thesis, and he read it all and replied that I was right in the center of the target. Then he pointed out one weak sentence where I could have been misread, and he included the following bit of free advice: "Most readers will misunderstand if you give them the slightest chance. (It's like driving cattle; if there's an open gateway anywhere on the road, they'll go into it!)"

Later I discovered that for a span of fifty years C. S. Lewis gave away pointers like that to both friends and strangers. He did this in personal letters; and, fortunately, many of them have survived.[2] I have dug out much of this writing advice, and I have grouped it into six generally chronological sets: letters to Arthur Greeves (Practice, Practice Practice), letters to other early friends (The Best Words in the Best Order), letters to children (Seeing One's Mistakes), letters to an American lady (As One Rhymester to Another), letters to a variety of adult correspondents (Simplify, Simplify), and letters to Sister Penelope (Raised in Print).

## Practice, Practice, Practice

All of C. S. Lewis's earliest advice about writing went to Ireland to his earliest friend, Arthur Greeves.[3] It seems that Lewis followed his own eager advice to Greeves far more than Greeves did. But we can be deeply grateful to Greeves for saving the letters all his life. He finally sent them on to C. S. Lewis's brother Warren, and Warren Lewis contributed them to the Wade Center in Wheaton, Illinois. Lewis's momentous decision against literary ambition is spelled out

---

[2]Some of these letters are in print, and others are available to researchers in the Bodleian Library in Oxford and in the Marion E. Wade Center at Wheaton College in Illinois.

[3]C.S. Lewis, *They Stand Together: The Letters of C. S. Lewis to Arthur Greeves* (1914-1963), edited by Walter Hooper (New York: Harcourt Brace Jovanovich, 1979).

in one place only: in a pair of 1930 letters to Greeves. But that was a turnaround in his maturity.

Just before his sixteenth birthday Lewis wrote from England that all he needed for his art was paper and pen, in contrast to Greeves' unfortunate need for a piano or a box of paints and drawing paper. Soon Lewis was urging Greeves to join him and become a writer.

In 1915 Lewis teased Greeves for his "gems of orthography" like "simpathise" and "phisically," admitting that his own spelling was almost as bad. A few days later Lewis criticized Greeves again and hit upon his lifelong theme: the first point for a letter writer to master is to make himself intelligible to his reader. For the next fifty years Lewis would constantly urge himself and others on toward the goal of clarity. That became his. hallmark.

When he was seventeen, Lewis was temporarily on guard against feelings. (He had lost his mother to cancer and had to put up with an emotionally stormy father.) He cockily told Greeves that feelings should be saved for literature and art, where they are delightful, and kept out of real life, where they are a nuisance. Several months later he decided that his own letters were becoming mawkish. He told Greeves that they should publish their letters some day in a book to be called *Lamentations*. (About sixty-five years later, his letters to Greeves really were published, under the title *They Stand Together*.)

At this point Lewis began seriously urging Greeves to try to make his mark in literature. "I cannot urge you too strongly to go on and write something, anything, but at any rate WRITE." He usually followed his advice to Greeves more than Greeves did. He advised Greeves not to try humor because it is a dangerous form of writing and there is enough humor in print already. (Ironically, Greeves comes across as rather melancholy; it was Lewis who developed a flair for wit.) Lewis obviously wanted an audience and companionship. He promised to tell Greeves the absolute truth about his writing and begged Greeves to do the same for him.

"Whenever you are fed up with life, start writing: ink is the great cure for all human ills, as I have found out long ago." Lewis was still seventeen when he wrote that. He was convinced that it didn't matter what they wrote at that age, just so they wrote continually, as well as they could. What Greeves needed, Lewis claimed, was practice, practice, practice. Lewis felt that every time he wrote a page of prose or verse, with real effort, he was making good progress as an author—even if he burned the page as soon as he finished it. On the other hand, he felt one can't write one's best if one never submits one's writing to a reader.

Lewis told Greeves that the beginning of his first story was superb and that only laziness could keep him from producing something good. Now that they were both writing and knew how much work there is in a short piece that can be read in a few minutes, they could both begin to realize the labor that went into writing a great and lengthy work.

On a practical note, Lewis advised Greeves to stop referring to the character in his story as "our young friend" or "our hero."

Greeves complained that he sometimes found the same word coming into his prose repeatedly; Lewis answered that this is the common experience of all writers. Greeves complained that he sometimes had to sit and think before he could go on writing; Lewis answered that good work is never done in a hurry. When one does write a good passage quickly, it always needs further work later, Lewis believed.

Lewis mentioned that he planned his writing in his head while he was walking; his imagination worked only when he was exercising.

Lewis hoped that Greeves would continue his story, but he admitted that authors rarely complete their first projects. By this time Lewis had begun and abandoned several. Further, he thought that Greeves gravely underestimated how much time it took Lewis to write.

At this point Greeves accused Lewis of flattering him about his story, and Lewis reminded him that he hardly let a sentence go past without picking holes in it. But Lewis's efforts were wasted; Greeves gave up on the story and decided to try a novel instead. At the same time, Lewis gave up on the epic poem he had been trying to write in antiquated English. He told Greeves that they had both gained valuable experience while their projects lasted, but Lewis didn't want much more of this kind of quitting.

"The Bible (which you don't read) has very hard things to say of people who put their hand to the plough and turn back," Lewis warned Greeves. (Greeves was proud of being a Christian, and Lewis was proud of not being a Christian.) Lewis thought it would be better to complete one small work than to begin and abandon twenty more ambitious projects.

Lewis felt an almost urgent need to be able to say that he had written a book and finished it, no matter how it turned out. Perhaps that was because of the First World War, which he and Greeves ignored in their letters. It was raging on, and Lewis would soon be pulled into it. (Greeves suffered from the idea that he had delicate health and never went to war or held a job.) When Lewis was eighteen, he was recruited. He intended to gather his poems and send them to a publisher before he was sent to France, he said, because if he died in France, his friends who knew nothing about poetry would be in awe of his book and believe that he had been a young genius. Behind his jaunty tone was the fact that literary immortality was the only kind that Lewis had any hopes for then.

Just before Lewis sailed for France he wrote to Greeves that thought can be expressed in a number of ways, and style is the art of expressing a thought in the most beautiful or rhythmical way. An example of poor style is "When the constellations which appear at early morning joined musical exercises and the angelic spirits loudly testified to their satisfaction." The same thought is expressed in good style in the King James Bible: "When the morning stars sang together and all the sons of God shouted for joy." With that point made, Lewis went off to the front lines.

Soon after Lewis returned to England to recover from war wounds, he was pointing out to Greeves how easy it is for readers to misunderstand a writer's words. Greeves had said that he was driven to town; he meant that someone took him in the car, but at first Lewis thought he was driven by circumstances.

At that point Lewis hired a typist to prepare his poems and began submitting the manuscript to publishers, starting with his first choice. Macmillan turned him down with a polite rejection letter; but Heinemann, his second choice, accepted his book. He was overjoyed. Later he wrote to Greeves that he was disappointed every week over the delay of his book. When it was published in 1919, he wrote to Greeves that he was NOT famous yet, but that perhaps he had slunk into a "modicum of notoriety." He was still urging Greeves to write and get published.

A decade passed. Lewis completed his lengthy education, became an Oxford professor of literature, and kept on writing.

In August, 1930, Arthur Greeves complained that he might be doomed to failure as a writer; and Lewis wrote an extraordinary letter in response. At this point Lewis had published two books of poetry that were almost completely ignored by the public, and Greeves had not come close to publishing anything. Both men were in their thirties.

First, Lewis declared that facing the possibility of being a literary failure, like facing the possibility of surgery, can drive a person crazy if he vacillates between hope and fear. It is better to resign oneself to the worst and deal with it.

The side of Lewis that longed for success as a writer, he admitted, was not the side that was worth much. (The desire to be a writer is another matter, because no one could stop Lewis and Greeves from writing.) Greeves no doubt believed that it would be bliss to have a book published, whether anyone bought it or not. But such an idea is an absolute delusion. If Greeves had a book that did not sell, he would soon be as disappointed as he was when he had no book. Lewis knew that from experience.

From the age of sixteen onwards Lewis had staked his whole contentment upon one single ambition: literary success. He had pursued that goal without wavering. And he had failed. He was an expert on suffering the pangs of disappointment as a writer; that was his special subject, his real profession. (He realized how absurd it is in such a world as this to dignify his disappointment with the word *suffering*.)

At this point in his life, Lewis believed in God and was on his way to becoming a Christian. He told Greeves that unless God has abandoned us, He will burn away our literary ambition someday. We need to endure the pain and be healed of our wish to outdo other people. When one gives up one's ambitions, one can for the first time have a restful state of mind and say with true sincerity, "Thy Kingdom come." In God's Kingdom there will be no competition, and a person must stop caring about status to enter there.

How difficult it would be to reach this stage after succeeding as an author, Lewis exclaimed. Perhaps God had been kind to Greeves and

Lewis by saving them from making literary success the center of their lives. Literary ambitions can be a dangerous idol.

Lewis shuddered to think what he would have given at one time to be a successful writer. One has to die to personal ambition. Greeves had written to Lewis for literary encouragment, and Lewis apologized for telling Greeves the moral truth instead. He said he had to.

Greeves thanked Lewis for his honesty, and Lewis took up the theme again. He said that since he had given up hope of publication and fame, his poetry had actually improved. The second book of poetry was not much noticed by the public, but he had got good out of writing it. Perhaps the true use of a book lies in its effects upon the author. Publication and sales are not the real test of the value of a book.

Some people are bound to write, just as a tree is bound to bear leaves, Lewis said; it is their way of growing. But for others, the desire to write is a form of vanity. When hope of literary success is gone, the former writers continue to write and the latter writers stop. Lewis believed that those who continue to work devotedly at their writing without success are not wasting their efforts; they or others, in this world or elsewhere, will eventually reap some kind of harvest from the work. That was Lewis's faith. And he included himself in that category. Perhaps unsuccessful writers like Greeves and himself, who used to think that the world was waiting for their words, were really ministering to something within themselves.

This very letter was an example of what he was talking about, Lewis exclaimed. He was writing to Greeves and trying to give something to Greeves; but by the time he finished, he had benefited himself so much that even if the letter became lost in the mail, it would not be wasted.

## The Best Words in the Best Order

As a young man at Oxford, Lewis found friends other than Greeves who were interested in writing, but he usually talked with them instead of sending letters. The first of these friends was Leo Baker, who eventually turned out to be an actor with the Old Vic Company rather than a writer. Before long Lewis and Baker and a third friend were putting together a collection of poems that they tried to publish.

Lewis advised Baker that struggling after originality is like trying to pull oneself off the ground by pulling up one's own suspenders—as if shutting one's eyes to the work of earlier writers would make one more likely to create new things. Homer and Virgil wrote great lines not for their own works alone, but for the use of all poets who followed them. The notion that one should not honestly refer to other authors and give to other authors is a heresy.

When a second publisher turned down the poems of the three friends, Lewis gave up on that project. But he reflected about what poetry really is. Coleridge had said that poetry is "the best words in the best order," but Lewis pointed out to Baker that this applies to any piece of good writing. "The train will leave at 7:30" gives us the best words in the best order and we can't improve upon them. Lewis made up a few lines of Wordsworthian poetry about the hissing locomotive and the laboring coaches and the grim chronometer, all worse words in a worse order. The real test of a poem is "Could this be said as well in prose?" If the answer is yes, the poem is not valid.

In another letter Lewis told Baker what he disliked about the prologue of a poem by Owen Barfield. In theory, a poet should be able to include anything he wants to in a poem; but in reality, some things make a reader squirm or laugh at the poet. Lewis complimented Baker for his use of the old phrase "God the father almighty" in one of his poems; he used it so skillfully that it seemed to become his own.

Another early friend of Lewis's at Oxford was A. K. Hamilton Jenkin, later known for his books about Cornwall. When Lewis learned that Jenkin had married, he sent him congratulations for marrying an author's daughter, because such a woman would probably already be accustomed to living with genius. Then he went on to condemn women' letters, full of so-called news about people going here and there. Lewis claimed to hate writing letters unless he was in the middle of an argument about ideas. Soon Lewis was begging Jenkin to find an excuse to come to Oxford for a visit. When that did not work out, Lewis wrote to Jenkin that he was by his absence a gap in Lewis's bookshelf and in the manuscript of his mind, as well as a drawn tooth in his psychic jaw and a broken lace in his spiritual boots. For Lewis, letters never served long as a substitute for talking with friends.

In 1929 Lewis first wrote to his fellow professor J. R. R. Tolkien with advice for improving some of his poems. Soon Tolkien was reading his fantasies to Lewis in person. "He was for long my only audience," Tolkien reflected later. "Only from him did I ever get the idea that my 'stuff' could be more than a private hobby." Lewis's unflagging enthusiasm finally pushed Tolkien into fame and fortune.

Sometime before 1939 Lewis drew to himself a circle of male friends including Tolkien who met weekly for literary discussion and response to each others' writing. At last Lewis had the writing companionship that he had been reaching out for all along, his personal critique group. By this time he had also started to receive letters from strangers who had read his books, and some of these were hopeful writers themselves. Lewis was especially helpful to American children.

## Seeing One's Mistakes

In 1956 C. S. Lewis wrote to an American girl named Joan that if she became a writer she would be trying to describe the indescribable essence of life always. Then he jumped from sublime thoughts to her practical question about correct English; *amn't I, aren't I* and *am I not*. Good English is whatever educated people speak in a given time and place, he told her. When he was a child, *amn't I* was good in Belfast and bad in London, and *aren't I* was just the opposite. Don't trust teachers, text-books, or logic in these matters, he warned her. Then he gave her five rules for writing:

1. Be clear, and make sure that your sentence can't be misunderstood.

2. Use plain, efficient words rather than long, vague ones. ("Keep promises" rather than "implement promises.")

3. Use concrete nouns rather than abstract nouns. ("More people died" rather than "mortality rose.")

4. Don't rely on adjectives like terrible and wonderful that tell the reader how to feel instead of making him feel that way. Such adjectives say to readers, "Please will you do my job for me."

5. Avoid word inflation; don't use "infinitely" when you mean "very." Save words for when you need them.[4]

A couple of years later Lewis responded to some stories from Joan. "One can learn only by seeing one's mistakes." In her animal fantasy the talking animals were still in our real world, yet they had lost their real relationships; the small animals were in no danger from the owl. That works only in a more thorough-going fantasy-world like Narnia. In Beatrix Potter stories, set in the real world, an owl is a threat to small animals. Reality and fantasy need to be mixed in one of the ways that work. Joan's spy story was better, but it was too condensed. And the police looked silly for failing to suspect the talented opera singer because he sang so well. Joan's poem had good content, Lewis said, but the verse "creaked" a bit.[5]

In 1959 he congratulated her about an Easter essay with sentences that were clear and taut and didn't sprawl. He said that she would be able to write good prose, but that she exaggerated her point in her essay's ending. She had claimed that her reader had everything he needed in his soul. Lewis told her that he certainly did not. Never exaggerate, he said. Don't say more than you really mean.

She had sent him two poems, and he told her that one of them was really just prose, but not so good as her ordinary prose, typed like verse. That was not good for her, he said. Ten years of writing strict, rhyming verse would be good for her before she ventured on into free verse.

In 1963 Lewis wrote to Joan that her poetry was developing. She would probably go too far with invented names for a while, but it would do no harm. It was like going through the measles. He mentioned to her that E.R. Eddison's invented name *silvamoonlake* had been spoiled for him recently by the advertising slogan "Drinkapintamilkaday" that everyone in England was tired of. Spelling counts as well as sound in creating a beautiful word. And of

---

[4]C. S. Lewis, *Collected Letters*, edited by W. H. Lewis (New York: Harcourt, Brace & World, 1966) 270-271.

[5]Lyle W. Dorsett and Marjorie Lamp Mead, ed., *C. S. Lewis: Letters to Children* (New York: Macmillan, 1985) 80-81.

course the beauty of the object itself plays a role. The lovely sound of *velvet* was spoiled for Lewis because he hated the fabric itself.[6]

In 1957 Lewis congratulated another girl, named Jane, for the excellent fantasy story she had sent him, and told her that her next book could be at least twice as good. He pointed out six mistakes she could avoid in the future, explaining that she would get plenty of bad advice, and so he felt he should send her some good advice:

1. In a fantasy land of enchantment the story should be high, reckless, heroic, and romantic—not like earth's humdrum politics and conflicts.
2. Commonplace technological luxury breaks the spell in fairyland.
3. Don't use adjectives and adverbs like "exciting" that tell readers how to feel. Make them feel the emotion you want them to feel.
4. Write by ear, not by eye. Test the sound of every sentence to make sure it is nice to pronounce and has the right texture or speed to go with its meaning.
5. Don't bore your reader with descriptions of ordinary clothes. Such habits can be picked up from reading poor-quality magazines. Read great fantasy books in order to pick up good fantasy-writing habits.
6. Fantasy names should be beautiful and suggestive, not merely odd.[7]

In 1954 Lewis wrote to an American boy named Martin that his story was good and kept Lewis guessing to the end. But a word about how the policeman felt (was he afraid?) and a name for him would help to make him more real.[8] Five years later, Lewis was still writing to Martin. "Remember this if you ever become a critic [book reviewer]: say what the work is like, but if you start explaining *how it came* to be like that (in other words, inventing the history of the composition) you will nearly always be wrong."[9]

Martin, a scholarly boy, had the idea of trying to translate some solemn Latin poetry into English and had chosen a rollicking rhythm that he liked. Lewis told him that his chosen rhythm was not

---

[6] *C. S. Lewis: Letters to Children,* 109-110.
[7] *Collected Letters,* 278-280.
[8] *Letters to Children,* 40.
[9] *Letters to Children,* 85.

appropriate for his lofty theme and wrote the following ditty to show him why:

> "A pound of that cheese and an ounce of the butter,"
> Aeneas replied with his usual stutter.[10]

Later in 1959 an American schoolgirl appealed to Lewis for writing advice, and he sent her a list of eight rules for good writing:

1. Turn off the radio [and television].
2. Read good books and avoid most magazines.
3. Write with the ear, not the eye. Make every sentence sound good.
4. Write only about things that interest you. If you have no interests, you won't ever be a writer.
5. Be clear. Remember that readers can't know your mind. Don't forget to tell them exactly what they need to know to understand you.
6. Save odds and ends of writing attempts, because you may be able to use them later.
7. You need a well-trained sense of word rhythm, and the noise of a typewriter will interfere.
8. Know the meaning of every word you use.[11]

Two weeks before he died, Lewis wrote to a young woman named Kathy about some "maddening experience" that she had just suffered as an author. (Perhaps she had worked hard on some project and it hadn't turned out well and she threw it away.) He assured her that this is one of the occupational risks of authorship and that the same sort of thing had happened to him more than once. "There is nothing to be done about it!"[12]

---

[10]*Letters to Children*, 86.
[11]*Collected Letters*, 291-292.
[12]*Letters to Children*, p. 113.

## As One Rhymester to Another

At the mid-point of the century, C. S. Lewis heard from an American widow who corresponded with him until his death, telling him her troubles and occasionally sending him a poem she had written. He analyzed one of her poems metrically for her, pointing out that where she collapsed into a 4-beat-rhythm it was not so good. He suggested that the ending, "God speed," was weak—especially because it seemed to be spoken by God, unaware that He was referring to Himself as humans do.[13]

When the woman sent Lewis a Christian poem by someone else, he found it very good Christianity but not good poetry. It was free verse (no rhyme and no metrical pattern). It had no rhythmic vitality, no reason why the lines should end where they did, and no melodious words. He admitted that he was old fashioned; he thought that free verse succeeded in only a few exceptional poems.[14]

The American lady mentioned the "cult of the obstuse" to Lewis, and he asked her frankly if she meant "abstruse," "obtuse," or "obscure."[15]

"The pen has become to me what an oar is to a galley slave; then (God be praised) influenza and long half-comatose days in bed," he wrote to her in 1955. A few months later he responded to another of her poems and added "Between ourselves, as one rhymester to another, it's a great pity that *world,* such a good important word and often so emphatically demanding to come at the end of a line, has so few rhymes in English. *Furled, hurled, curled*—none of them very serviceable—and what else is there. Let's invent a verb *to churl* (behave churlishly).[16]

In 1956 Lewis let off steam about book reviewers. "The review is of course a tissue of muddles and direct falsehoods—I don't say 'lies' because the people who write such things are not really capable of lying. I mean, to lie = to say what you know to be untrue. But to know this, and to have the very ideas of truth and falsehood in your head, presupposes a clarity of mind which they haven't got. To call

---

[13]Clyde S. Kilby, ed., *Letters to an American Lady* (Grand Rapids: Eerdmans, 1967) 18.

[14]*Letters to an American Lady,* 27.

[15]*Letters to an American Lady,* 29.

[16]*Letters to an American Lady,* p. 40.

them liars would be as undeserved a compliment as to say that a dog was bad at arithmetic."[17]

"People in real life are often so preposterous that one would not dare to put them in a novel"[18]

## Simplify! Simplify!

C. S. Lewis sprinkled snippets of advice about writing throughout his correspondence that is yet unpublished. I have collected some samples.

On August 3, 1943, Lewis wrote to J. B. Phillips thanking him "a hundred times" for making *Colossians* more clear with his modern paraphrase. Lewis said it was like seeing a familiar picture after it had been cleaned. The only complaint Lewis had was about the phrase "Life from nothing began with Him." It was a bit ambiguous and could be misread to mean that Christ was created out of nothing.

On January 3, 1944, Lewis sent Phillips a list of suggestions for improving the manuscript of his next paraphrased epistle. First, Lewis advised Phillips to use fewer exclamation marks. Many of Paul's sentences call for them, but together in print they tend to give a childish or hysterical appearance to the letter. Similarly, "Never!" might be better expressed as "Not at all," or "By no means."

"Filial duty" is too hard, Lewis claimed; how about "duty to parents"? "Believe on Him" is not modern English; we use "in Him." "*Ipso facto*" would puzzle some readers, and Latin often annoys people. "Your *members*" is archaic; would "organs" do? "A commonplace metaphor" could be replaced by "an illustration from ordinary life." "What *fruit*" would be more clear as "What was your harvest?" or "What sort of crop did you raise?" "Erstwhile" is too archaic. "Who have written this epistle" would be more clear as "to whom he's dictating this letter." Again and again Lewis pointed out what uneducated readers might misunderstand and suggested that even more clarity was needed. He was highly enthusiastic about the project.

On March 29, 1952, Lewis wrote to Miss H. D. Calkins of Los Angeles that he had read her book manuscript *India Looks* and found

---

[17]*Letters to an American Lady*, 49.
[18]*Letters to an American Lady*, 80.

it as interesting as an adventure story. He would not write a preface for it because he was not qualified; for all he knew, the book could be a mass of errors (although he was sure it was not). Aside from that, Miss Calkins spoke well of Lewis in her book, and it would look like a mutual admiration society if he wrote the preface.

Lewis wrote out a list of 13 suggestions for improving her book. Some of them were about getting quotations and facts exactly perfect and avoiding false impressions. He also advised her to write "enamored of," not "enamored with" and "Christocentric" rather than "Christ-centric;" and he told her not to write that *the reason* for something *was because*...One can correctly use either "*The reason* for his reluctance *was that*..." or "He was reluctant *because*..." The latter is better because it is more concrete and less abstract, and this helps to avoid "gobbleydegook."

Lewis found two sentences in Calkins's book that conveyed no clear meaning at all to his mind. A knot of abstract nouns (such as aspect and framework), he warned, is usually a danger signal. Simplify! Simplify! But Lewis cited a sentence that he particularly liked and ended his letter by saying that that's the way to write.

On June 10, 1952, Lewis wrote to mystery writer Katharine Farrer that he greatly enjoyed her book *The Missing Link*, although he was an inexperienced reader of whodunits. Then he told her that her dialogue needed improvement. Lewis himself found dialogue frightfully tricky to write for two reasons. First, his own characters tended to talk too much; and second, because what works in real conversation often looks different in print. "Huntin'," without the *g* at the end, takes on unwanted significance in print that it does not have in real conversation. The word reminded Lewis of all the odious literature by authors who admire those people who say "huntin'" and all the more odious literature by authors who dislike people who say "huntin'." Then Lewis came up with the idea that authors would be wise to re-read all their dialogue as it might be read by a dull, vulgar, or hostile reader. That would be a test. And he concluded with the idea that the hardest dialogue to write well is light dialogue such as banter between lovers or small talk at a party.

On February 3, 1954, Lewis wrote to Mrs. Farrer praising another book of hers and finding fault with the fact that a certain character giggled. Even if she would have giggled, he said, the word is too damaging. He was always reminding people, he said, that nothing gets into literature without becoming a word, and that sometimes the *things* are O.K. but their *words* are not. For example, no matter how deeply one feels about Czechoslovakia, it is impossible to use the word in a lyric poem. Then he scolded Mrs. Farrer for describing a moon, which we have all seen, by likening it to something that most of us have not seen—the white face of an idiot lost in the wood. This was disrespectful to the moon; if he were her spiritual director, he would make her learn Psalm 136 by heart. (He knew Mr. and Mrs. Farrer; Austin Farrer was a theological author.)

On August 14, 1954, Lewis wrote to a Mrs. Donnelly telling her that he thought she had a mistaken idea of a Christian writer's duty. We are all obligated to avoid writing anythng that will increase in our readers lust, pride or the ambition to outdo others; but we are only obligated to use the particular writing talent we have, not one we don't have. Not all Christian writers are called to write specifically Christian works, and it is a mistake to tack on bits of Christianity. A good story and a good meal are both innocent pleasures that don't need Scripture verses tucked in. The first job of a story is to be a good story; and if God wants the story to carry a Christian message, that will come in of its own accord. Lewis believed that some writing that is not obviously religious may do more good than some that is.

Lewis concluded his advice to Mrs. Donnelly by saying that first we must fulfill whatever duties life imposes on us, and then we are to do well whatever job our natural talent points to. Any honest work can be done to the glory of God, whether it is making stories, shoes, or rabbit hutches.

On February 2, 1955, Lewis wrote to Father Milward, who sent him thanks for his writing, that all teachers know that those who needed their help least are the ones who acknowledge it most fully. Then on Christmas day in 1959 Lewis wrote to Milward that he used to carry on deep discussions with friends in letters when he was young, and it was much like writing a book. But when he was actually a writer of books later, it finally became too hard to keep up discussions in letters. One shouldn't fill one's leisure with the same activity that is one's major work. Both Lewis's mind and his hand got tired.

On March 7, 1960, Lewis sent some preaching advice to Milward. The joints in the sermon or lecture cannot be made too clear (We have finished point A; now for B...). And if you want people to weep at the end, make them laugh at the beginning. Lewis added that he agreed with Milward that "the greater the author, the less he understands his own work."

One day after his first letter to Father Milward, on February 3, 1955, Lewis wrote to a Mrs. Johnson in Canada that many people don't seem to understand what fiction is. If a writer says what is untrue with the intention of making people believe it, that's lying. But if he says it with no such intention, that's fiction. Fiction is apt to express an author's deepest thoughts, speculations, dreads, and desires. Writing a story is only imagining out loud.

On September 2, 1956, Lewis wrote to I. O. Evans that he had done a frightful thing. He read the galleys of a story that Evans had sent him before properly reading the Evans letter that came also, and tore up the galleys. Then he saw that Evans wanted the galleys back. Lewis had never heard of an author keeping his galleys before. He had no ashes on hand because he heated his house with gas, he said, but he could order himself a little sackcloth. He signed his letter "Yours abjectly."

On April 19, 1958, Lewis wrote to Jane Douglass of New York that he did not find her dramatic adaptation of *The Lion, the Witch and the Wardrobe* very promising, but he assumed she would get other advice before deciding. He didn't want her to waste any more time than necessary on the project. Our lives are littered with false starts, he said; at least his was.

On March 29, 1962, Lewis wrote to his old friend Owen Barfield about his exciting new book and added, "Your language sometimes disgruntles me." He didn't like Barfield's word *polyvalence* and his phrase "He bases on..." instead of "He starts from..." Lewis preferred plain English.

## Raised in Print

Sister Penelope, a Church of England nun, had come into C. S. Lewis's life in 1939 and became a friend of his. She lived in a convent at Wantage. When C.S. Lewis dedicated a book to Sister Penelope and her fellow nuns, he used the words "To Some Ladies at

Wantage." The Portuguese translation accidentally changed it: "To Some Wanton Ladies." Lewis enjoyed that story.

Sister Penelope had first contacted Lewis with a letter of praise and a copy of her book *God Persists*. He said he didn't know how to respond to praise from his readers; he trusted that someday he could enjoy such compliments with the same innocence as if the compliments were for someone else. "Perfect humility will need no modesty." He was becoming a successful writer, and he saw pride as a continuing threat. He complimented Sister Penelope on her own book and told her that her phrase "God sat again for His portrait" (the New Testament) was daring and good.

He also told her that convincing good characters are uncommon in fiction because in order to imagine a man worse than himself an author only has to stop doing something [pushing back evil]. To imagine one better than himself, an author has to do something new [come closer to goodness]. He also told her that it is hard to invent something that isn't there already. He had learned to his surprise that some of his invented words in *Out of the Silent Planet* resemble real words in Arabic.

A couple of years later Lewis sent Sister Penelope a disreputable-looking copy of his *Screwtape Letters* for safe-keeping. The only other copy was with his publisher in London, and there was a danger that it might be destroyed in the London bombing. He did not say so to Penelope, but it is a matter of record that Lewis expected to be executed if the Germans took England. He no doubt thought that until publication his manuscript would be safer with her in her convent than with him in Oxford.

In 1942 Lewis answered Penelope that he used "all right' to mean that all items in a group are right, but "alright" to mean "perfectly right." It is an old Anglo Saxon custom to double the l for the long sound at the end of a word but to use a single l for the shorter sound in the middle of a word like already. (This distinction is not observed in the United States, where "alright" has usually been judged incorrect.)

Penelope had also asked Lewis about people making up myths, and he told her that he thought they really come from good and bad spiritual sources. And what *is* the process we call "making up," he

asked her. He agreed with her praise of a book by his friend Charles
Williams, and he too wished that Williams would write more clearly.

In February 1943, Lewis found himself sharing Sister Penelope's
frustration about book publication. His *Perelandra* was delayed at the
bindery, and her book on St. Athanasius had been sent back for rewriting. He advised her to try different publishers first. "Do fight."
He likened their frustrations about their delayed books to the long
waiting of God through the centuries to see His plan for mankind
work out. When will the divine books he meant us to be actually lie
on God's table in perfect form without faulty text or printer's errors?
An author's desire for a perfect book is like God's desire for us, Lewis
believed.

Human authorship is not real creation, of course. We only re-
arrange elements that God has provided. We can't imagine a new
primary color, a third sex, a fourth dimension, or even a monster that
does not consist of bits of previous animals stuck together. That is
why we can't control exactly what our writing means to other people.
And we can never know the entire meaning of our works. The
meaning we never intended may be the best and truest one. Writing a
book is like planting a garden or begetting a child; we are only one
cause among many in the flow of events.

"But how dull all one's books are except the one you are waiting
for at the moment!" Lewis observed. The author is like a shepherd,
and the delayed book is like a lost sheep.

Later in 1943 Lewis read some radio dramas Sister Penelope wrote
to teach the Bible to children. He suggested that she should not have
characters say "Alas," which is not living language in our day, unless
the entire play is in antiquated language. She should avoid trying to
sneak descriptive matter into the dramatic dialogue. And she should
try to keep her writing simple and concrete instead of abstract. Even
if Ezra were the kind of man who would talk about the "agricultural
aspect" of a ritual, that term seems a poor choice for children. "The
parallel is as close as possible" also sounds too lecture-like for such a
play. Victims of the Assyrian conquest would not have said that they
were ground under the enemy's heel; they would have named specific
terrors and cruelties. Lewis compared these weaknesses to surface
stains that could be easily removed; he encouraged Penelope in her
work and also urged her to have a rest.

Lewis was six chapters into his book *Miracles* at this point and told Penelope that he was surprised to find that writing about the Supernatural turned out to include much praise of nature. "One never knows what one's in for when one starts thinking."

Lewis couldn't offer Sister Penelope much advice about publishers, although he had had many manuscripts rejected and accepted. He sent his books to one publisher after another, in the order of his choice, and he found it a great distraction to have to do so. He disapproved of her publisher's plan to alter her radio plays "not to disturb the children's minds." What staggered him about publishers, he said, was not their wickedness ("in fact they may not be wicked at all"), but their muddle-headedness.

Twelve years later, it turned out, Lewis would announce to Sister Penelope that he had put himself into the hands of a good literary agent and would never deal directly with publishers again. He advised her to do the same. When news got out that Lewis was in touch with an agent, one of his publishers went all the way from London to Cambridge and offered to raise the terms on all his previous books if he would promise not to hire an agent. Lewis took that as a sign that he should do so. An agent means increased royalties, but he also means relief from work and thought and frustration that is not good for an author. "Study to be quiet...!" he reminded her.

In May 1948, *Out of the Silent Planet* was temporarily out of print, and Lewis explained to Penelope that his pestering the publisher would do even less good than anyone else's pestering.

She had sent Lewis a story idea that intrigued him, but it lacked a good ending. He suggested several endings for her and exclaimed, "What fun it is writing other people's books!" He didn't know if she was capable of writing a good novel or not, but he encouraged her to try. In a couple of months she sent him the beginning of the novel, and he was so excited about it that he answered at once. He thought that the first two chapters might need to be rewritten later, after the story was finished. The readers should be kept guessing about the nature of the odd experience in the first chapter instead of finding out the truth almost before their curiosity was aroused. One character's wife should be left out unless she was going to play a real part in the story; there were already two good female characters, and this housewife seemed to add nothing. There was too much guidebook information in the first chapter. The priest tended to lecture when he would have done better to hint. And people don't say "my boy" or "my friend" to another person now.

Lewis's main point was that Penelope needed to go through her manuscript and remove adjectives of praise, replacing them with adjectives of description. It is no use telling the reader that things were lovely, exquisite, and superb, because the reader won't believe it. The writer must tell the reader about the color, texture, size, shape, or motion of the shadows instead of saying they are lovely.

"God speed!" Lewis concluded warmly after all his advice.

A month later Lewis congratulated Penelope on her progress and pointed out some more weaknesses that he compared to skin troubles, not heart disease. First, he claimed that the word *tense* had been overworked by cheap writers, and so "a voice tense with interest" didn't work well; and it didn't need to be said anyway. Second, "had nothing outward seen" in dialogue was unclear and didn't sound like ordinary spoken English. That was true of some other odd-sounding phrases in the dialogue also. "If so be that the difference in size...." should be replaced by "If it's really true that the difference in size." Lewis pointed out that a certain bad sentence managed to be as clumsy as real conversation and at the same time as stiff as a lecture.

"Does a grin really go through a telephone?" Lewis wondered.

When the adult male hero made remarks like "it was just topping" and "I just loved..." he sounded too much like a child. In real life he might say those words, but the impression would be modified by his mature face and voice. On the printed page one doesn't have those and must be more careful. Lewis revised some of those sentences to show how to make them seem like what a grown man would say.

It is useful for an author to imagine dialogue being read aloud or acted on the stage. Listen for anything that an actor would find difficult to say or that one would feel embarrassed at in front of a large audience. The fictional dialogue must always sound like real conversation but must always be clearer and more concise than in reality. "Literature is the art of *illusion*."

Six months later, at the beginning of 1949, Sister Penelope was considering a pen-name, and Lewis suggested a couple. The first he mentioned was Pevensey. She did not use it, but a few months later

Lewis used it himself—as the name of the four children who entered the land of Narnia.

He told Penelope that all he could suggest for possible publication of her novel was stocking up on postal supplies and fortitude, finding a magazine that might want to publish it as a serial, or putting it aside in order to rewrite it in a few years. Rewriting it would probably be impossible in the near future, but he suggested that the story would be better without its improbable coincidence. *Real* life isn't often probable, but stories have to seem probable.

Next Penelope titled her story "The Morning Gift" and hoped for a preface from Lewis himself. He said no, that he had written too many prefaces already. Later that year he read the entire manuscript and said that it was better than he had expected. His curiosity about the story kept him up past his usual bedtime. Once again he told her what he liked and how she could make the novel better.

One of the characters was not much more than a mouthpiece for doctrine. What he said was interesting, but he was not interesting. The ideas could just as well have come from a book that the main character was reading. Anything, even oddities, to bring this character to life would be a great gain. Perhaps she could draw him in part from a real person. Lewis told her not to be timid, to let her imagination and humor go to work. He also suggested that her new convert should perhaps not find churchgoing entirely pleasant at first and that there should be a clear reason for the bride and groom's decision that they would never consummate their marriage. This sacrifice was artistically right in the story, but the reading public would dislike it; and it seemed to have no ethical or theological basis.

The style was now satisfactory, Lewis said, except for cliches. He advised Penelope to cut out stale phrases such as "all too little," "sands of time running out," and "three score and ten." But her image of Jesus leading an old man down to age like an old horse brought tears to Lewis's eyes. "I wish I had thought of it myself."

Early in 1950 Lewis expressed sorrow that Penelope had no luck finding a publisher for her novel, and he reminded her that many a book that succeeded later was first rejected by several publishers. He said he couldn't help her to revise it. He congratulated her on the status of her Biblical plays, which had done him good. "They may be, in a way, your most important work."

At this point Sister Penelope asked Lewis what he would think about other people bringing out their own Screwtape Letters, using his idea. He told her that a literary idea ought to belong to anyone who could use it and that exclusive ownership of literary ideas is a kind of Simony—the misuse of holy things for financial profit. However, he said, his publisher might not hold his view.

Finally in 1956 Penelope wrote to Lewis and asked for permission to sell the manuscript of *Screwtape Letters* that he had entrusted to her fifteen years earlier during the bombing of London. He replied that he hadn't the faintest notion that she had it, or that it existed. She was welcome to sell it if she could find a buyer and to use the money for any pious or charitable purpose she liked.

Then he asked her if it had ever occurred to her that the replacement of the scrawled old manuscript by the clear, printed book in mint condition was an excellent symbol of our bodily resurrection. "It is sown in inky scratches, it is raised in print."

In 1960 Reverend E. T. Dell wrote from Massachusetts and asked C. S. Lewis to consider writing a book about death. Lewis answered on March 5 that it was a tough proposition, but he would think about it. The idea that death is a hideous enemy is Scriptural, he told Dell; and the idea that there is no death or that death doesn't matter is blah. He was starting to write the book already, he half-joked.

It never got written. His health was sinking fast.

In 1963 Lewis found himself slowly parting with the inky old manuscript of his mortal life. One of the last letters he wrote before his death was to Sister Penelope. He concluded their long correspondence with some final thoughts on life and death and closed with the message,

> "It *is* all rather fun—solemn fun—isn't it?
> Yours always, C.S. Lewis."

That could stand as his last word on creative writing as well. It is all rather fun, solemn fun.

23

# MINING DANTE:
## *DIVINE COMEDY* DISCOVERIES
## FOR EVERYONE

*There are still discoveries to be made in* The Divine Comedy, *and to my surprise I seem to have made a few dozen myself. I think they are understandable and interesting, even for people who have never read* The Divine Comedy.

American poet John Ciardi pointed out once in *Saturday Review* "It is true that Dante writes in depth. But if the gold of Dante runs deep, it also runs right up to the surface. A lifetime of devoted scholarship will not mine all that gold; yet enough lies on the surface—or just an inch below—to make a first reading a bonanza in itself."

Ciardi's claim was not hyperbole. Although the story in *The Divine Comedy* took place exactly 700 years ago and scholars have been mining it for over 650 years, more is still there for the taking. The main reasons for this are, in my opinion, Dante's condensed and elliptical style, his audacious new uses of the material at hand, his dizzying displays of synthesis and double meaning, his spectacular intelligence, and his extraordinary familiarity with the Bible.[1]

---

[1] Richard Wilbur (United States Poet Laureate, 1987-1988) said "I admire Dante and his Comedy for a great many reasons: a brilliant, intricate architecture

Dante's mind was even more steeped in Scripture[2] than most of his commentators realize, and to miss any of his sometimes intricate and convoluted biblical allusions and spiritual insights is to miss part of his passion and artistry. Too many academics and literary critics today are content to treat *The Divine Comedy* as a great secular work of art encrusted with an almost inconsequential residue of outdated Christianity. But even Dante lovers who are also Bible lovers have failed to notice the full extent of his immersion in the Bible and how it permeates his *Comedy*. Although most biblical references in the *Inferno* and *Purgatory* are well documented in commentaries, many in *Paradise* have been overlooked. (*Paradise* is the most complex, challenging, and ambitious of the three books, and as a result it is the least explored.)

To my surprise and delight, as an enthusiastic amateur I have found fifty previously overlooked nuggets (some large and some miniscule) of what I consider Dantean gold.[3] My favorite discoveries are biblical, but the non-biblical ones are of broader interest. Topics of these non-biblical discoveries involve, among other things, astronomy, animal husbandry, geology. geometry, sexual ethics, metaphysics, and church politics. Although some are complex, no one has to have a background in Dante studies or *The Divine Comedy* to understand them.[4]

---

that's wholly serious, and wholly justified in its intricacy; profound knowedge of the heart and soul; sinewy spareness of style; a superb range of intonations." (From an interview in *Image*, Issue 12, Winter 1995.)

[2] The Bible that Dante used was the Latin Vulgate (translated circa 400 A.D.). For this essay I am omitting the Vulgate and limiting myself to the Authorized Version (1611) or the New International Version (1984).

[3] I failed to find these nuggets in any of the excerpts or essays I read, or in the commentaries for the entire *Comedy* accompanying the seven translations I used—those by Carlyle-Wicksteed, John Ciardi, Henry Wadsworth Longfellow, Allen Mandelbaum, Mark Musa, Dorothy Sayers (with Barbara Reynolds), and Charles Singleton. Needless to say, in 650 years of Divine Comedy scholarship, some insights and discoveries have been forgotten or overlaid along the way; my ideas may have surfaced before.

[4] A more thorough treatment of Dante's allusions would require quoting his lines in Italian as well as in English. All of my quotations are from my prose rendition in *Dante's Divine Comedy, Journey to Joy: Inferno* and *Purgatory* (Macon: Mercer University Press, 1997) or *Paradise* (Macon: Mercer University Press, 1998).

## TWENTY NON-BIBLICAL DISCOVERIES

### 1. Dante and Jacob

One of the first questions that confronts us in the *Inferno* (Canto 2, lines 100-102) was passed over in all the commentaries I have read.[5] I wondered why Beatrice, who lived in Italy from 1266 to 1289 A.D. and died in her early twenties, was seated in heaven next to Rachel, who lived in the Middle East circa 1800 B.C., died in middle age or later, and was somewhat of a schemer, like her husband Jacob. The two women would not appear to have anything in common, and for years I assumed that Dante put them together by chance; but eventually their connection dawned on me. I propose that Dante links Beatrice to Rachel because they are two of history's most ardently loved women. Thus Dante intentionally associates himself and his love for Beatrice with Jacob and his love for Rachel; as a poet of the Courtly Love tradition, Dante could hardly have overlooked the parallels between Jacob's love and his own. Confident that his *Comedy* was a masterpiece, he undoubtedly foresaw that because of it Beatrice would have a place as high as Rachel's in the literary pantheon of love. (See "Closing the Brackets" near the end of this essay.)

### 2. Loving in Return

Canto 5 of the *Inferno* (lines 79-142) includes the single most famous scene in the *Comedy,* that of the doomed lovers Paolo and Francesca. Because they had committed adultery, they were killed by Francesca's vengeful husband and were swept about forever by winds in the second circle of Hell. This scene is rightly pointed out as an example of Dante's compassion and tenderness.

Francesca explains to Dante, "Love, which kindles quickly in a gentle heart, seized him because of my lovely body that has been stolen from me. (That theft still grieves me.) Love, which excuses no one loved from loving in return, caused me to delight in him so

---

[5] In addition to the seven translations of the entire *Divine Comedy* that I used, I also consulted those by Francis Cary, Robert Pinsky, and Elio Zappulla.

strongly that even now I love him. Love led the two of us to one death." Dante (the allegorical traveler) is still naive at this point in the story of his spiritual education; thus he is swept away with sympathy for the charming, self-centered Francesca. But in real life Dante the author is warning readers about such naivete. As Charles Williams and Dorothy Sayers put it, Dante included this scene to show the sweet desirability of the first small surrender of the soul to Hell. If they had been honest, Francesca and her handsome brother-in-law Paolo would have realized that they were flirting with disaster as well as each other when they spent time alone reading about love and adultery. There is a difference between true innocence and this kind of poor judgment. Here Dante the author is warning about the step-by-step seductiveness of all sin, not just the sin of adultery; but many readers are so taken by Francesca that they miss Dante's point completely.

Even the commentators who understand Dante's point pass over the powerful irony of Francesca's key phrase, "Love, which excuses no one loved from loving in return..."[6] The entire *Comedy* is about God's "primal, perfect Love" and our response to it; but instead of loving God (and His available forgiveness), Francesca loves only her love affair with Paolo. Incidentally, the dramatic irony of her words is similar to that in the words of Caiaphas the High Priest in John 11:50: "...it is expedient for us that one man should die for the people, and that the whole nation perish not." Neither Caiaphas nor Francesca knew the true meaning of their words.

## 3. Voyeurism

In Canto 30 of the *Inferno* (lines 141-148) Virgil rebukes Dante for listening to two sufferers squabbling in Hell, then advises him, "Know that I am always at your side, in case it ever happens that Fate brings you to where people are squabbling like this again. To enjoy listening to such talk is really gross." In my opinion, this is a good example of Dante's very sly wit; on one level Dante (through Virgil) is

---

6 Barbara Reynolds points out that the inevitablity of loving where one is loved was a theme in Dante's (earlier) love poetry and that of his contemporaries. (For example, in section XX of *La Vita Nuova* [Poems of Youth], he cited the wisdom of Guido Guinizelli, who said the gentle [noble] heart is the abode of love and has no option but to respond to love with love.)

tweaking everyone who dutifully and attentively reads the malicious bickering. After all, Dante wrote this quarrel to be read, not skipped. He has set a little trap for his readers, and I think he did it in playful, mischievous spirit. Nevertheless, Virgil's rebuke can serve as a valid warning against voyeurism.

## 4. Postojna Caves

It is common knowledge that in the *Inferno* Dante descends into Hell, occasionally encountering an underground stream, until he reaches an icy cavern (where Satan is trapped in the center of the earth) in Cantos 31-34. There is no doubt that Dante was alluding to Virgil's portrayal of an underground hell (70-19 B. C.), as Virgil was alluding to Homer's (circa 750-700 B. C.); but I assumed that Dante's far more detailed image of Hell was *sui generis*. Then I happened to learn about the Postojna Caves, a 14-mile labyrinth of underground passages, channels, and chambers located in a part of Slovenia that used to be Italian, then Yugoslavian. According to geologists, millions of years ago water flowed above ground from the Pivka basin to the Planina basin; but eventually the Pivka River cut and filtered its way underground, and there it eroded enormous caverns, including one white-frosted chamber sometimes called Snow Mountain because it looked like ice and snow. A half century before Dante's birth, Italian visitors were already inscribing their names and dates inside the Postojna caves. Because Dante was a frequent traveler with great interest in geological formations, I strongly suspect that his description of Hell was based on the memorable Postojna Caves; in fact, I enjoy imagining his visit there.

## 5. Astronomical Convergence

In the first Canto of *Paradise* (lines 37-42) Dante says "The lamp of the world rises for mortals by various routes; but from the one which joins four circles and three crosses it rises with a better course, linked to a happier constellation, and warms and stamps our earthly wax to be more like its own nature." As commentators explain, Dante is referring to four great astronomical circles. The first three are the equator, the ecliptic, and the colure (a great circle that intersects both poles and which is the longitudinal circle of a given place). These all cross the fourth circle, the horizon, and the sun rises at different points on the horizon as seasons change; hence, three crossings. As Dante knew, at the spring equinox in Florence the three crossings actually take place at the same point on the horizon. With this display of learning, Dante is alluding to the four cardinal (human) virtues and the three theological (divine) virtues. In my opinion, he is also alluding to the human and divine nature of Christ, where the seven virtues converge. The sun in this analogy is God, who warms and imprints us to be more like His own nature.

## 6. Family Pride

In Canto 16 of *Paradise* (lines 16-180) Dante exclaims to the spirit of his distinguished ancestor Cacciaguida, "You are my father. You make me bold to speak. You uplift me so that I am more than I." As commentators explain, in Italian this plural form of the pronoun *you* expresses respect; for this reason Dante addresses Cacciaguida with this pronoun three times in a row. Then he claims that (being descended from) Cacciaguida has made him more than himself alone. As I see it, Dante feels figuratively expanded by his connection to this illustrious ancestor, foreshadowing Cacciaguida's warning about dangers of hubris and over-expansion.

## 7. Tetragon

In Canto 17 of *Paradise* (line 24) Dante assures Cacciaguida "I feel I am set foursquare to withstand the assaults of fate..." Using the term tetragon, which suggests the English adjective foursquare, Dante refers to geometry for the third time in two sentences. Longfellow is unique among commentators I have consulted in pointing out that Dante must be alluding to the following statement from Aristotle's *Ethics*, "Always and everywhere the virtuous man bears prosperous and adverse fortune prudently, as a perfect tetragon." Neither Longfellow nor other commentators I consulted mention the second definition of tetragon in the *Oxford English Dictionary*: a square fortress. I have not ascertained that such a definition existed in Italian in Dante's day, but it fits perfectly Dante's hope to be like a tetragon in withstanding the assaults of fate. I thinks the four sides of Dante's tetragon are the four cardinal virtues that the Church adopted from Plato and Aristotle: prudence, temperance, fortitude, and justice.

## 8. See, Will, and Love

In Canto 17 of *Paradise* (lines 103-105) Dante seeks advice from Cacciaguida "like a man in doubt who seeks advice from someone who sees and rightly wills and loves." I suspect that Dante believed that man is designed to reflect the triune nature of God he expressed elsewhere: the Son (wisdom) sees, the Father (power) wills, and the Spirit (love) rejoices. This divine and human triad is implicit in the following prayer of St. Augustine: "O God, you are the light of minds that know you, the joy of hearts that love you, and the strength of wills that serve you. Grant us so to know you that we may truly love you, and so to love you that we may freely serve you, whom to serve is perfect freedom."

## 9. The Vatican

Canto 18 of *Paradise* (lines 118-123) ends with Dante railing against disgraceful church leadership in Rome, particularly that of Pope John XXII. Jupiter is the locus of just leadership, and Dante prays to God (the Mind in which the planet Jupiter originated) for Him "to watch the place that issues smoke that dims [Jupiter's] rays; then His wrath will be kindled again against the buying and selling in the temple whose walls are built by miracles and martyrdoms." Everyone agrees that Dante is bitterly attacking the abuse of office by greedy, dishonest church leaders; but I suspect that Dante is specifically referring to release of white smoke by the College of Cardinals to signal their selection of a new pope. According to *Europe A History* by Norman Davies, this custom began in 1271; Dante was eleven years old then. He saw that some of these selections obscured and diminished justice. (The papacy was transferred to Avignon in 1305, before Dante wrote *Paradise*; but Dante's fictitious visit to the heaven of Jupiter took place in 1300, before the transfer. Furthermore, Dante was convinced that the papacy would soon return to Rome; and in contrast he was convinced that his *Comedy* would endure for centuries.)

## 10. The Mystery of Creativity

In Canto 20 of *Paradise* (lines 37-42) Dante sees the spirit of King David ("the Holy Spirit's songwriter") shining brightly and is told

"Now he knows the value of his songs, insofar as they were his, because of his commensurate reward." David's reward, presumably, is joy about the role his art played in God's plan for blessing the world. Dante was interested in the mysterious way that God's will and human will work together in creativity. It seems to me that although Dante was concentrating on David here, he was also commenting on all artists and artisans.

In Canto 28 of *Paradise* (lines 133-135) Beatrice's seemingly contradictory attributions of *The Celestial Hierarchy* first to the author's hard work ("Dionysius set himself to contemplate these orders with such zeal that he named them and described them") and then to revelation ("And you need not be amazed that a mortal man dispensed such secret truth on earth; for one who saw it up here reported it to him...") strike me as parallel to her previous statement "the allotment of sight is according to the righteousness bestowed by grace and by good will [correct choice]." In my opinion this is Dante's way of telling how he wrote *The Divine Comedy*: it was the product of years of extremely enthusiastic and intense labor, but it was also a gift of God's grace. Throughout, Dante depended upon divine assistance. At the beginning of *Paradise* he wrote "...for this crowning task make me an adequate channel of your power... Enter my heart and breathe..."

## 11. Two Pairs of Doves

In Canto 25 of *Paradise* (lines 19-24) Dante reports "As it is when a dove alights by its mate and they express their love for each other by circling and cooing, so I saw one great, glorious prince greeting the other, praising the banquet that they feast on above. But when their greeting was completed they both settled silently before me, burning so brightly that they overwhelmed my eyes." Although commentators I consulted don't say so, I am convinced that this image is designed to contrast with the image of lovers Paolo and Francesca in Canto 5 of *Inferno*, who were like doves swept hither and yon by a dark wind amidst the noisy screaming and crying of other unrepentant souls. (Hell is all darkness, misery, and noise; Heaven is all light, joy, and peace.)

## 12. Teeth That Bite

In Canto 26 of *Paradise* (lines 49 - 63) St. John interrogates Dante theologically about spiritual love and asks him, "As human wisdom and authorities concur, of all your loves the highest is for God. But tell me also if you feel other cords pulling you toward Him, in order to identify the various teeth with which this correct love bites you." Dante answers, "All the bites which have power to make the heart turn to God work together in my love... drawing me from the sea of wrong love and placing me on the shore of correct love." John Ciardi ventures that such an erotic figure of speech is necessary to express the ardor of the love of God, "about which there can be nothing bland." Mark Musa notes the origin of this metaphor in the writings of mystics. Barbara Reynolds proposes that the teeth are those on a ratchet, which dredged Dante from the sea of wrongful love. In his essay "Imagery in the Last Eleven Cantos of Dante's *Comedy*," C. S. Lewis names and categorizes the images in cantos 22-33 according to topic; but although he does that with the cords, he fails to categorize or comment on the teeth that bite.

None of the commentaries I consulted mentioned what seemed obvious to me: that this is one of Dante's pastoral and agrarian metaphors. I think St. John is referring to the ministrations of sheep dogs, which nip at the animals they are herding in order to guide them safely in the right direction. George MacDonald was a lover of *The Divine Comedy*, and I suspect he recognized Dante's sheep dogs for what they were. In "The Voice of Job" (*Unspoken Sermons, Second Series*), he wrote, "[A soul] has a claim to be compelled to repent; to be hedged in on every side: to have one after another of the strong, sharp-toothed sheep dogs of the Great Shepherd sent after him..." Could Dante have intended the teeth as double imagery, both agricultural (sheep dogs) and mechanical (a ratchet)? I think so.

## 13. The Words of Mortals

In Canto 26 of *Paradise* (lines 136-138) Adam told Dante, "Before I descended to Hell's anguish, J [Yahweh] was the earthly name of the Supreme Good that wraps me in gladness; but later He was called El [Elohim]. And this is fitting, for the words of mortals are like leaves upon a branch; one falls and another replaces it." Adam seems to me to indicate that the specifics of language are mere accidents of history and not ordained by God or nature. (As Barbara Reynolds points out, the image of words as leaves is from "Ars Poetica" by Horace, lines 60-62.) Although I have not seen the idea elsewhere, I suspect that this foray into etymology might also be Dante's allusion to the following statement by Thomas Aquinas in *Summa contra Gentiles*: "...the reality of the names predicated of God and other things is first in God according to His mode, but the meaning of the name is on Him afterwards. Wherefore He is said to be named from his effects." Perhaps this puts Dante's special deference for the names Jesus and Christ in his *Comedy* into perspective; the words themselves are earthly artifacts.

### 14. Rotten Fruit on the Tree of Time

I believe that in Canto 27 of *Paradise* (lines 88-120) Dante is suggesting that humans experience historical reality in the created dimensions of space and time, but blessed spirits experience higher reality ("the mind of God") in the eternal dimensions of light (our experience of Christ) and warmth (our experience of the Holy Spirit), beyond space and time. After this subtle metaphysical lesson about "the nature of the universe," Beatrice ends by deploring human greed (lines 124-126): "The human will blossoms well; but a continuous downpour turns the fine plums into spoiled fruit." Even in *Paradise*, Dante's polemics about corruptive greed are bitter; Dante was a social activist and reformer, and greed is the destroyer of the fruits of time he cherished. His exclamation about the papacy applies also to the human race and to Satan himself; all three began well but fell. In her commentary Barbara Reynolds remarks, "Men have become degenerate as a result of their abuse of time, so that progress is turned into regress, the innocence of childhood being quickly lost with the passing of the years." In my opinion this concept accounts for the way Canto 27 treats the relationship of greed and time as if it is obvious.

In Canto 32 St. Bernard is completely absorbed in his contemplation of Mary, but he is free to instruct Dante about the seating arrangement in the circular amphitheater. This seems to me to demonstrate that just as the blessed souls can (in our terms) be in two or more places at once because they are no longer limited by space, they can also be doing two or more things at once because they are no longer limited by time.

## 15. Untying the Knot

In Canto 28 of *Paradise* (lines 16-87) Beatrice displays mysteries of space and time to Dante and tells him "If your fingers are unable to untie such a tight knot, don't be surprised; it is this tight because no one has ever tried to loosen it." By the time she finishes, Dante has untied the knot: "my mind cleared when my Lady provided me with her clear answer; and the truth was seen like a star in the sky." Unfortunately, Dante does not explain what the truth was that he saw, but I think I know. In addition to light and warmth, he often focuses on spatial magnitude and intensity of speed—which symbolize magnitude of goodness and intensity of desire. Spiritual reality (the Empyrean) transcends space and time, and so perhaps knowledge (of goodness) and love are its real dimensions. (Barbara Reynolds explores much but not all of this idea in her notes.) Thus I believe that in both Cantos 27 and 28, Beatrice has enlightened Dante about the relationship of physical reality to spiritual reality.

## 16. Laughing at Himself

In Canto 28 of *Paradise* (lines 133-135) Dante endorses the system of angelology expressed in *The Celestial Hierarchy*. In his earlier book *Convivio* he had endorsed instead the angelology of Pope Gregory I (590-604), but between *Convivio* and *The Comedy* Dante obviously changed his mind. In my opinion, Dante's portrayal (through Beatrice) of Gregory gently laughing at his own error when he saw Heaven for himself is not only a tribute to Gregory's buoyant humility, but also an intentional display of Dante's. And considering the errors in the medieval view of the physical universe that Dante had to use in his *Comedy*, I think it is fair to assume about Dante what he assumed about Gregory: "as soon as his eyes opened in Heaven he laughed at himself."

## 17. The Ocean of Light

In Canto 30 of *Paradise* (lines 61, 90) Dante is shown a river of light and then sees it revealed as an ocean of light. I believe this ocean of light is the very sea that Piccarda spoke of in Canto 3. There she told Dante that the essence of Heaven is the ocean of rest that is God's will. "In His will is our peace. It is that sea to which everything moves."

## 18. The Celestial Rose

In Cantos 30-31 of *Paradise* Dante visits the highest heaven and sees a vision of it as a gigantic pure white rose. (In Canto 30 the angels appeared as frolicking sparks of topaz flying back and forth beween a river of dusky golden light and river banks covered with spring flowers; and in Canto 31 white-robed angels with golden robes and faces like flames fly in and out like bees, seeing and singing the glory of the One who arouses their love.) In my opinion, Dante's visual ascent into the fragrant white rose is meant to remind readers of his earlier descent into the foul darkness of the Inferno. (In Cantos 21-22 of *Inferno* Dante visited a ditch where thick tar boiled, coating the rocky banks with glue. Two angry demons who fell into the boiling tar stuck fast, cooked within black crusts, and had to be fished out with grappling hooks.) At the bottom of the pit Dante and Virgil saw and touched Satan himself, the frozen negation of love and beauty. In contrast, God is blazing above the rose and is the archetypal sun.

Upon previewing these insights, Nancy-Lou Patterson suddenly had an insight of her own: the frolicking sparks of topaz are a mirror image of the fiery sparks that rain onto the skin of scorched and charred souls in *Inferno* (Canto 14). In return, I noticed that Paradise's river of dusky golden light and its banks covered with spring flowers are a mirror image of Hell's river of boiling blood with rocky banks (Canto 14). As if to hint at this connection, Dante links the sparks to bees when he opens Canto 16 by saying that when three souls running through the rain of painful torture left the others, he could already hear the rumble of boiling water falling down into the next level of Hell, a waterfall that sounded like the heavy hum of a bee-hive. Thus the metaphorical bee/sparks in *Inferno* are bees that sting terribly, and those in *Paradise* are those that make honey.

## 19. Celestial Seating

In canto 32 of of *Paradise* (lines 27-33) Bernard tells Dante "Just as on one side of the circle the partition is composed of the glorious seat of the Lady of Heaven and the seats below it, so on the other side the partition is composed of seats assigned to great, ever saintly John (who endured the wilderness and martyrdom and then two years in Hell)..." Thus John, Christ's cousin and his baptizer, holds the pre-Christian seat of honor, equivalent to his aunt's seat of honor in the Christian section. John's martyrdom mentioned by Dante occurred when an evil woman had his head cut off and brought in on a platter. This is the second beheading alluded to in Canto 32 and the reverse of the first one; Judith, who is seated below Mary in the line of Hebrew women across the amphitheater from John, heroically saved Israel by cutting off the head of Holofernes and carrying it back to her people. Dante focused on such correspondences and contrasts.

In lines 133-138 Bernard shows Dante that Anna sits across the amphitheater from her daughter Mary, immediately to the right of her nephew John; and Lucy sits on his left. Because of the significance that Dante invested in meaningful symmetry of his celestial seating plan, I looked for the link between Anna and Lucy. I think Lucy and Anna are paired because Anna doesn't take her eyes off her daughter Mary on the far side of the amphitheater, and Lucy is the patron saint connected with good vision. According to Canto 2 of *Inferno*, Mary had summoned Lucy across the amphitheater and committed Dante to her care; then Lucy had commissioned Beatrice to rescue him, which she did by recruiting Virgil. Lucy is also the last saint Dante will see in Paradise before looking directly at God; thus she represents both the clear vision and the spiritual enlightenment that Dante desperately needed in the first sentence of *Inferno*: "Midway on life's journey, I woke up and found myself in a dark wood, for I had lost the path." With the help of Lucy, he finds his path and ascends to the ultmost light.

Similarly, I think I see the link between the two saints seated on both sides of Mary—St. Peter and Adam. As I see it, Adam caused the human race to be locked out of Paradise, and Peter was entrusted with the keys to open Paradise.

## 20. *Squaring the Circle*

In Canto 33 of *Paradise* (lines 133-135), Dante likens a unified perception of the two natures of Christ to "squaring the circle" (constructing a square with the same area as a given circle). This was a goal in geometry for many centuries; but it would have required discovering a correspondence between the radius of a circle and the side of a square with the use of no more than a straight edge and a compass. The task was eventually proved to be impossible, as Dante foresaw, like the task of intellectually reconciling the two natures of Christ (his humanity and his divinity). In Canto 31 of *Purgatory* Dante had seen Christ's two natures seem to alternate, as reflected in the eyes of Beatrice; in Canto 33 of *Paradise* he sees the two simultaneously. The circle, like the sun, is a traditional symbol for God: "God is a circle whose center is everywhere and whose circumference is nowhere." In my opinion, Dante chose a square to symbolize Christ's human nature because He was the perfect manifestation of the four cardinal [human] virtues.

# THIRTY BIBLICAL DISCOVERIES

## 1. *Three Wild Beasts*

In the first canto of the *Inferno* (lines 31-54) Dante tries to ascend a holy hill and finds his way blocked by three animals: a leopard, a lion, and a wolf. Commentators rightly relate these creatures to Jeremiah 5:5-6: "'So I will go to the leaders and speak to them; surely they know the way of the Lord, the requirements of their God.' But with one accord they too had broken off the yoke and torn off the bonds. Therefore a lion from the forest will attack them, a wolf from the desert will ravage them, a leopard will lie in wait near their towns to tear to pieces any who venture out, for their rebellion is great and their backslidings many." Jeremiah laments social evils.

Many *Comedy* experts think the three beasts represent certain personal sins as well as social evils, and I agree. (The leopard represents worldly pleasure and lust, sins typical of youth; the lion represents pride and ambition, sins typical of adulthood; and the wolf represents greed and avarice, sins typical of age.) But although it must have been noted before, none the commentaries I consulted mentions the fact that Dante's three beasts relate to Isaiah 11:6, "The wolf also shall dwell with the lamb, and the leopard shall lie down with the kid; and the calf and the young lion and the fatling together; and a little child shall lead them." The peaceable kingdom that Isaiah foresaw is a symbol of Paradise.

## 2. Seven Golden Candlesticks

At the beginning of Canto 29 of *Purgatory* a maiden named Matilda told Dante to look and listen. (That is Dante's clue to readers to be alert, and I don't think they have adequately heeded his advice.) Then Dante saw the air blaze and heard the sweet chanting of a choir. From that point on, his experience in Canto 29 (lines 15-154) loosely reflects the experience of John in Revelation 4.

Dante watches an allegorical procession that represents the history of divine revelation. Seven blazing golden candlesticks float ahead of the parade and cast great bands of colored light into the sky. The candlesticks are followed by twenty-four elders (referred to in Revelation 4:6-8) who are like actors who play the parts of all the books of the Old Testament (as counted in a condensed way by Jerome). The song of the elders echoes words spoken to Mary in the first chapter of Luke, implying that the Old Testament is a preparation for the Incarnation. The twenty-four elders are followed by four symbolic beasts that represent the gospels of Matthew, Mark, Luke, and John. Next come two old men representing the book of Acts and the Pauline epistles, followed by four humble men representing the epistles of James, Peter, John, and Jude. Last but not least, a solitary old man resembling a sleepwalker represents the book of Revelation.

Commentators agree about the meaning of the biblical figures in the procession, and they agree that the seven candlesticks correspond to the seven lamps in Revelation 4:5. Most also agree that the bands of colored light correspond to the rainbow in Revelation 4:3 and represent the attributes of God. (I suspect that Dante also had in mind Genesis 9:13, "I do set my bow in the cloud, and it shall be for a token of a covenant between me and the earth.")

But in my opinion commentators have overlooked Dante's obvious rationale for placing these lights at the head of the procession:

the seven candlesticks represent the seven days of creation. According to Paul in Romans 1:20, creation is God's original, universal revelation, preceding the books of the Bible: "For since the creation of the world God's invisible qualities—his eternal power and divine nature—have been clearly seen, being understood from what has been made, so that men are without excuse." Revelation 4, which forms the basis of Canto 29, ends with the creation theme also: "You are worthy, our Lord and God, to receive glory and honor and power, for you created all things, and by your will they were created and have their being."

When Dante first sees the light of the candelabras, he hears sweet voices chanting "Hosannah." Hosannah means "Save, we pray," and it is what the crowd shouted to Christ at his triumphal entry into Jerusalem (see Matthew 21:9). The procession Dante watches in Canto 29 is indeed a triumphal entry, replete with Christ's triumphal chariot located in the midst of the four gospels.

Who was chanting Hosannah at the beginning of this triumphal entry? I believe Dante was alluding to God's words in Job 38:4-7 "Where wast thou when I laid the foundations of the earth? declare, if thou hast understanding. Who hath laid the measures thereof, if thou knowest? or who hath stretched the line upon it? Whereupon are the foundations thereof fastened? or who laid the corner stone thereof; When the morning stars sang together, and all the sons of God shouted for joy?" At the beginning of the procession Dante heard the morning stars singing Hosannah at the dawn of creation.

### 3. Color Scheme

In *Purgatory* 29 (lines 121-129) Dante says "Three maidens moved forward, dancing in a circle by the right wheel; one so red she would hardly be visible in a fire; the next as green as if her flesh and bone were made of emerald; the third like new–fallen snow. Now the white one seemed to lead the dance, and now the red; and from the red one's song the others paced their dance slowly or quickly." Commentators agree that the white dancer is faith, the green dancer is hope, and the bright red dancer is charity (love). Paul said in I Corinthians 13:13 "And now these three remain: faith, hope and love. But the greatest of these is love," and Dante's red maiden leads the other two dancers. The colored wreaths on the figures representing the books of the Bible (lines 82-84, lines 91-93, lines 133-144) have the same allegorical significance: white lilies represent the faith of the Old Testament, green leaves represent the hope of the Gospel, and red roses represent the love of the New Testament.

As I see it, these three colors (which became the colors of the Italian flag five centuries later) correspond to the red and green in Revelation 4 and Revelation 21. In Revelation 4:2-3 John says "At once I was in the Spirit, and there before me was a throne in heaven with someone sitting on it. And the one who sat there had the appearance of jasper and carnelian [both red]. A rainbow, resembling an emerald [green], encircled the throne." In Revelation 21:10-11 John says "And he carried me away in the Spirit to a mountain great and high [Dante's Mount Purgatory], and showed me the Holy City, Jerusalem, coming down out of heaven from God. It shone with the glory of God, and its brilliance was like that of a very precious jewel, like a jasper, clear as crystal." Verses 18-20 continue, "The wall was made of jasper, and the city of pure gold, as pure as glass." The foundations of the city wall are overlaid with precious stones, including emerald.

### 4. Bread of the Angels

In Canto 2 of *Paradise* (lines 10-12) Dante says "You other few, who have already raised your heads for the bread of the angels which sustains life but is never filling..." He is quoting Psalm 78:25, "Man ate of the bread of the angels; he [God] sent them food in abundance." On the surface, this psalm refers to the manna that God provided to hungry wanderers in the wilderness (see Exodus 16), but Dante is referring allegorically to truth, especially the truths of philosophy and theology. I suspect that Dante is also alluding to the way Christians raise their heads and open their mouths to receive the consecrated bread in a traditional Communion service (Mass). In that sense the bread of the angels is Christ, whose words in John 14:6 are "I am the way and the truth and the life. No one comes to the Father except through me."

### 5. A Dancing Ruler

In Canto 7 of *Paradise* (lines 1-9) Dante describes the light of Justinian whirling in dance and singing. "'Hosanna, Holy God of

Hosts, You who light the blessed fires of these realms with Your shining.' Thus I saw that pure being sing, revolving to his own music with twin lights above him. Then he and the rest of the dancers, like sparks that shoot away, quickly disappeared behind the veil of distance." In my opinion, Justinian's dancing before Dante is meant to bring to mind the account of King David's festive dancing in 2 Samuel 6:14-22. David, wearing a linen ephod, danced before the LORD with all his might. His wife Michal accused him of making a fool of himself in public, but he replied "I will celebrate before the LORD."

## 6. Sparkling like Sunlight

In Canto 9 of *Paradise* (lines 115-120) a resident of the third heaven tells Dante "You want to know who is within the light that sparkles by me like sunlight in pure water. Know, then, that in it Rahab has peace; know that by joining our order, she became our highest-ranking member." He explains that when Christ visited Hell immediately after the crucifixion and rescued many souls, Rahab (a Hebrew ex-prostitute) was the first soul rescued. Dante is emphasizing the biblical truth that it is ultimate response to God, not circumspect living, that determines eternal destinies. In my opinion, Dante wrote this canto with Romans 8:28-29 in mind, "And we know that all things work together for good to them that love God, to them who are called according to his purpose. For whom he did foreknow, he did also predestinate to be conformed to the image of his Son, that he might be the firstborn among many brethren. Moreover, whom he did predestinate, them he also justified: and whom he justified, them he also glorified."

## 7. The Role of Rahab

The most complicated and delightful biblical allusions I found in *Paradise* involve Rahab in Canto 9 and King Solomon in Canto 10, and they have been overlooked in all the commentaries I consulted. According to Canto 9 of *Paradise* (lines 121-125) "it was fitting for [Rahab] to be a palm here of the lofty victory which was achieved with two palms, because she helped toward Joshua's first glorious victory in the Holy Land..." Rahab was a Canaanite prostitute in approximately 1250 B.C., and she saved the lives of spies that Joshua had sent into Jericho. When the Hebrews conquered Jericho she gathered her relatives into her house, and in her window she hung a skein of scarlet thread (a signal given to her by the spies); thus the lives of her family members were spared. I believe Rahab's signal to the invaders symbolized the blood on the doorpost that had miraculously saved the Hebrews from death at the occasion of the first Passover and that to Dante it symbolized Christ's saving blood. Dante commentators refer readers to the account in Joshua 2-6 but leave out the salvific red thread and its Christian meaning. Furthermore, they usually leave out the crucial fact that later, as a married woman, Rahab actually became an ancestor of Christ. None that I know of mention that from Dante's point of view both Paul (who stressed the importance of faith in God) and James (who stressed the importance of good works) praised Rahab in the New Testament, in Hebrews 11:31 and James 3:25.[7]

This sentence about Rahab is an ingenious and profoundly meaningful knot of wordplay and ideas, typical of Dante. In his youth countless brave and devout pilgrims spent months trekking to the Holy Land; they were called palmers because they usually brought home palm fronds as trophies from the long, arduous trip. Rahab serves as a "palm" in Heaven, a trophy of Christ's journey to Hell and back after the crucifixion. Thus Dante begins this sentence by likening the crucified Christ to a palmer who has journeyed to the "unholy land" of Hell and back. Next he audaciously switches definitions and attributes Christ's victory over the kingdom of sin and death to Christ's two nail-pierced palms. Dante considers Rahab an especially appropriate trophy of Christ's pilgrimage because of her role in Joshua's victory over the kingdom of Canaan. In my opinion the key to this claim is the fact that the name Jesus is a Greek version of the Hebrew name Joshua, which means "Yahweh [God] is salvation." Dante is accomplishing a remarkable literary sleight of hand by juggling the identities and victories of the two Joshuas in the receptive reader's mind while juggling the salvific Passover blood on the doorpost with Rahab's red thread and the bleeding hands of God on the cross.

---

[7] Through the years, I might have seen some of these points about Rahab made by Bible expositors; otherwise, they are my own perceptions.

## 8. Chasteness, Harlotry, and Spiritual Adultery

At the conclusion of Canto 9 of *Paradise* (lines 127-142), Dante declares "Thus the attention of the pope and cardinals is narrowly focused, and they never turn their thoughts to Nazareth, where Gabriel once spread his wings. But the Vatican and Rome's other burial sites of the brigades that followed Peter shall soon be freed from such adultery." Although I haven't seen the following ideas elsewhere, I believe they are key to this brief passage, which is in reality a vital link between the complexities of Rahab and those of Canto 10.

Dante's suggestion that Gabriel spread his wings when he told the virgin Mary that she would conceive a child is a daring allusion to the mythological impregnation of the virgin Leda by Zeus in the form of a swan. (As an art lover, Dante might have been familiar with depictions of Leda, unclothed and supine, beneath the wings of a huge swan at the moment of conception. And he was certainly familiar with depictions of Mary, chaste, robed, and a discrete distance from Gabriel at the moment when she was impregnated by the Holy Spirit.) The contrasts between the two stories hardly need to be stated.

Illicit sex is a metaphor Dante borrowed from the Old Testament, where it appears almost fifty times in verses from Exodus to Nahum. (In the Authorized Version the word adultery is used this way eight times; the word whoredom, eighteen times; and the word harlot, about twenty times.) I haven't come across any Dante commentaries that mention this allusion or the rest of the interwoven sexual aspects of Canto 9. In *Paradise* Dante repeatedly condemns inordinate earthly loves but praises Rahab, an ex-prostitute; then he closes Canto 9 by prophesying the 1305 transfer of the Papacy from Rome to Avignon and charges church leaders who love money instead of God with adultery.

## 9. King Solomon

Dante used another ingenious and profoundly meaningful knot of wordplay and ideas at the end of Canto 10 of *Paradise* (lines 109-114). This canto begins with a prologue about the Trinity. God the Father (Power) and Christ the Son (Wisdom) breathe forth eternally the Holy Spirit (Love). The Father is indescribable, but the Son is described as light and the Holy Spirit is described as heat. In the Heaven of the Sun Dante discovers twelve intellectual Christian souls set in a circle like a clock, singing and rejoicing; and Solomon is one of them. Because the sun is our chief natural means of measuring time, the chief theme of this canto is timekeeping. Mechanical clocks, one of the latest wonders of advanced technology, were such a new invention when Dante wrote this that few people had seen one or learned about the cogged wheels inside that run them.

Some commentators express puzzlement about Solomon's inclusion in the circle of Christian intellectuals, and Barbara Reynolds suggests perceptively that he is included because of his famous ability to judge truth and error; but I believe his prominence in the *Comedy* rests primarily upon his writing about love. (One of the twenty-four elders in the procession in Canto 29 of *Purgatory* represents the books of Solomon, and in Canto 30 that elder sings out the words "Come, bride of Lebanon," from the Song of Solomon 4:8.) His connection to Cunizza and Rahab in Canto 9 is that on earth he had too many lovers.

One of the twelve spirits says to Dante: "...the Ray of Grace shining in you (from which True Love is kindled, then grows and multiplies in you by loving) has guided you up the [heavenly] stairways..." The Ray of Grace is the Son, and True Love is the Holy Spirit. Like lightning that can set a forest on fire or a light beam from a magnifying glass that can set paper on fire (and like the tongues of flame at Pentecost that set the world on fire), understanding bestowed by grace has lit Dante's ascent through Paradise.

The last sentence in Canto 10 is "Then like a clock calling us when God's Bride rises to sing her morning song to her Groom to encourage His love—in which the clock parts pulling and pushing each other, 'Ting-ting,' resound with sweet chimes that swell the willing one with love—that is how I beheld the glorious circle revolve and link voice to voice in such harmony and sweetness that it can only be known where joy begets joy eternally." Although I saw no analysis of it in several commentaries I consulted, I was struck by this surprisingly erotic multiple metaphor that combines an echo of the imagery of carnal love in the Song of Solomon (tenth century B.C.) and the imagery of the newly invented mechanical clock (thirteenth century A.D.) with the imagery of Christians attending a traditional morning prayer service—all to describe allegorically the relationship of the Church to Christ, in order to describe the state of being of twelve specific spirits in Paradise who are in turn Dante's allegorical illustration of truth about ultimate love. This rather playful exhibition of Dante's intellectual complexity at the conclusion of a passage about a dozen intellectuals who had ascended from intellectual complexities to ecstatic love strikes me as quintessential Dante. His writing is so compressed that if a reader blinks mentally he is apt to miss a display of Dante's virtuosity.

## 10. *The First Commandment*

In Canto 12 of *Paradise* (lines 73-75) Dante refers to "Christ's prime admonition." Previous Dante commentators think this means that the first counsel of Christ was poverty or humility. (They cite Matthew 19:21, "Go, sell what thou hast, and give to the poor," or Matthew 5:3, "Blessed are the poor in spirit...") I have not found one commentator who suggests Matthew 23 37-38, "Thou shalt love the Lord with all thy heart, and with all thy soul, and with all thy mind. This is the first and greatest commandment." This commandment is especially pertinent in all of Canto 12, and it is indeed Christ's prime admonition; He said so.

## 11. *Burdens*

In Canto 18 of *Paradise* (lines 4-6) Beatrice comforts Dante about the injustice of his exile: "...remember that I am close to the One who lightens every unfair burden." I think this is a reference to the words of Jesus in Luke 11:46, "Woe to you authorities in the law, because you weigh people down with burdens they can hardly carry..." and in Matthew 11:30, "My yoke is easy and my burden is light."

## 12. *The Wealth of Ethiopians*

In Canto 19 of *Paradise* (lines 106-148) the souls of just rulers declare "But many cry 'Christ, Christ,' who at the judgment shall be even farther from Him than those who don't know Christ; and the Ethiopians shall put them to shame when the two groups are separated, the one forever rich, the other poor..." Ethiopians are those who have not heard about Christ. Although no other commentators mention it, I think it's obvious that the riches described here are those described by Wisdom in Proverbs 8. Wisdom declares, "To you, O men, I call out; I raise my voice to all mankind.... Counsel and sound judgment are mine; I have understanding and power. By me kings reign and rulers make laws that are just; by me princes govern, and all nobles who rule on earth. I love those who love me, and those who seek me find me. With me are riches and honor, enduring wealth and prosperity. My fruit is better than fine gold; what I yield surpasses choice silver. I walk in the way of righteousness, along the paths of justice, bestowing wealth on those who love me and making their treasuries full. For whoever finds me finds life and receives favor from the Lord. But whoever fails to find me harms himself; all who hate me love death." This teaching and the teaching that faith in Christ is the only way to Heaven seem mutually exclusive; but the Bible has it both ways—and so does Dante.

## 13. Overcoming with Benevolence

In canto 20 of *Paradise* (lines 94-96) the souls of just rulers tell Dante "The Kingdom of Heaven suffers violence from ardent love and living hope that can overcome the eternal Will—not in the way men overcome each other, but because it wants to be overcome, and, being overcome, overcomes with benevolence." Commentators agree that Dante is alluding to Matthew 11:12, "From the days of John the Baptist until now the kingdom of heaven suffers violence, and the violent take it by force." Although this verse refers to evil powers, the Eagle quotes from it to explain that God wills that human love and faith in Him can prevail over the justice that excludes all unbelievers from Heaven. I suspect that Dante is also alluding here to Revelation 17:14, "They will war against the Lamb, but the Lamb will overcome them because He is Lord of lords and King of kings; and His called, chosen and faithful followers will be with Him."

## 14. Salvific Reversals

In Canto 22 of *Paradise* (lines 88-96) St. Benedict tells Dante, "Peter began his gathering without gold or silver, I began mine with prayers and fasting, and Francis began his with humility; but if you look at the beginning of each one and look at how it has strayed, you will see how the whiteness has darkened. Yet a rescue here would not be such an amazing sight as the Jordan flowing backwards [Joshua 3:14-17] and the parting of the sea at God's will [Exodus 14:21-29]." About 2,800 years after the reversal of the flow of the Jordan (circa 1500 B.C.), Benedict hopes that God will reverse the tragic course of monasticism (circa 1300 A.D.), and he is surely referring to the opening verses of Psalm 114: "When Israel came out of Egypt, the house of Jacob from a people of foreign tongue, Judah became God's sanctuary, Israel his dominion. The sea looked and fled, the Jordan turned back; the mountains skipped like rams, the hills like lambs. Why was it, O sea, that you fled, O Jordan, that you turned back..." Thus God twice reversed the natural flow of water in order to rescue His people from apparently hopeless situations, and in his typical style Dante has Benedict reverse the chronological flow of the narrative by switching the two exodus events.

### 15. A Threshing Floor

In Canto 22 of *Paradise* (lines 150-153) Dante looks down at the world: "And as I circled with the eternal Twins, the little threshing-floor that incites our ferocity was entirely visible to me, from hills to shores..." All the commentators I have consulted assume that a threshing floor is mentioned here simply because it is a small and humble area, as the earth is a small and humble planet; but I believe this misses Dante's main point, which is the overwhelming cosmic significance of the earth. There are almost forty references to threshing floors in the Bible, both historical and symbolic, and an amazing array of biblical events took place at these little plots of land—ranging from courtship and human slaughter to angelic visitations. In fact, the great Jewish temple was built on a threshing floor. The final mention of a threshing floor in the Bible is Christ's warning in Luke 3:17: "His winnowing fork is in his hand to clear his threshing floor and to gather the wheat into his barn, but he will burn up the chaff with unquenchable fire." Clearly, in my opinion, in both Luke's gospel and Dante's *Comedy* the threshing floor is the earth, the farmer is God, the grain is human souls, the fire is Hell, and the barn is Paradise itself. (Barbara Reynolds points out that in medieval writings it was not unusual to refer to the inhabited parts of the earth as a threshing floor. I suspect that this custom was based upon Christ's words in Luke 3:17.)

Although the adjective feroci (plural of feroce) is commonly translated as savage, it can also mean proud; and I wonder if Dante might have had that in mind. He considered pride his own besetting sin and the most basic sin of all humanity. *The Divine Comedy* teaches that souls will be completely cleansed of the taint of pride on their way to Paradise.

### 16. Seedsowers in Babylon

In Canto 23 of *Paradise* (lines 130-133) Dante exclaims "What great wealth is stored in these treasure chests for those who were faithful seedsowers on earth! Here they live in joy with the treasure they earned by weeping in exile in Babylon, where gold was scorned." Although no commentators I have consulted mention it, Dante seems to have Galatians 6:8 in mind: "Be not deceived; God is not mocked. For whatever a man sows, that he will also reap." The Babylonian exile represents life on earth, where we are aliens and strangers. I believe that Dante is referring here to the famous passage about Old and New Testament heroes of the faith in Hebrews 11:13, "All these people were still living by faith when they died. They did not receive the things promised; they only saw them and welcomed them from a distance. And they admitted that they were aliens and strangers on earth." 1 Peter 2:11 is a fitting corollary: "Dear friends, I urge you, as aliens and strangers in the world, to abstain from sinful desires, which war against your soul."

### 17. Birth and Babyhood

In Canto 23 of *Paradise* Dante begins with the image of a mother bird sheltering her brood, then gives a series of related images upon which I've found no commentary. These include an enfolding cloak, intensely bright light and learning to see, sweetest milk, a glad face, and (in lines 121-123) an infant who stretches his arms toward his mother when he has had his milk. Needless to say, aside from breathing, these are the most dramatic experiences of a newborn baby.

I believe that Dante had in mind the following Bible verses: John 3:3 "In reply Jesus declared, 'I tell you the truth, no one can see the kingdom of God unless he is born again,'" John 3:7, "You should not be surprised at my saying, 'You must be born again,'" and 1 Peter 1:23, "For you have been born again, not of perishable seed, but of imperishable, through the living and enduring word of God." For the entire *Comedy* he probably had in mind Matthew 18:3 "And he said: 'I tell you the truth, unless you change and become like little children, you will never enter the kingdom of heaven.'"

Only four wombs are specifically mentioned in Dante's *Comedy*: those of Dante's mother, Jacob's mother, Christ's mother, and Dominic's mother. The latter is mentioned because of the dream Dominic's mother had that foretold her baby's future, and a mention of Mary's womb was to be expected in this masterwork. In my opinion, the other two wombs, those that nurtured Dante and Jacob, are intentionally mentioned in *Paradise* because of the monumental loves those two men bore for Beatrice and Rachel.

In my opinion an underlying theme throughout *Paradise* is an innate spiritual longing in humans to "return to the womb" of their origin, the Mind of God. (The Empyrean is like the womb of the entire cosmos.)

## 18. The Rose and Lilies

In Canto 23 of *Paradise* (lines 73-75) Beatrice points Dante to a garden and says "There is the Rose in which the Divine Word made itself flesh; there are the Lilies whose fragrance guided people to the right path." As commentators have suggested, the rose represents Mary and the lilies represent apostles. I feel sure that Dante was alluding to the Song of Solomon 2:1, "I am the rose of Sharon, the lily of the valleys," and 2 Corinthians 2:14, "But thanks be to God, who always leads us in triumphal procession in Christ [related to the triumphal procession in *Purgatory* 29, where twenty-four Old Testament elders wore wreaths of lilies and seven New Testament elders wore wreaths of roses] and through us spreads everywhere the fragrance of the knowledge of him."

## 19. Light and Heavy

In Canto 23 of *Paradise* (lines 37-39) Beatrice says to the spirit of St. Peter, "O light eternal of that great man to whom our Lord brought down and entrusted the keys to this miraculous joy, test this man, as it pleases you, on light and heavy principles of the faith that once enabled you to walk upon the sea." In my opinion, Beatrice asks Peter to question Dante about his faith because Peter is the most famous person who ever answered a question about his faith. In Matthew 16 Christ asked the disciples who they believed He was, and Peter answered, "You are the Christ, the Son of the living God." Christ responded by announcing that Peter would receive the keys to the Kingdom of Heaven. I suspect that Beatrice injected the terms light and heavy into her request because according to Matthew 14 the faith of Peter (whose name meant stone) once made him light enough to walk on water.

## 20. Bountiful Rain

In Canto 24 of *Paradise* (lines 91-92) Dante answers St. Peter's question about the origin of his faith by saying "The bountiful rain of the Holy Spirit that showers on the old and new scriptures is proof that has convinced me..." Dante says the Old and New Testaments, inspired by the Holy Spirit, are the source of his faith. From Genesis to Revelation, there are by one count 85 references to rain in the Bible. In my opinion, two that Dante had in mind here are Deuteronomy 32:2, "Let my teaching fall like rain and my words descend like dew, like showers on new grass, like abundant rain on tender plants" and Acts 14:17, "Yet he has not left himself without testimony: He has shown kindness by giving you rain from heaven..."

## 21. From Vine to Thorn

In Canto 24 of *Paradise* (lines 109-111) Dante says to Peter "when you were poor and fasting you entered the field and sowed the good plant that was a vine—but has now become a thorn." Dante acknowledges Peter's role in the wonderful growth of the Christian Church, but he laments again (as he did at the end of Canto 23) its corruption. In my opinion he draws this vineyard image from Jeremiah 2:21, "I had planted you like a choice vine of sound and reliable stock. How then did you turn against me into a corrupt, wild vine?" and Micah 7:-1-4, "What misery is mine! I am like one who gathers summer fruit at the gleaning of the vineyard; there is no cluster of grapes to eat... The godly have been swept from the land; not one upright man remains.... Both hands are skilled in doing evil;

the ruler demands gifts, the judge accepts bribes, the powerful dictate what they desire—they all conspire together. The best of them is like a brier, the most upright worse than a thorn hedge...."

## 22. Not Here

In Canto 25 of *Paradise* (lines 122-123) the spirit of St. John says to Dante, "Why do you blind yourself trying to see what is not here? My body is now earth in the earth, and there it shall remain with all the rest until [the resurrection]." John knows that Dante is trying to see if the story is true that when John died his body went directly to Heaven with his spirit. (It did not.) I believe that John's words are meant to be a mirror image of Luke 24: 5-6, in which the women who went to Christ's tomb to anoint His body were addressed by two shining men who said, "Why do you look for the living among the dead? He is not here; he has risen!" (Barbara Reynolds responded to this opinion of mine by pointing out that the words of the Vulgate are "non est hic." Dante's words are "qui non ha loco," which are quite near the Latin.) Christ's followers who thought His body was earthbound were mistaken, and later followers who thought John's body was not earthbound were mistaken.

## 23. Great Weight of Glory

In Canto 25 of *Paradise* (lines 38-39) the spirit of St. James said to Dante "Look up and be confident, for it befits anyone who ascends here from the mortal world to ripen in our radiance." In my opinion, James, the symbol of hope, might be comforting Dante with the hope that during his spiritual journey his pride is being replaced by humility, obviating his need to be cleansed of pride after death. "This comforting word from [James] caused me to lift my head up toward the mountains that had bent me down with their great weight." This is, of course, an allusion to Psalm 120:1, "I will lift up my eyes to the mountains, the source of my help." Peter and James are the two mountains Dante was looking to for help, but he was in such awe of their radiant majesty that he bent his head as if the weight of their light (glory) was more than he could bear. I suspect that this is an allusion to 2 Corinthians 4:17, "For this slight momentary affliction is preparing for us an eternal weight of glory beyond all comparison..." (In his sermon "The Weight of Glory," C. S. Lewis wrote, "The load, or weight, or burden of my neighbour's glory should be laid daily on my back, a load so heavy that only humility can carry it, and the backs of the proud will be broken.")

## 24. The A and Z of Love

In Canto 26 of *Paradise* (lines 16-18) Dante says to St. John, "The Good that fills this royal residence is the Alpha and Omega of all the writings that love has read to me, whether softly or loudly." God is the true beginning and end, the A and Z, of all there is to know about love. As I see it, Dante is referring to John's teachings about love in his epistles (such as "God is love" in 1 John 4:8), and he is also referring to John's report in Revelation 1:8 and 21:6 that God is the Alpha and Omega, the beginning and the end. (It was assumed that these books were all by one author named John.)

## 25. God So Loved

In Canto 26 of *Paradise* (lines 55-60) Dante identifies for John three things that have caused his heart to turn to God: "[1] the world's existence and my own existence, [2] the death He endured that I might live, and [3] every believer's hope, along with mine..." I think Dante is consciously referring, point by point, to John's most famous teaching about love, John 3:16: "[1] For God so loved the world, [2] that he gave his only begotten Son, [3] that whosoever believeth in him should not perish, but have everlasting life."

## 26. Ravening Wolves

In Canto 27 of *Paradise* (lines 40-55) Peter says, "The bride of Christ was not nourished by my blood and that of Linus and Cletus so that she might later be used for gain of gold.... From up here we can see ravening wolves dressed like shepherds in all the pastures." (Barbara Reynolds has pointed out that the metaphor of ravening wolves was very common in medieval writings about the greed of priests.) In my opinion, Peter is alluding not only to Christ's warning in Matthew 7:15, but also to Paul's warning in Acts 20:29, "I know that after I leave, savage wolves will come in among you and will not spare the flock" and his related admonishment in verses 33-35, "I have not wanted anyone's silver or gold or valuable clothing. You all know that my manual labor has supplied my needs and those of my companions. In all that I did, I showed you that by hard work we must help those in need, remembering Jesus' words 'It is more blessed to give than to receive.'" When Paul said that, he was well aware that he was going to die soon for his faith. Thus Acts 20 is the most eloquent rebuke possible to greedy, worldly, hypocritical church leadership.

## 27. Grace, Knowledge, and Love

In Canto 28 of *Paradise* (lines 106-114) Beatrice tells Dante, "And you should know that bliss is allotted according to how deeply anyone sees into the truth in which every intellect finds rest. From that, one can see that being blessed is the result of seeing—not of loving, which is its result. And the allotment of sight is according to the righteousness bestowed by grace and by good will." In my opinion, Dante is referring to Paul's teaching in Philippians 1:9-11, "And this is my prayer: that your love may abound more and more in knowledge and depth of insight, so that you may be able to discern what is best and may be pure and blameless until the day of Christ, filled with the fruit of righteousness that comes through Jesus Christ—to the glory and praise of God." Ultimately it is grace, the unmerited favor of God, that enables his creatures to see, understand. and love spiritual truth; but created beings must choose to cooperate with this grace.

## 28. Nurse and Be Satisfied

In Canto 30 of *Paradise* (lines 73-74) Dante enters the Empyrean, and before his eyes adjust Beatrice tells him, "But before your great thirst [to see more] can be quenched, first you must drink of this water." Dante tells his readers, "No baby who awakens far later than usual ever turns his face toward his milk faster than I turned." Although I have not found this idea in commentaries, I am convinced that he was greatly influenced here by Isaiah 66:10-13, "Rejoice with Jerusalem and be glad for her, all you who love her; rejoice greatly with her, all you who mourn over her. For you will nurse and be satisfied at her comforting breasts; you will drink deeply and delight in her overflowing abundance.' For this is what the LORD says: 'I will extend peace to her like a river, and the wealth of nations like a flooding stream; you will nurse and be carried on her arm and dandled on her knees. As a mother comforts her child, so will I comfort you; and you will be comforted over Jerusalem.'" For Dante this prophecy was about Heaven, the New Jerusalem, the eternal City of God. See also 1 Peter 2:2, "Like newborn babies, crave pure spiritual milk, so that by it you may grow up in your salvation." I believe that Dante's driving thirst for insights, likened to that of a newborn baby for milk, is at heart a thirst for reality.

In addition to the image of a baby eager for milk, Dante has five images of milk in other cantos of *Paradise*. First, in Canto 5 Christians are urged not to wander away from their mothers' milk like silly lambs. Second, in Canto 11 he cites the shortage of milk that occurs when sheep (clergy, perhaps) go astray. Third, in Canto 23 (lines 55-57) he gives a rather startling image of poets whom the Muses "have ever enriched with their sweetest milk." Fourth, at the end of Canto 30 Beatrice prophesies against Italy and Pope Clement, "The blind greed that bewitches you has made you like a little child dying of hunger who pushes away his mother's breast..." (Dante began Canto 15 by stating that benevolence is the essence of genuine love, "just as selfishness is the essence of malice." Maternal love is obviously an image of God's benevolence and the opposite of malicious selfishness.)

Fifth, in Canto 33 (lines 106-108) Dante said "From here on my language is even more deficient for what is in my memory than that of an infant who is still bathing his tongue at the breast." Once again, for the last time in his *Comedy*, Dante returns to babies, their inborn thirst for mother's milk, and language development. In addition to comparing his verbal inadequacy to that of a baby, I think Dante is implicitly comparing his spiritual thirst to a baby's physical thirst, comparing the Empyrean to a mother, and comparing the light of God (itself a metaphor) to mother's milk. Several lines earlier, Dante wrote of sweetness still showering on his heart, an image of refreshing and fructifying rain; now he returns to the familiar image of being embraced and nourished, of his human thirst being quenched.

## 29. Bees and Honey

In Canto 31 of *Paradise* (lines 7-12) Dante has a vision of angels "like a swarm of bees that first plunge into flowers and then return to where their toil is turned into sweetness..." In his elliptical style, Dante refers to honey and beehives here without using the actual words. Dorothy Sayers pointed out that Dante's bee image was an allusion to Virgil, but commentators I consulted do not mention its Scriptural basis. Honey is mentioned from Genesis to Revelation. (Best known is the promise in Ezekiel 20:6 of "a land flowing with milk and honey, the most beautiful of all lands.") I find Song of Solomon 4:9-12, which mentions honey and honeycomb, highly relevant to all of Canto 31 in several ways: "You have stolen my heart, my sister, my bride; you have stolen my heart with one glance of your eyes, with one jewel of your necklace. How delightful is your love, my sister, my bride! How much more pleasing is your love than wine, and the fragrance of your perfume than any spice! Your lips drop sweetness as the honeycomb, my bride; milk and honey are under your tongue. The fragrance of your garments is like that of Lebanon. You are a garden locked up, my sister, my bride; you are a spring enclosed, a sealed fountain."

In fact, in my opinion Dante wrote Canto 31 in response to that passage, and all of *Paradise* in response to the Song of Solomon.

## 30. Closing the Brackets

In Canto 32 (lines 10-12) of *Paradise* Dante beholds the ranks of the saints in the vast amphitheater of the highest part of Heaven. On the female side of this amphitheater, three Hebrew women (plus Beatrice) are seated just below Mary (mother of Christ), and Eve (mother of humankind), above all other women in heaven. These three women are Rachel, Sarah, and Rebeccah, in that nonchronological order. Sarah was the beautiful wife of Abraham [circa 2000 B.C.], mother of Isaac, and mother-in-law of Rebeccah. (See Genesis 11-23.) Rebeccah was the beloved wife of Isaac, the mother of Jacob, and the mother-in-law of Rachel. (See Genesis 24-28.) Rachel was Jacob's beloved wife and the mother of Joseph and Benjamin. (See Genesis 29-35.) Jacob's other name was Israel, and from him the twelve tribes of Israel descended; so these three women—Jacob's grandmother, mother, and wife—were the foremothers of Judaism. Many commentators identify the three in a cursory way as individuals, without noting their relationship to Jacob and without suggesting why Dante placed Rachel above the other two—with Beatrice (the only one of them not a famous mother) seated next to her. Dante considered this arrangement so important that he bracketed *The Divine Comedy* with it—in the next-to-first canto of *Inferno* and the next-to-last canto of *Paradise*.

In light of Dante's extraordinary penchant for making connections, I like to think that as he completed his masterpiece at what turned out to be the very end of his life, he enjoyed the fact that just as Jacob had willingly labored for his father-in-law for fourteen years in order to fulfill his love for Rachel by marrying her, so Dante willingly labored for fourteen years to fulfill his love for Beatrice by immortalizing her in his *Comedy*.

## CONCLUSION

In his introduction to *Studies in Words* C. S. Lewis cautioned about dangers besetting an overconfident and under-informed reader of old literature. "His mind bubbles over with possible meanings. He has ready to hand unthought-of-metaphors, highly individual shades of feeling, subtle associations, ambiguities—every manner of semantic gymnastics—which he can attribute to his author. Hence the difficulty of 'making sense' out of a strange phrase will seldom for him be insuperable. Where the duller reader simply does not understand, he misunderstands—triumphantly, brilliantly. But it is not enough to make sense. We want to find the sense the author intended. 'Brilliant' explanations of a passage often show that a clever, insufficiently informed man has found one more mare's nest."

In the *Comedy*, however, Dante himself bubbled over with possible meanings. Dante had "ready to hand unthought-of-metaphors, highly individual shades of feeling, subtle associations, ambiguities—every manner of semantic gymnastics." To explore the *Comedy* adequately one must have an eager imagination and risk an occasional mare's nest. (In terms of John Ciardi's metaphor, one must risk finding fool's gold.)

Perhaps my interpretation of the following passage is fool's gold, but I don't think so. In Canto 27 of *Purgatory* Dante went to sleep, and in his dream he seemed to see a fair young woman in a meadow gathering flowers and singing: "Whoever wants to know my name, know that I am Leah, working with my lovely hands to make myself a garland to enjoy in my reflection in the mirror. But my sister Rachel never stirs from her mirror, and sits there all day. She prefers to gaze into her own bright eyes, as I prefer to adorn myself with my hands. She finds joy in seeing; I find it in doing." The sisters Leah and Rachel were Jacob's two wives described in Genesis 29. Leah, who had weak eyes (Dante allegedly had weak eyes), bore him more children; but Rachel, who was more beautiful, was his favorite. Leah and Rachel were forerunners of Martha and Mary in the New Testament (Luke 10 and John 11). In both stories the active sister produced more good works, but the contemplative sister chose the better way.

Dante was by nature a busy activist like Leah and Martha. I strongly suspect that his image of Leah gathering flowers and weaving them together into a garland is at one level an intentional portrait of himself writing the *Comedy*. He spent the last fourteen years of his life gathering the flowers of his known world and ingeniously, intricately weaving them together to produce the *Comedy*.

NOTE: I am grateful to *Divine Comedy* authority Barbara Reynolds for reading the first draft of this essay and offering many valuable suggestions.

# INDEX